In Search of the Ultimate High

Dedicated to Nicholas Saunders who died on 3 February 1998 in
South Africa, whilst travelling to research this book.
May he have reached the Ultimate High.

In Search of the Ultimate High

Spiritual Experience Through Psychoactives

Nicholas Saunders

Anja Saunders

Michelle Pauli

RIDER

LONDON · SYDNEY · AUCKLAND · JOHANNESBURG

1 3 5 7 9 10 8 6 4 2

Copyright © Anja Saunders 2000

Anja Saunders has asserted her right to be identified as the Author of this work in accordance with the Copyright, Designs and Patents Act, 1988.

First published in 2000 by Rider
an imprint of Ebury Press, Random House,
20 Vauxhall Bridge Road, London SW1V 2SA
www.randomhouse.co.uk

Random House Australia (Pty) Limited
20 Alfred Street, Milsons Point, Sydney, New South Wales 2061, Australia

Random House New Zealand Limited
18 Poland Road, Glenfield, Auckland 10, New Zealand

Random House South Africa (Pty) Limited
Endulini, 5A Jubilee Road, Parktown 2193, South Africa

The Random House Group Limited Reg. No. 9954009

Papers used by Rider are natural, recyclable products made from wood grown in sustainable forests.

Printed and bound by Mackays of Chatham plc, Kent

A CIP catalogue record for this book is available from the British Library

ISBN 0-7126-7087-4

Contents

Acknowledgements

We would like to thank Ann and Alexander Shulgin for their wise words in the preface of this book. We would also like to thank Alex Grey for the use of his painting 'Universal Mind Lattice' which appears on the front cover. This painting was inspired by a mystical psychedelic experience that unveiled the interconnectedness and unity of all beings and things.

Given the controversial subject matter of this book, many of the people who helped us have chosen to remain anonymous. So, rather than include a partial list of names, we send our thanks out to all the people who generously shared with us their accounts of spiritual experiences and psychedelic journeys. We apologise to you if we have not been able to include your account in the book due to restrictions on space, but reading your experience was part of the path of inspiration that made this book happen.

We would like to thank the many people who encouraged us to write this book, and continued to believe in us finishing it after Nicholas's death – friends, family, and all the open-hearted people we met in spiritual gatherings.

Thank you for your trust.

Preface
by Alexander and Ann Shulgin

There are many people, particularly in the Western world's scientific and medical community, who regard the entire concept of a so-called 'spiritual' level of existence as self-deluding nonsense. They are comfortable with a belief system that says, in essence, 'We are born, we live our lives, and we die, and that's all there is to that; nothing of us continues after death; no consciousness, no awareness, no identity. All experiences of out-of-body consciousness, of mystical bliss states, or encounters with some entity not contained in a physical body are delusions, brought about by a refusal to accept the simple truth about our universe: there is no great 'meaning' to life; it arose out of an accidental fusing of certain molecules, and there is no spiritual mystery to be explored.'

Yet, strangely and even incredibly, these same people are able to accept without unease a theory called the Big Bang, which involves the explosion of Everything out of an exquisitely small point floating in Nothing. If this is not a supreme mystery, what in heaven's name is? Those who feel comfortable negating all meaningfulness and anything called God, the Ground of Being, or the Great Mind (among many other names) insist that we will, some day, under-stand how this explosion of matter out of nothing came about. It's simply a matter of time before we have the answer, and until that happens, we can just accept that it did take place without any divine intervention or thought or purpose. There's no need for spirit or the spiritual; it will all be resolved in a few years, by physicists and chemists and astronomers. End of story.

So these words are not for those people. They are welcome to their material world, devoid of spirit, while we remain aware of the interpenetration of another dimension – or many other dimensions – in every corner of the physical world. Few of us know what and how and why; we just know there is a spiritual energy and intelligence within us and within everything that sur-rounds us.

Many humans are born with the ability to sense and sometimes see and hear the flow of spiritual energy throughout our world. For most, the ability to perceive this companion reality is lost with the firming of ego and focusing of the physical senses which come about when babyhood grows into child-hood. Three- and four-year-olds often speak of past lives, but their memories dim and eventually fade as they participate more and more in the busy world of the five- and six-year-old child. As adults, they usually have no conscious access to these early experiences, unless something happens to allow the memories of long ago to resurface.

One of the ways in which the early memories of a spiritual reality can be recaptured is by the ingestion of a psychedelic drug. It is certainly not the only way. The practice of meditation, holotropic breathing and yoga – to name a very few – can also release these memories, as well as making it possible for the adult to see again the emissions of light from plants and the flow of atoms across surfaces. How often have we who make use of psychedelics heard the phrase, 'I found myself in a world that was completely familiar, although I had forgotten it for years!'

We all know, but it has to be said again and again, that these special con-sciousness-expanding drugs are not for everyone. For a young adult who hasn't yet fully formed and firmed his core self, and who has not yet made the vital decisions about who he intends to be, with whom he will ally himself, and what he wishes to accomplish, these drugs may produce more confusion than insight. But decisions about such a person taking a psychedelic are not often left in the hands of wise elders. He himself will usually decide to experiment with friends, out of curiosity and a desire to win the approval of his peers. The results can sometimes be frightening, disturbing or even dangerous, for instance if a state of psychological inflation takes hold, or if the Place of Sorrow and Meaninglessness is the first to open up to him.

When an adult is ready to use a psychedelic drug to open doors within his psyche, the experience can be – and often is – one of the most important of his life. Not only may he feel the warmth of familiarity, a sense of coming home, but an interior landscape seen and felt only in the deepest dream states can appear to the inner eye. He might experience one of the most treasured states known to humankind, that of knowing himself to be a participant in the great River of Life, being connected on many levels with all other living beings, and being engaged in a process filled with intense meaningfulness. He may find himself filled with cosmic laughter and taken over by immense love and deep joy.

Many, although not all, psychedelic drugs or visionary plants produce insight into ones' self, one's direction in life, and previously unconsidered alternatives which might steer one in a different and more productive direction. The best and most friendly drug or plant of this kind will also allow the searcher to feel acceptance and love for himself, warts and all, and this may be truly the most valuable experience: love and validation of his own existence, and the ability to forgive mistakes and inadequacies of the past.

The spiritual path that makes use of visionary plants and psychedelic drugs is full of pitfalls and even dangers, which is why the wise traveller will always have a knowledgeable and experienced friend by his side when he embarks on such an journey. This minimises the threat of despair that may arise if one of the dark places is opened and the psyche delivers the message that this, too, is part of the universe and must be acknowledged. The friend will know that the traveller is not obliged to stay in a place of greyness and sorrow, but is meant to find his way through and out, back to the world of Kwan Yin, the goddess of mercy and compassion, the Christ, bringer of love and light, and the Buddha, the archetype of wisdom, cosmic laughter and forgiveness.

Nicholas Saunders was a wise and gentle searcher, a person of immense compassion and active involvement in his world, always doing whatever he could to ease the problems of others and bring light and joy to those caught in depression and darkness in their lives. He knew that the spirit invades every cell of our physical world, and because of his own nature and the nature of his experiences on this particular path of development, he maintained an integrity of soul and purpose which could be felt by anyone meeting and greeting him. His work – on both the material level and the spiritual – will shine for the rest of us, and for thousands of others, for a long, long time to come. We bless him and ask him to bless us. It was an honour and an immense pleasure to have known Nicholas in this world and, for the two of us, it has been an honour and pleasure to write these words for his book.

Introduction

by Anja Saunders

All men die,

but not all men

truly live!

William Wallace

About this book

Throughout history people have taken mind-expanding substances. Whether it is out of curiosity, a need for development or a deep longing for something bigger than themselves, people have always been searching the realms beyond the here and now. Psychoactive substances have for many been the guides they chose on this path. There is no reason why it should be any different now, or any different in the future. Every society has had its own spiritual medicines and ours has them too.

This book deals specifically with the spiritual quest through the use of psychoactive substances. We do not intend to promote the general or symptomatic use of drugs and this book is not about the substances themselves, but about their spiritual use. It considers psychoactives as powerful medicines that deserve to be handled with respect by the taker. They should not be used as a distraction to life, but only taken with clear positive intent to learn from and experience the spiritual life more to the full. Preparation of oneself and one's environment are required before a psychoactive is taken. A caring and safe atmosphere whilst taking 'the sacrament' is also needed, and an integration of the process afterwards.

The accounts we have selected for the book reflect this. We have chosen to give much space to personal accounts. As well as being fascinating stories in themselves, we hope that they will help people who have had a spiritual experience on a psychoactive to better understand it through identifying with someone else's experience. The accounts are written by people who feel they had a spiritual experience facilitated by a psychoactive substance, which gave them insights that were useful to their lives. They are people who honestly seek spirit and truth, who use psychoactives not as an escape route, but as a way to en-spirit, to inspire their lives.

Whilst this book does not deal specifically with the problems of drug abuse, it is an aspect that cannot be ignored entirely. Many societies suffer from its consequences. Poverty and hopelessness have driven many to the abuse of drugs. The need to escape from the daily burden of life has become so great for some people that they are even prepared to drug themselves and others to destruction. We see this in inner cities and we see this in the countryside. We see it in the Western world as well as the developing worlds. It is often precisely the lack of spirituality, the lack of purpose and belonging that causes people to abuse drugs. This was illustrated in an article in the *Observer* news-paper about the recent development of drug abuse amongst native American Indians.

> Police officer Stanley Star Comes Out was involved in investigating a
> juvenile homicide that involved two young Lakota. He believes such
> incidents arise because of factors such as drug abuse, but also because
> young Lakota do not receive a 'spiritual preparation' for life.[1]

The drugs involved in these situations bring symptomatic relief, often at a great price. It is mostly drugs like heroin and cocaine, and their derivatives, that are used for this purpose. In many parts of the world they are cheap and offer a 'quick fix'. Different substances, tryptamines and mescaline in particu-lar, can have different effects, but it is the intention with which a psychoactive substance is used that makes all the difference. Drug addicts act out of des-peration rather than choice and find themselves lost rather than found through the use of drugs. We would like to make it clear that none of the contributors to this book are drug abusers. They are all people who lead responsible lives, are not drug dependent and use these substances intentionally to connect with spirit.

The reader should be under no illusion that most of the substances men-tioned in the accounts are illegal and can be dangerous. To reduce the potentially harmful effects various precautions need to be taken.

Addiction is a common disease in our society and affects those who take psychoactives equally. Some people are by nature more susceptible to addic-tion than others and therefore may be more vulnerable to dependency behaviour. Timing is another critical factor. Psychoactives taken at the wrong time in one's life or in the wrong place or circumstances can do a great deal of harm. Where people have reported a spiritual experience, they typically speak of a sense of dissolving, of boundlessness, of oneness with the Source. It is a good idea to have a sense of self, boundaries and structure in one's life before embarking on a psychoactive journey. The substances that people use for spiritual development have the capacity to break habits in thinking and perception. This can lead to the frightening state of total loss of control as well as bringing new perspectives in possible ex-static (out of static) states.

Lack of guidance is one of the main problems one encounters and so a whole chapter of this book is devoted to the subject of guidance, preparation and integration. Those who are attracted to the path of psychoactives to experience the sacred do not easily find spiritual guides within conventional settings, since most churches do not recognise psychoactives as having a role within spirituality. Even though the role of established churches has diminished, people have not stopped searching for spirit and keep looking for new ways, which may be even closer to the very old ways.

In 'primitive' cultures, guides and safe spaces were always available to connect with spirit. Indigenous peoples in many parts of the world are now getting more attention. The threat to the rainforests and an increased awareness of the need to look after the earth has made many people look at what we can learn from indigenous cultures. When we look at how they live it is immediately clear that they don't make a sharp division between matter and spirit. The spirits of nature are honoured as part of daily life, as are ancestors. The unseen world is not excluded – it is a reality, and death is not the end. The presence of spirits is an accepted fact and to learn to work with them and use them as guides is seen as a useful practical skill. Charles Tart emphasises that 'many primitive peoples...believe that almost every normal adult has the ability to go into a trance state and be possessed by a god; the adult who cannot do this is a psychological cripple'.[2]

In indigenous cultures all over the world, plants have been used as teachers and to help form a bridge between the seen and the unseen worlds. In some cultures only the shamans or shamanas, the medicine people, take the plants. In other cultures everyone in the tribe uses the plants as teachers. Whether it be the Aztecs or Siberian shamans who use mushrooms, or the Huichol Indians who take peyote, whether it is ayahuasca taken in the rainforest, or San Pedro in the mountains, the plant teacher is always treated with respect. Plant medicine is used to understand more about life on this earth and its connection to the worlds beyond.

In our society loss of control or becoming ex-static is a problem, because we do not have the structure to deal with it. There are other cultures who do seem to handle this 'out of mind' state quite gracefully. The spiritual teacher Ram Dass gave an example in one of his lectures:

> Here when you lose your ground, when you forget your zipcode, you get
> put in a mental hospital. In India, when you do that, they see the

distinction between someone who is caught in another ego trip and someone who is really on another plane of reality and just lost their ground and they call these people god intoxicants. They treat them with honour and reverence and they help them through that process. Like Ananda Maima who was a great woman saint in India. She was a very conservative Bengali woman and then the Shakti, the kundalini went and she started doing cartwheels and throwing off her sari but instead of saying 'poor Ananda' they just took care of her, her husband became her devotee and as a result for forty years or so after that she was one of the great feeding sources of India. There was a society that had an institutional structure that allowed for those people and saw their benefit for society as a whole.[3]

There are not many people who can act as guides, given the illegality of psychoactives and general unfamiliarity with these altered states of consciousness. People who have been there before and have come back; who can hold the hands of those going through a growing experience with psychoactives. People who can tell stories of how it was for them. People who can be supportive when fears and doubts need to be faced bravely by those under the influence of psychoactives. Spaces that are safe can be hard to find in public: places where people can be surrounded by love and care from friends, without fear of the opprobrium of society or the dangers of the black market; safe places where the sacredness of psychoactives can be guarded. This book cannot replace a caring guide or create a safe space, but it may be a stepping stone to finding one.

Why use the word psychoactive?

The word 'drug' has many negative connotations and it also covers both medical and recreational drugs. This book deals with the use of drugs for spiritual purposes and it may be helpful in this context to choose a different name, one that is not so loaded. So what to call them? 'Medicine' is a term used in shamanic circles, 'psychedelics' seems to belong to the hippie culture, 'entheogens' is a brilliant word, meaning: *'gen – generating, theo – god, en – within –* generating the god within – but how many people have heard of it? Various terms will be used in the accounts in this book, but for our purposes we have chosen 'psychoactive substances', or 'psychoactives' for short. This is a neutral and definable term, meaning activating the psyche. We can count a whole variety of substances under this title, but have restricted ourselves to the ones we know to be used for spiritual purposes.

Why spiritual?

Spiritual is a broad term and we did not want to limit ourselves to our own definition. We have accepted each contributor's own definition of what they perceived as spiritual as far as the accounts are concerned. In the first chapter we look in more depth at various concepts of spirituality, but for now it is enough to say that a spiritual experience goes beyond the physical and emotional realm.

Why beyond the physical? People report the most wonderful sensual experiences with psychoactives. Feeling comfortable in one's body and being relaxed can facilitate the spiritual experience. Being in touch with one's body is also valuable in integrating the experience afterwards. However, the spiritual experience is not confined to the physical.

Why beyond the emotional? Feeling uneasy, depressed, confused or fearful is not helpful when taking psychoactives. With the guidance of an experienced therapist it is possible to use psychoactives to work through emotional blockages and this can open the way to spiritual experiences. However, psychotherapy work is not directly spiritual. We saw many accounts of people who came across psychological issues on their inner journeys. The substances can give insight into the perceptions of oneself that are getting in the way. For example, I remember one session when I realised I was getting exhausted by constantly being strong and independent, totally overlooking my connectedness with other people and cutting myself off from the help that was offered all the time. This insight has helped me to open myself up, which may have brought me closer to spirit. A necessary step for me – but this was not a spiritual experience.

So here we look beyond the physical, emotional and mental into the transpersonal realm where we connect with something that expands our entire sense of self.

Where did the idea come from?

This book is largely based on an idea by Nicholas Saunders, who died in a car accident in Feburary 1998. He was a man who had always come up with new ideas, from writing a book called *Alternative London* in the 1970s to setting up a dozen alternative businesses in Neal's Yard, London in the 1980s to getting involved in the dance scene and writing several informative books on the drug Ecstasy in the 1990s. Nicholas had been walking around with the idea for a 'spiritual book', as we called it in passing, for a while. After his success with his Ecstasy books a monk suggested that he write one about the spiritual aspects of drug taking. He was not quite sure if he was the right person to write such a book. Although brought up as a Catholic, he had left religion a long time ago and felt it was not for him. Neither was he convinced that there was a whole book in it, or even that the subject would appeal to enough people. I was quite keen on it, though. I do not belong to any religious group, but my work in healing has connected me to a world that is not restricted to my day-to-day reality. I feel there are parts of me that extend beyond my ego and my life is influenced by forces greater than myself. Is that a spiritual belief? The word itself is off-putting, since it evokes so many images relating to weird ritual practices or people losing their connection with reality. Nicholas and I both hated that kind of thing, but were curious about the part of life that is more than just what is in front of us. Nicholas had been using psychoactives for longer, and more frequently, than I had, but the exploration of altered states of consciousness had been of interest to both of us long before we met. I thought that writing the book could provide another meeting ground for us, and Nicholas envisaged some great travels together researching the book.

And great adventures we shared, inner and outer journeys. We met many interesting people, from sorcerer shamans, drunk and surrounded by parts of the human skeleton to the most gentle open-hearted people who welcomed us as part of their own family. Our relationship grew and intensified beyond measure in the last two years through embracing the search for the ultimate high. This did not mean spacing out together, but the seeking of an exquisite quality of life: to experience and to understand it as well as to share as much of it as we could in our day-to-day life. Of course we had many dull days and the travelling was not anything like as romantic as we had imagined at first. Spending hours stuck in airports or searching for days in a town for a John who was supposedly a great healer was not very exciting. The inner journeys are not for the faint-hearted and, at times, we were frightened and struggling together, but the way we used psychoactives did help us to deepen our love.

The lead up

It is remarkable how Nicholas's own life story illustrates the different phases in society that led up to the current interest in spirituality and the use of drugs as part of this.

Nicholas was in many ways a classic hippie. He came from a well-to-do family, had a good education, went to university and was all set up for a respectable career. He took LSD in the 1960s and, like so many, saw there was more to life than he had been led to believe. Through his LSD experience he became aware of an aspect of life that went beyond the material world. An appetite for the mystical was born as well as a spiritual longing, which was still there when I met him years later.

Nicholas wrote this about his LSD experience:

I first took LSD in the mid-Sixties while I was an engineering student. I dropped out of college, travelled overland to India and explored a variety of mystical paths. An observer might well assume that I was yet another sheep following the prevailing fashion, yet for me the experience was profound and my motives sincere.

My first exploration of LSD was to be a scientific observation, so I equipped myself with an observer, notebook and stopwatch; but nothing happened as I had been sold a dud. This may have been a blessing in disguise as next time I was far more relaxed as I took the supposedly ––– micrograms while visiting two fellow students, and when nothing happened half an hour later, casually took another.

The first thing I noticed was that things seemed different out of the corner of my eye, but when I turned to face them, all was normal. My caring friends kept asking how I felt, and after a while I found I was looking down on them; not only as though from physically above them but also I felt that their questions were, well, trivial. So much so that I felt it pointless to answer, and instead I allowed myself to become absorbed in more important things: in this case, the weave of the bedspread. I was fascinated watching each thread weaving its way over and under in superb rhythm and with great significance and beauty, a beauty that I knew was always there: it was simply ignored by insensitive people such as my friends, and by myself before then. I was enjoying myself enormously. I felt freed from the restraints of normal life, free to do anything I wanted. I knew that I had the power to fly or create or destroy just by willing it, but to do so would have been to test myself and that would have implied doubt, and as I had no doubt I was content to bask in the glory of my power. But the most important lesson of the experience was the certain knowledge that this consciousness was on a higher level and provided not just a different, but a broader perspective than normal. I saw my world for the first time in all its glory as though my previous view of it had lacked reality, like watching television.

The event was profoundly important for me, and certainly changed my life in spite of the fact that I found it impossible to describe or even remember with any clarity. The immediate effect was to destroy the ambitions and values I had been brought up with. We were insignificant and our lives so absurdly short that nothing was worth doing: anyone who was enthusiastic about anything was either blind to the truth or kidding themselves to avoid facing it. This made me dissatisfied and determined to find something meaningful in life, hence I got involved with one mystical group after another.

The 1960s generated an interest in Eastern religions and alternative spiritual practices on a unprecedented scale. In many circles it became the most common thing to sit in the lotus position, sing Krishna mantras, meditate on emptiness or surround oneself with pictures of the Maharishi. The sometimes very unearthly quest for spirit was enhanced by the sweet fragrance of incense, little bells and various drugs. Not everyone managed to come out of this period unscarred, but those who did often still speak fondly of a time when life was uniquely expanding or deepening. At that time Nicholas included in his chapter on drugs in *Alternative London* (a guide to 'surviving and thriving' in London of the 1970s) the following extract from *Alice in Wonderland*, which illustrates the enquiring state of mind which prevailed at the time:

The Caterpillar and Alice looked at each other for some time in silence: at last the Caterpillar took the hookah out of its mouth, and addressed her in a languid, sleepy voice.

'Who are *you*?' said the Caterpillar.

This was not an encouraging opening for a conversation. Alice replied, rather shyly, ' I – I hardly know, sir, just at present – at least I know who I *was* when I got up this morning, but I think I must have been changed several times since then.'

'What do you mean by that?' said the Caterpillar sternly. 'Explain yourself!'

'I can't explain *myself*, I'm afraid, sir,' said Alice, 'because I'm not myself, you see.'

'I don't see,' said the Caterpillar.

'I'm afraid I can't put it more clearly,' Alice replied very politely, 'for I can't understand it myself to begin with; and being so many different sizes in a day is very confusing.'

Questions about the meaning of life, and who we are, have always been asked but, in contrast to the 1960s, we entered a time in the late 1970s and the 1980s where it felt as if material concern prevailed. Maybe 'way-out' concepts of the 1960s needed to ground themselves, and Nicholas did this with the development of a 'community' of businesses in Neal's Yard in London. These were set up with ideological principles in mind and all were financially successful. However, as time went on, the ideology faded and he found himself in a somewhat depressed state. Like so many people he started once again to ask the questions: 'What is it all for? Is this all there is to life? Where has the dream gone? What is the dream anyway?', existential questions that have led many back to the spiritual quest.

The second wave

The end of the 1980s produced a second wave of people who were looking for more in life than simply material reward. Unemployment and social divisions had left many disillusioned. Whilst the churches emptied, new age ideas were thriving. The desire to explore different ways of thinking and living led many to creative visualisation, meditation, positive thinking, complementary medicine, ecology and holistic living. Those who had left religion did not seem to have abandoned a search for spirit. The religious 'middle men', like priests and gurus, became less popular, but there was an increased desire to have a direct personal connection with God or the Source or the Spirit, however one wants to name it. The use of mind-altering substances was once again seen as a path to fulfilment.

With the more widespread use of Ecstasy (MDMA), Britain saw, in 1988, the 'second summer of love'. The rave movement took off. A whole new spiritual imagery appeared in clubs, much of it drawn from shamanic roots. The music and the names of many bands and tracks directly referred to the shamanic cultures of the Americas. Whereas in the 1960s the Eastern religions were the centre of attention, now the native American Indians were the inspiration. The rave awakened a sense of tribal belonging. The vast numbers of people, often in big open spaces, the beat of the music, trance dancing, and the open heart connection that Ecstasy brings about, gave people a renewed sense of connectedness with each other. There was a revived interest in ritual. 'A secular society does not train people in ritual experience. The rave brings some of that back,' as Professor Roger Griffin put it.[4]

Nicholas was also part of this movement. He took Ecstasy in 1988 and he always said it changed his life, and for the better:

> When we got off the train I took deep breaths; the air felt wonderful and I realised that I was simply allowing myself to enjoy what had always been there. I looked back and saw that what I had come to accept as my normal state over the past few years was actually a mild depression. For me the experience was just the tonic I needed; ever since, I have felt more positive and healthy...
>
> ...I turned up at midnight just as the E I had taken was coming on. I got into dancing in my usual rather self-conscious way, keeping an eye on what other people were doing and well aware that I was thirty years older than nearly everybody else. Then, imperceptibly, I gradually relaxed, melted into it and knew I was part of it all. There was nothing I might do that would jar because everyone else was simply being themselves, as though they were celebrating their freedom from the constraints and neuroses of society. Although everyone was separately celebrating in their own space, when I looked around I would easily make eye contact – no one was hiding behind a mask. There was virtually no conversation or body contact except for the occasional short hug, but I experienced a feeling of belonging to the group, a kind of uplifting religious experience of unity that I have only felt once before, when I was part of a community (Christiania)* that was

*Christiania is an alternative community in Copenhagen, Denmark, which still exists.

threatened with closure. It was as though we belonged to an exclusive tribe bonded by some shared understanding, yet full 'membership' was mine for the £10 ticket and £15 tablet.

Nicholas decided he wanted to know more about Ecstasy and found that the media were not giving unbiased, or even correct, information. His philosophy in life had always been that adults should be able to make their own choices about what they do with their lives and in order to do so it is important to have access to objective information. So he set out to find out what MDMA was really all about and self-published three books on the subject. New technologies, especially the growth of the World Wide Web, were also at the forefront of this 'second wave', and Nicholas involved himself in this area when he set up the Internet site ecstasy.org, which is the most respected site on the subject in the world, with over three million visits a year.

What is the search for the ultimate high?

There seems to be an inherent longing in people to make sense of, to give sense to, to deeply sense life. To be alive. This state, once experienced, is so profound – as we can see from the accounts in this book – that it at once brings us to the centre of all that is life as well as expands our states of consciousness to embrace the vastness of life. The psychoactives teach us of the world beyond ourselves and at the same time show us the depth within us. They can bring us awareness and promote an awakening.

The breeze at dawn has secrets to tell you
don't go back to sleep
you must ask for what you really want
don't go back to sleep
people walk back and forth across the doorsill
where the two worlds touch
The door is round and open
don't go back to sleep

(Rumi)

Psychoactives can wake us up to the world beyond. Is this world really beyond? Time and space seem to lose their meaning in altered states of consciousness. Linear time is no longer there: there is no sense of 'now is life' and 'later is death'; no sense of 'I am here on earth and cut off from life and souls in other dimensions'. There is a connection to other realities which often seem more real than what we experience in our daily material world. Plato gave us the image of life on earth as living in a cave. All we see are shadows. When we get outside, in the bright light, we see things as they really are. Traditions that do not push death away, in the way that we do in the West, tell us that this is what we experience after we die. The image of the all-illuminating light is a common theme in many spiritual traditions.

It seems to me that the search for the ultimate high involves dying and being reborn. It involves learning about our shadows and our light. It involves facing fears of the unknown and letting go of what does not stand the test of space and time. The practice of letting go of matter and being reborn into spirit. Breathing out and breathing in.

It fascinates me that Nicholas died while searching for the ultimate high. Researching this book, he was on his way to a ritual with a special guide, which he hoped would make sense of many of his previous experiences with psychoactives. He was in the happiest time of his life, he wasn't confused, and he had no desire to escape. He died in a car accident in 1998, no substances involved. 'Just' an accident. He died instantly, in Free State near Kroonstad in a place about which Nelson Mandela said: 'When I visit there, nothing can shut me in. My heart can roam as far as the horizons.'

In 1996 Nicholas had a 'peak experience'. He wrote:

After my first psychedelic trip, I had an even more profound experience on LSD. The setting was perfect: I was with Anja out in the country in a beautiful secluded place on a perfect summer's day. We had made love and were in love, felt calm, relaxed and open to one another. At one point I felt that I was able to let go completely, like never before, and the result was to allow my 'essence' to flow out and to rejoin its source. It was like 'coming home' but far more so. It was incredibly 'right' and joyful and I wept with joy.

We were camping, and that night I stayed awake, savouring the experience and trying to keep it in mind without using words to describe it.

I valued the experience so much that I did not want to describe it in words that might debase it, so I tried hard to think of ways of identifying what happened so that I could recall it, yet without using words with a connotation, like 'soul'.

I also contemplated the experience, and it felt 'natural' in that I felt sure that this was something essentially human, and that it had been experienced by people of all cultures throughout time. In fact, I had the insight that mankind invented religions in order to provide an explanation, or framework, for such experiences, so as to give them validity in our normal consciousness. That is what religions are for, and why people believe in them. I saw how my experience related to the Christian teachings of everlasting life, with God in the other realm of consciousness and Jesus as the link between realms of consciousness.

When he died, would he have recognised the lessons previously taught? Was he able to let go of matter and allow his essence to rejoin its source?

I feel sad that he is not here in body, but somehow manage to feel a happiness when I think of him.

I don't know where he is, but my own experience of life, and the medicine teachers I have had, taught me that there is more than the material reality, visible in daily life.

> life is eternal
> and love is immortal
> and death is an horizon
> and what is an horizon, but the limit of our view?[5]

Psychoactive substances have truly helped many to explore the limits of their views.

A Guide to this Book

To see a World

in a Grain of Sand

and a Heaven in

a Wild Flower,

Hold Infinity in the

palm of your hand,

And Eternity in an hour.

William Blake

*I*n Search of the Ultimate High is a book for people who want to know more about the spiritual uses of psychoactives. The focus is on exploring the *spiritual quest through the use of psychoactives*, rather than focusing on the psychoactives themselves. Throughout the book much space is given to personal accounts. As well as being fascinating stories in themselves, we hope that they will help people who have had a spiritual experience on a psychoactive to better understand it through identifying with someone else's experience.

In the first chapter we look at what is generally understood by the term 'spiritual experience'. We argue that the conventional wisdom that drugs and spirituality are incompatible is misguided if one looks at history, at advances in scientific knowledge, and at contemporary accounts.

We then move on to the various settings in which psychoactives are used. 'A Different Kind of Church' looks at religions which use a psychoactive in a sacramental way. Churches covered range from the well-established ayahuasca churches in South America and the peyote-using Native American Church to the Temple of True Inner Light in New York and the iboga-using Bwiti religion in Gabon. The history and beliefs of each church are described, along with personal accounts from those who have attended services.

The use of psychoactives within world religions such as Christianity, Buddhism and Islam, which is considered in our next chapter, is a subject which is little explored due to the taboo on drug use in most long-established religions. A number of practitioners, such as Buddhist and Benedictine monks, as well as practising Christians, speak out about the way psychoactives have aided them in their chosen path.

In 'Contemporary Shamanism for Westerners' we look at the pleasures and pitfalls of searching for a shaman, the opportunities for 'entheotourism' in the Amazon, and the phenomenon of workshops in the West which incorporate shamanic teachings. We then focus on those psychoactive explorers who seek a spiritual experience outside of the structure of a church or workshop. Many of the accounts in 'Home Users of Psychoactives' come from a survey which was placed on the Internet, and a wide range of experiences and psychoactive substances are covered.

'Rave Spirituality' is the subject of the next chapter. The feelings of over-

whelming love and unity experienced at raves are expressions of a most contemporary form of spirituality. Could that spiritual energy be transforming
society on a wider scale?

'Before, During and After' discusses guidelines that may help to facilitate
and integrate a spiritual experience.

The last part of the book contains more practical information. Sections
on legal and medical aspects can be found here, together with contacts for help
and more information. We provide a short glossary of terms used in this book
and conclude with an extensive annotated bibliography.

Our wish is for this book to provide an insight into the different ways that
psychoactives are used by those who see them as a valuable aid on their spiritual path. In doing so, we aim to contribute to an open discussion about the
potential of psychoactives within spiritual practice.

1

Drugs and Spirituality?

There are more things in heaven and earth, Horatio, than are dreamt of in your philosophy.

William Shakespeare

*I understand,
you are in the grip
of the ineffable
inexpressible...*

J. Caleb Donaldson

Put the words 'spirituality' and 'drugs' together and drop them into ordinary conversation and the immediate reactions from those listening tend to be predominantly surprise, disbelief, even anger. Comments on the utter incompatibility of the two usually follow.

The human search for transcendence, for a glimpse of a different reality, for a touch of the divine, is universal and has always been with us. Seeking to change the chemistry of the brain by a variety of means is a feature of every human society throughout time. It is little wonder that people have sought to combine the two.

Some, such as physician and writer Andrew Weil, believe that the desire to alter consciousness is an innate, normal drive. It can be seen in the way children hold their breath until they faint, or whirl around until overcome by light-headedness. Discouraged from these forms of play, children learn that by crossing the boundaries of consciousness they are entering forbidden territory. In adulthood the desire to suspend ordinary consciousness is often satisfied through socially acceptable means such as alcohol. While awareness of the drive may fade, it will always find outlets, whether through daydreaming or chemicals or a whole variety of means, and Weil believes that

> to try to thwart its expression in individuals and society might be psychologically crippling for people and evolutionarily suicidal for the species. I would not want to see us tamper with something so closely related to our curiosity, our creativity, our intuition, and our highest aspirations.[1]

There are many paths to an altered state of consciousness. For example, fasting, drumming, meditation, sleep deprivation and trance dancing have all been employed throughout history and are still used today. Ingesting perception-altering substances is another long-standing method which has been used for spiritual purposes throughout history in tribal ceremonies, in elaborate religious rituals, and as part of individual spiritual quests. It is only relatively recently that the boundary between drugs and spirituality has been as fixed as it is today.

The Eleusinian Mysteries

1

Three thousand years ago in ancient Greece a mass religious event took place every year in which a sacred brew was drunk by initiates in a ritual setting.

Blessed is he who, having seen these rites,

undertakes the way beneath the Earth.

He knows the end of life,

as well as its divinely granted beginning.

Pindar

The Mysteries were celebrated at Eleusis, from around 1500 BCE to the fourth century CE, in honour of the goddess Demeter and her daughter Persephone. After Persephone's abduction by Hades, god of the underworld, Demeter left Olympus and vowed never to return, nor to allow crops to grow on earth until she and her daughter were reunited. Demeter found refuge in the palace of the king of Eleusis, Keleos, and as a mark of gratitude, she founded a temple there. Fearing that humankind would become extinct without food, Zeus ordered that Persephone be returned so that Demeter would also go back. Before Demeter returned to Olympus she instructed the kings of Eleusis, Keleos and Triptolemus, on how to celebrate the rites in her temple, which were to be 'Mysteries' (secret teachings).

Up to 3,000 people were initiated each year – any Greek-speaking person who had not committed a murder could present themselves once for initiation. Among those initiated were Aristotle, Sophocles, Plato, Cicero and a number of Roman emperors such as Hadrian and Marcus Aurelius. The celebration of the Mysteries began in the autumn, with four days of rites and festivities in Athens. On the fifth day, a solemn procession to Eleusis began, during which rites, sacrifices and purifications took place. On the sixth night, cloaked in secrecy, the climax of the Eleusinian ceremony took place in the inner sanctum of the temple, into which only priests and initiates could enter.

The initiates often experienced in vision the congruity of the beginning and the end, of birth and death, the totality and the eternal generative ground of being. It must have been an encounter with the ineffable, an encounter with the divine...[2]

Before the climax of the initiation, a sacred potion made of barley and mint and called the *kykeon* was administered. The possible psychoactive ingredients in *kykeon* have been hotly debated. It has been suggested that the mint in the mixture might have provided the mind-altering element as the sage family contains the plant *Salvia divinorum*, used by the Mazatec Indians of Mexico in a divinatory context. Terence McKenna has suggested that *Stropharia cubensis*, or another psilocybin-containing mushroom, might be the key.

The most convincing theory about the nature of *kykeon* results from extensive research by Gordon Wasson, Albert Hofmann and Carl Ruck. In *The Road to Eleusis* they argue that the parasitic fungus ergot, found growing on certain wild grasses, is the psychoactive component of *kykeon*.[3] It would have been simple for an Eleusinian priest to collect ergot from the wild grass growing near to the temple, grind it into a powder and add it to the *kykeon*. The theory is further supported by the fact that ergot is commonly found on grain (especially rye), Demeter was the goddess of grain, and ears of grain featured prominently in the ritual.

LSD is a modern synthetic derivative made from components of ergot, providing an intriguing link between the Greek religious rituals of many thousands of years ago, and today's entheogenic explorations.

As Albert Hofmann – inventor of LSD and investigator of the Eleusinian Mysteries – puts it:

> If the hypothesis that an LSD-like consciousness-altering drug was present in the *kykeon* is correct – and there are good arguments in its favour – then the Eleusinian Mysteries have a relevance for our time in not only a spiritual – existential sense, but also with respect to the question of the controversial use of consciousness-altering compounds to attain mystical insights into the riddle of life.[4]

What do we mean by 'a spiritual experience'?

The actual psychoactive ingredient in *kykeon* may still be the subject of debate, but the descriptions of the visions seen by some of those who drank the brew could just as easily have been written today by an ayahuasca-drinking member of the Santo Daime Church or by someone who has had a peak experience on

LSD. So what is it about the experience that can link a Roman emperor and a late twentieth-century spiritual seeker?

Any attempt to define what a spiritual experience is faces an immediate problem in that such experiences are usually deemed to be beyond words (ineffable). However, for a subject which is so intensely personal to those who have experience of it, there is a surprising consensus in the general literature about what constitutes a spiritual or mystical experience.

William James was the first to put the phrase 'religious experience' into general currency with his book *Varieties of Religious Experience* in 1902. He was primarily concerned with the private experience of the individual rather than that of organised religious groups (James defined religion as 'the feelings, acts, and experiences of individual men in their solitude, so far as they apprehend themselves to stand in relation to whatever they may consider the divine'.) He argued that personal religious experience has its 'root and centre' in mystical states of consciousness and identified four main features of a mystical experience:

- ineffability: it cannot be put adequately into words: 'it follows from this that its quality must be directly experienced; it cannot be imparted or transferred to others. In this peculiarity mystical states are more like states of feeling than states of intellect';
- a noetic quality: mystical states also seem to those who experience them to be states of knowledge: 'they are states of insight into depths of truth unplumbed by the discursive intellect';
- transience: mystical states cannot be sustained for long;
- passivity: although a mystical state can be facilitated and prepared for through meditation or other techniques, 'when the characteristic sort of consciousness once has set in, the mystic feels as if his own will were in abeyance, and indeed sometimes as if he were grasped and held by a superior power'.

Mysticism is concerned with the experiential. Some argue that mysticism is at the core of religion, and religion could be seen as the social expression of the inner experience. Even religions which emphasise the separateness of God have a mystical branch which emphasises the feeling that all things are One, from the Sufis within Islam to Kabballah in Judaism to the Rhineland school of Meister Eckhart in Christianity. It can be an uneasy relationship, with mystics throughout history denounced as heretics.

The mystical experience is described by writers and students in all-encompassing terms. Walter Houston Clark,[5] for example, talks of the 'experience of the sacred, the encounter with the holy, which not so much logically, but intuitively, or non-rationally, the subject recognises as that which links him with the seers and the saints of today and yesterday', and Brother David Steindl Rast (a Buddhist monk and writer who now lives a life of solitary contemplation on a mountain) describes the essence of mystical awareness as 'an overwhelming sense of unconditional belonging'.[6] The same feelings have been expressed by people of different ages, from different cultures and different backgrounds.

While the elements of the experience itself appear to be universal, interpretation is dependent on the context within which it takes place. A Christian might interpret the experience as an ascent of the soul or as a coming closer to communion with the saints. A Buddhist, meanwhile, might describe it as reaching a state of eternal nothingness. But the context does not need to be pre-existing belief in a particular faith. While some feel led to convert to a religion after their experience, this is by no means always the case.

> The only faith I had when I had my first spiritual experience was faith that there was no God, only science. At 17 I was a complete doubter, and actually had a long conversation with my brother the night before this one particular trip about how I was so sure that religion was developed to protect the weak from the strong. I figured that the weaker and smaller people made up religion so their butts wouldn't be kicked all the time. Ha!
>
> The next day (April Fool's Day, 1978, my awakening day) we waited for a guy we knew to get home with a fresh batch of moonshiner LSD. When he arrived my brother and I split three hits, it was purple microdot.
>
> We drove around for a while and picked up a friend who was hitchhiking that had just eaten some too. We went down to an elementary school nearby and lay down in the grass. At first the effect was a visual cartoon, like the Flintstones. I started to have auditory hallucinations, soft fart noises, bubble noises and so on. This was the highest I had been till this time and I was very high indeed.
>
> As I was lying there on the grass, I saw the trees around me kinda waving at me. I had one trip before where trees talked to me and told me they loved me. In that trip I saw feet on the bottoms of the trees, and they had eyes all over them. I wrote that trip off as a hallucination, but now it was happening again. So the trees started to communicate with me telepathically,

1

again telling me that they loved me. I was in awe, and started to accept that they were actually communicating with me. They went on and began to rub their leaves together: when doing this a fine gold dust started to fall. It fell to me and covered me, I was covered in shining gold dust. Rainbows filled the sky, grass was reaching to touch me, it felt really neat.

Then, all of the sudden I realised that there is a God, a living spirit from the earth, and it loved me. I couldn't understand that at all, I was so against religion that I was preaching atheism to all my friends. But this experience was so powerful that I was changed in a moment. I was being blessed by these trees, and they kept telling me how they loved me and would protect me. I would not have anything to fear as long as I knew that trees were my friends. They were so happy that I could hear them. I was blown away. Where I had no faith, now I had an unshakeable faith that never left me. What was strange to me was that evolution was one of the main reasons I hadn't believed in God, but the trees kinda explained how science is fact, but it fits in perfectly with God, it is God's thing. It is the Church that is screwed up. I now could see how true this was. The trees were speaking for the earth, and they were speaking directly to me. I was special to them, but they said we all are and that I was only lucky because I could hear them. They would be my friends for ever, and now I have found that all plants and cacti are my friends. So, faith may help in spiritual experiences, but it is definitely not required. If the spirits find it appropriate, no faith in anything is needed. It was the LSD that opened my eyes, but the trees were the ones that taught me about spirituality. I've never had such vivid visual hallucinations like that since. Whatever the reason, it changed my life within an hour. Trees have talked to me on occasions since, and other plants have too. In fact rocks and cliffs have spoken to me also. The earth is alive, and I'm not sure if I can even say it's faith that I believe this is so, it's more like seeing is believing. No force on earth could ever tell me it's not true. I know better, and when trees speak to me I listen. Funny thing is they always have positive things to say. They do love us all.

It was several years later I read that Indians talked with trees and thought it funny that white people couldn't hear them. Well, one white kid heard them in 1978 and never forgot what they said. They can be pretty convincing. Sure are pretty, too.

(Jim, aged 36, USA)

A contemporary view of mystical experience is provided by the Alister Hardy Religious Experience Research Centre in Oxford. Since 1969 the centre has been collecting and analysing written accounts of religious experiences from 'ordinary people'. Alister Hardy, a Darwinian biologist, was fascinated by the way that many people have profound transcendental experiences in which they become 'aware of the presence of a non-physical power which appears to be far greater than their individual self'. He felt that there was little organised knowledge of the phenomenon and set out to explore the subject as objectively as possible. Through articles in newspapers and information leaflets, within the first few months he gathered over 1,000 accounts, which he then classified and stored.

In 1975 the centre conducted the first national survey of reports of religious experience in Great Britain. They asked, 'Have you ever been aware of or influenced by a presence or power, whether you call it God or not, which is different from your everyday self?' Over a third of the population aged 16 and over answered yes to this question.

Today, the centre has over 6,000 accounts and supports local groups that hold discussion meetings about spiritual experience. They continue to collect accounts and now tend to use a looser definition to elicit them, relying more on self-definitions of spirituality rather than Alister Hardy's 'presence of a non-physical power'. Their research seems to indicate that such experiences are widespread, but that the real level of their incidence is hidden because they tend not to be discussed voluntarily by those who have had them. This might be because of the difficulty in talking about such intense, personal events, but also because they are not seen as suitable subjects for discussion in our society. Many of those who sent accounts to the centre said that it was the first time they had talked about their experience, having felt before that they might be seen as odd or crazy, and that they had a sense of great relief in being able to share what had happened to them.

Internet survey of spiritual experiences

For the first-hand accounts in this book we have also chosen to use self-defined notions of what constitutes a spiritual experience. A survey aimed at people who had had a spiritual experience was placed on two Internet sites and over a hundred responses were received. The first question asked was:

'Spiritual' can mean a variety of things. What does it mean to you?

The **transcendent nature** of the experience, the aspect Alister Hardy felt to be of prime importance, was emphasised in many of the replies:

> Spiritual would define for me states in which our centre of reference or core identity is no longer limited to our physical bodies or psychological egos...any hierarchy above our physical reality in a nested hierarchy set would be by definition spiritual, but one feels that the orientation in spiritual states is towards the highest (all-inclusive) one.
>
> By 'spiritual' I mean, in essence, that which goes beyond my personality and the space/time location where my individual consciousness seems to reside.

There was generally a **feeling of 'truth'** or 'rightness' about spirituality – 'you can feel it in your body and mind and it just clicks'. Spiritual experiences were found to be both intense and significant. Their significance lies partly in the idea, articulated by many of the respondents, that they must contain a transformative element. One person described it as 'a kind of "Eureka!" for the subconscious, in which you have no choice but to view/interact with the world in a slightly different way'.

For some the sense of **transformation** is the defining element in spirituality:

> The single most important factor which decides if an experience is spiritual or not, is its mental and emotional effect. If you need 2+ months to digest the experience, if during the trip you have been shown things which make you seriously consider everything you've ever thought about yourself and life in general, it probably was a spiritual experience.

Yet another described how a spiritual experience showed him the path he should take:

> For the last ten years of my life I was plagued with those eternal questions: where do I come from, why am I here? The answer was right under my nose, that I was the answer to my own questions. I *am* here...there is no why, only a choice: spread love and acceptance every day because that is

the kind of world I want to live in...or fumble around looking for some universal truth to make sense of it all. I chose the former.

There came a strong sense from the respondents that spirituality is drawn from within oneself rather than having an external source in a god or supreme power.

> Spirituality to me is not getting in touch with some supreme being or power that lies outside myself. Instead, my spiritual experience has come from getting in touch with power that lies inside self. Realising my potential, who I am, where I fit in this world, all of these are things I consider spiritual.
>
> I am talking about the core of my being...For me it has nothing to do with institutionalised religion.
>
> Spirituality, to me, is getting in touch with the base part of our being, the essence of the spirit. The centre and balance point within us all, that we all have come from and will eventually find again.

For some, the experience was a purely **positive state**:

> To enter a transcendent state where you lose all earthly worries, fears, anticipation...a state of complete contentedness. A state of clarity where thought can happen free of any earthly constraints...
>
> Spiritual to me means having no inhibitions or bad feelings or thoughts about a person, place or thing. Being spiritual to me means total acceptance and trust and, above all, truth.

Others, however, felt that a spiritual experience could also be frightening or disturbing. These people emphasised its **imperative nature**:

> For me spiritual experiences are those experiences which teach one fundamental things about oneself, life and the universe...spiritual experiences don't have to be nice or positive but must feel true. A spiritual experience teaches you what you need and not always what you want.

More about this survey can be found in the chapter 'Home Users of Psychoactives'. For now it is sufficient to note that these respondents describe their experiences in ways William James, Alister Hardy and others would recognise. And all the answers to this first question in the survey come from people who claim to have had a spiritual experience *while on a psychoactive drug*. Each of the respondents regards their experience as truly spiritual, regardless of the fact that it was facilitated by a drug. Drugs and spirituality are clearly not as utterly incompatible as one might suppose.

1

Brain chemistry

The 'incompatibility' argument is also being eroded from another direction. Although much of the workings of the brain remain a complete mystery, recent developments in the field of neuroscience have started to shed light on what happens in the brain when a person is having a peak experience. Research is also being undertaken on the location of the 'God-lobe', as it has been described.

The human brain consists of two distinct hemispheres that can operate independently of each other. The left brain deals with intellect, logic, numeracy and speech; the right with visual–spatial awareness and emotion. Dr Peter Fenwick, a neurophysiologist at the Maudsley Hospital in London, points to the fact that components of a mystical experience such as ineffability, loss of boundaries, intensity of colour, sense of significance and time distortion are all functions of the right hemisphere of the brain.

In the 1930s and 1940s Wilder Penfield conducted pioneering brain-mapping studies by electrically stimulating different parts of the brains of patients who were undergoing neurosurgery. He found that stimulation of the temporal lobes led his patients to report vivid dreamlike memories, feelings of peace, hallucinations and out-of-body experiences. Dr Michael Persinger at Laurentian University in Canada has taken this research one step further. He has developed a method whereby electrical currents can be precisely focused on a particular part of a subject's brain – the temporal lobes – while the subject is sitting in a sensory deprivation chamber wearing a helmet. The outcome is often to induce a mystical experience, of some kind, in the subjects, with visions commonly being reported.

Another area of consciousness that has been the subject of research is sleep and dreaming. Sleep is an altered state of consciousness experienced consistently by all humans and is vital for normal mental health. Dr Serena Roney-Dougal, a parapsychologist, believes there are similarities between the altered state of consciousness that is dreaming, and what happens in the brains of people who have taken the plant-drug ayahuasca. Her theory centres around a small gland in the middle of the brain known as the pineal gland. During sleep the pineal gland also makes a substance called pinoline, which prolongs the action of the neurotransmitter serotonin in the brain by reducing its re-uptake into nerve cells and hence its eventual destruction and has actions somewhat similar to the harmala alkaloids contained in the vine used in ayahuasca. Various tryptamines are formed in the brain, of which DMT (dimethyltryptamine) is one. DMT is also the main psychoactive substance in ayahuasca tea, where it is combined with the harmala alkaloids necessary to protect it against destruction metabolism in the gastrointestinal tract, so making it active when ingested. The drinking of ayahuasca promotes an altered state of consciousness used for insight and healing. If Dr Roney-Dougal's ideas are correct it seems that the brain produces a psychoactive substance in order to reach this state every night.[7]

However, this theory is a controversial one. Dr Jace Callaway of the University of Kuopia, Finland, was the first to look into this hypothesis in 1988. He now feels that the amount of pinoline produced would be too weak to be effective and that there is no existing proof for a 'psychedelic or 'dream' locus. However, his research into 'the kind of stuff that dreams are made on' contin-ues and he believes that:

> it seems a natural function of psychedelic substances, whether
> endogenously produced or exogenously administered, may be to restore a
> sense of inner balance in the mind. The need to enter altered states of mind
> is underscored by the fact that sleep deprivation quickly results in psychotic
> symptoms...The commonality of the psychedelic experience indicates that
> the healthy mind has a capacity and function for such states.[8]

Dr David Nichols of Purdue University believes that it is unnecessary to claim that an endogenous molecule such as DMT is produced in the brain during sleep when it is possible that the brain chemistry simply changes during sleep:

> I am not convinced that there is any unusual molecule produced during
> dreaming that is responsible for the process. I think that the brain is rather
> like a large symphony orchestra. During the daytime it plays melodies by
> 18th century English composers, and during the night, symphonies by

1

dissonant 20th century American composers... All the instruments are there at both times, but depending on the arrangement of the composition, entirely different music comes out. I think that the brain rearranges its neurochemistry at different times so that serotonin released in a particular area in the daytime has an entirely different effect than serotonin released in the same area during the night.[9]

Some might condemn the kind of research detailed here as denying the God-given element of faith. However, exploring the process of how mystical experiences might work within the brain does not have to mean discounting religious experience. Michael Persinger, aware that his work could be seen as reductionist, commented:

It all goes back to your philosophy of reality. Johannes Müller once stated that you are only aware of the states of your nerves. So if a psychotropic drug, or a maintained electrical series of seizures, or even a tumour, effectively induces new connections in the brain, then you may indeed perceive things hidden from others. Even the fact that we can actually insert a God experience doesn't change the fact that the process is there for some functional or evolutionarily significant reason. If one accepts that God created the universe, then why not have a brain mechanism whereby these experiences take place?[10]

As the biochemistry of the brain becomes better understood, the demarcation lines between what is natural and what is unnatural are becoming blurred. Whereas taking drugs might once have been seen as the introduction of an unnatural substance into the human organism, it is becoming increasingly clear that it is more a case of adding chemicals (which may mimic the action of those already in the brain) into an already existing biochemical structure.

Drugs and the search for spirit

We have argued that altering one's consciousness is a normal and necessary desire and can lead to spiritual experience. Seeking to achieve this state through natural or synthetic drugs is one method. However, there are a number of conventional objections to the synergy of drugs and spirituality, beyond the knee-jerk reaction that they are simply incompatible.

Even if the potential link between drugs and spirituality is accepted, it is then commonly argued that it is too easy to have a spiritual experience on drugs and so the experience has less worth than one achieved through hard graft. This is a questionable argument given that there is no evidence that mystical experiences are more likely to occur after arduous spiritual practice. They can equally occur unpredictably and suddenly. Besides, using drugs with serious intent is not necessarily easy, as is shown in many of the accounts later in the book. Mentally, one may be forced to confront difficult personal issues. Physically, nausea, vomiting, stomach cramps and dehydration are among the delights in store for drug-using spiritual seekers.

A variation on the 'too easy' argument is that drugs provide a quick route to a mystical state which by its very speed can cause difficulties. This is a more serious objection. The loss of previously taken-for-granted certainties can cause real problems. A sudden dissolving of the ego, common to both spiritual experiences and powerful drug journeys, can be terrifying. As the spiritual teacher Ram Dass points out: 'you've got to have a somebodyness before you can have a nobodyness. Drugs for kids aren't so cool because they screw around with nobodyness too soon and then they don't know where they are. You've got to have a somebodyness to come back to.' Later in this book we discuss ways to help avoid the difficulties caused by a sudden paradigm shift. Careful preparation, where possible, and integration of the experience afterwards are key factors in turning difficult situations into valuable experiences.

Finally, the danger of physical illness or addiction, or mental breakdown as a result of drug use – the reasons cited by governments for the illegality of psychoactive drugs – tend to come up in debates about the value of mixing drugs and spirituality. Drugs *do* have the potential to cause great harm. Used out of hopelessness or helplessness, poverty and desperation, as an escape route, they can ruin lives. Addiction, and the damage caused by addiction, is a serious problem in most societies.

But the picture is not as simplistic as that generally painted by governments and the media. The differences between drug *use* and drug *abuse* has to be recognised. Differences between various types of drug must also be recognised. Simply lumping them all into the same bag does not provide for a reasoned, informed debate.

In this book we are talking about very specific drug-using situations and also a specific class of drugs. Psychoactives such as LSD, magic mushrooms and ayahuasca are not known to be particularly addictive. Certainly, they are regarded as having far less addictive potential than such socially sanctioned drugs as nicotine and alcohol. They are even used to help sufferers out of addictions to heroin, alcohol and cocaine.*

Clearly, not all spiritual experiences are drug-induced, and not all drug experiences are necessarily spiritual. We are talking about drug use as a path, a technique, which has been used for thousands of years as a way in which to enter a state that aids mysticism. Not every LSD trip is spiritual, in the same way that one would not expect to have life-changing communication with the divine every time one struck a yoga position or played bongo drums. Andrew Weil again:

> Drugs are merely means to achieve states of non-ordinary awareness and must not be confused with the experiences themselves. They have the capacity to trigger highs; they do not contain highs. Moreover, the experiences they trigger are essentially no different from experiences triggered by more natural means. Many of the dangers attributed to drugs have no basis in fact but arise entirely from our own fears.[11]

Putting it to the test: the Good Friday Experiment

Spiritual experiences can occur out of the blue but they can also be facilitated. This can be seen in the Good Friday Experiment, one of the most significant psychedelic experiments in the scientific literature. It used scientific methods to test the hypothesis that psychedelic drugs can help facilitate spiritual experiences when used by religiously inclined people in a religious setting. As well as data and conclusions from the original experiment, there is also now a long-term follow-up study providing further support to the original findings.

The experiment took place on Good Friday 1962 at Boston University. At that time, there was no law against psychedelic drugs, or even much public prejudice about them. In fact, LSD was seen as an exciting new drug with great

* Both ibogaine and ayahuasca are currently being used to treat drug addiction. There is more information about this in the chapter 'Contemporary Shamanism for Westerners'.

therapeutic potential and in Britain over 10,000 psychiatric patients were treated with it.

The subjects in the experiment were postgraduate students studying theology at Boston University, and the experiment was conducted by Walter Pahnke, a physician and minister, as part of his PhD in 'Religion and Society'. None of the students had taken a psychoactive drug before, so they were prepared for the effects by attending classes given by experienced assistants who were careful not to use any religious terminology. The classes were designed principally to build trust between the participants, allay their fears and encourage them to go with the experience.

The Good Friday service was conducted by a charismatic preacher in the main chapel of the university, and broadcast into the self-contained basement chapel that contained an altar, pews and stained-glass windows. By anchoring the experiment within the existing framework of the participants' beliefs, Pahnke was aiming to create an atmosphere similar to that achieved by tribes who use natural psychedelic substances in religious ceremonies.

One and a half hours before the service, all twenty volunteers were given identical-looking capsules. However, while half the capsules contained psilo-cybin (an extract from psychoactive mushrooms), the others contained placebos. The experiment was conducted in standard double blind fashion: neither researchers nor participants knew who had the 'real thing'. But this was even more clever than usual, as the placebo was 'active': it contained nico-tinic acid, a drug which was not psychedelic but produced a feeling of warmth and tingly skin. The result was that all participants felt something, and were equally expectant.

Immediately after the experiment the participants were given a ques-tionnaire to evaluate their experience, and again six months later. The result was that eight out of ten of those who had psilocybin were evaluated as having had a strong spiritual experience. None of the controls had high scores, but some did appear to have had mildly spiritual experiences. This may have been due to 'contact high',[12] or it may simply be that they would have had them anyway, given the setting.

So, how was the mystical experience measured? Pahnke designed a ques-tionnaire which included these categories:

Unity: loss of ego or sense of underlying oneness. This meant remaining fully conscious of surroundings while becoming unaware of oneself; or it could mean that all living things shared the same energy.

Transcendence of time and space. The experience was not ruled by clock time or geographical location. Sometimes this was described as eternity or infinity.

Sacredness: a feeling of awe. No religious beliefs or terminology need be involved.

Paradoxicality: this quality meant that the experience had to have elements that are logically contradictory.

Ineffability: or the inability to describe the experience adequately in words.

Transiency: the experience is transitory, does not last.

Positive mood: a deeply felt sense of well-being, with the most universal elements being joy, blessedness and peace.

In addition, a test was devised to see whether the experience produced positive life-changing behaviour. This was assessed at the six-month follow-up by asking the subjects whether they had experienced an increase or a decrease in their feelings of happiness, joy, peace, reverence, creativity, anxiety and so on. They were also asked if they had experienced changes in their relationships with others and whether they thought their behaviour had changed in positive or negative ways.

The results clearly supported Pahnke's hypothesis that psilocybin, when taken in a religious setting by people who are religiously inclined, can facilitate valid spiritual experiences. He also found that the subjects who received the psilocybin experienced positive and persisting effects in attitude and behaviour.

In the six-month follow-up, Pahnke found that:

life-enhancing and enriching effects similar to some of those claimed by mystics were shown by the higher scores of the experimental subjects when compared to the controls...the experimenter was left with the impression that the experience had made a profound impact...on the lives of eight out of ten of the subjects who had been given psilocybin. Although the psilocybin experience was unique and different from the 'ordinary' reality of their everyday lives, these subjects felt that this experience had motivated them to appreciate more deeply the meaning of their lives, to gain more depth and authenticity in ordinary living, and to rethink their philosophies of life and values.[13]

Time magazine summarised these results by saying that: 'All students who had taken the drug psilocybin experienced a mystical consciousness that resembled those described by saints and ascetics'. This was actually an exaggeration, as one subject had freaked out completely and was tranquillised using Thorazine, but Walter Houston Clark declared that 'there are no experiments known to me in the history of the scientific study of religion better designed or clearer in their conclusions than this one'.[14]

A follow-up to the Good Friday Experiment was carried out about twenty-five years later by Rick Doblin of the Multi-disciplinary Association for Psychedelic Studies (MAPS). He managed to get seventeen of the original twenty subjects to answer the same questionnaire again, and also recorded personal interviews. Many of these people had been clergymen for over twenty years, and some had had spiritual experiences since, both with and without drugs. Rick Doblin found that:

> All psilocybin subjects participating in the long-term follow-up, but none of the controls, still considered their original experience to have had genuinely mystical elements and to have made a uniquely valuable contribution to their spiritual lives. The positive changes described by the psilocybin subjects at six months, which in some cases involved basic vocational and value choices and spiritual understandings, had persisted over time and in some cases had deepened.
>
> The overwhelmingly positive nature of the reports of the psilocybin subjects are even more remarkable because this long-term follow-up took place during a period of time in the United States when drug abuse was becoming the public's number one concern, with all the attendant social pressure to deny the value of drug-induced experiences. The long-term follow-up interviews cast considerable doubt on the assertion that mystical experiences catalysed by drugs are in any way inferior to non-drug mystical experiences in both their immediate content and long-term positive effects.[15]

Drugs and spirituality

In 1953 the writer Aldous Huxley took mescalin. He had an overwhelming experience which he later described in *The Doors of Perception* and *Heaven and Hell*, books which are now classics of drugs literature.

He wrote of his experience:

> I am not so foolish as to equate what happens under the influence of mescalin or of any other drug, prepared or in future preparable, with the realisation of the end and the ultimate purpose of human life: Enlightenment, the Beatific vision. All I am suggesting is that the mescalin experience is what Catholic theologians call 'a gratuitous grace', not necessary to salvation but potentially helpful and to be accepted thankfully, if made available. To be shaken out of the ruts of ordinary perception, to be shown for a few timeless hours the inner and outer world, not as they appear to an animal obsessed with survival or to a human being obsessed with words and notions, but as they are apprehended, directly and unconditionally, by Mind at Large – this is an experience of inestimable value to anyone.[16]

Nearly fifty years after Huxley wrote this, the 'inestimable value' of the psychedelic experience with regard to spirituality is still not accepted in society. This is despite the fact that people have been altering their consciousness by taking psychoactive substances for many thousands of years, and spiritual experiences induced by drugs are clearly as 'authentic' as spiritual experiences facilitated by any other method.

However, developments within biochemistry and neuroscience are breaking down boundaries and challenging previously accepted orthodoxies in many different (and equally controversial) areas. Research into the role of endogenous chemicals in the brain, into the existence of a 'God-lobe', into the nature of consciousness itself should lead to a body of knowledge being built up in this field which will support the case that drugs are not alien to the body but part of it.

It may be that it is through scientific arguments, allied with growing knowledge of the practices of indigenous people and interest in more individual modes of religious expression, that drugs and spirituality are no longer seen as incompatible.

2

A Different Kind of Church

Our birth is but a sleep and a forgetting:

The Soul that rises with us, our life's Star

hath had elsewhere its setting

And cometh from afar;

Not in entire forgetfulness,

And not in utter nakedness,

But trailing clouds of glory do we come

From God, who is our home.

William Wordsworth

What guarantee is there that the five
senses, taken together, do cover the whole
of possible experience?...
There are gaps between the fingers;
there are gaps between the senses.
In these gaps is the darkness which hides
the connection between things...
The darkness is the source
of our vague fears and anxieties,
but also the home of the Gods.

Alan Watts

Whilst mainstream religions generally shy away from the use of drugs, there are organised religious groups who base their beliefs and rituals around the use of a psychoactive substance. Many of those which originate in South America have their roots in shamanic beliefs and practices but have also incorporated Christian elements, in part due to the influence of Christian missionary activity in that part of the world. Three of the churches covered here have that history and all use the rainforest plant brew, ayahuasca. These are the Santo Daime, Barquinha and Uniao do Vegetal churches. All three started in Brazil, but the Santo Daime and Uniao do Vegetal now have churches all over the world.

Other, much smaller, groups also use the visionary ayahuasca tea but have moved further away from the shamanic/Christian path to embrace other beliefs such as Hinduism and Buddhism. An example is the Gnostisismo Revolutionario de la Concienca de Krishna, a small spiritual community based in the Colombian rainforest and founded on Gnostic principles.

Another example of the mix of indigenous and imported beliefs is the Bwiti religion in Gabon, West Africa. The sacrament used – iboga – comes from the root bark of a shrub, and is a relative newcomer to the Western psychedelic scene. The Bwiti initiation rite takes up to a week and involves the initiate consuming massive amounts of iboga and entering a near-death state. The Bwiti has been called 'an exemplary case of "psychedelic", or, better, "entheogenic" religion' by Giorgio Samorini, who was the first white man to be initiated into a Bwiti sect. We include parts of his account of the initiation experience in this chapter.

Moving on to North America, the peyote cactus-using Native American Church is perhaps the best known 'psychedelic religion'. It holds a unique position in the American legal system, and peyote ceremonies and vision quests are held all over the world.

Another very well-known plant-using religion is Rastafarianism, in which marijuana is considered to be a holy herb. Originating in Jamaica, there are now Rastafarians worldwide.

In contrast to these syncretic churches which use plant-based psychoactives, the Temple of the True Inner Light in New York City uses a synthetic substance, dipropyltyramine. Later in the chapter, the executive editor of *High*

Times magazine offers his personal description of a visit to the Temple.

These religions, spanning different continents, using different substances and incorporating different beliefs, give an indication of the wide variety of active psychedelic religions which currently exist.

In many ways, taking a psychoactive with spiritual intent along with others who have the same commitment, in a religious environment, can be an ideal situation for some people. There will be experienced elders who can provide support and new attendees usually receive guidance before the ceremony. It is likely to be a very safe setting in which to take a psychoactive in terms of spiritual and material support.

2

Generally, these religions prefer new people to be introduced on a personal recommendation from another member, and will expect someone attending a ceremony for the first time to be able to give clear reasons as to why they want to attend, what their previous experience with psychoactives is, and what they expect from the ceremony. People who go expecting a workshop-style experience may be surprised. It should not be forgotten that these are religious groups with particular religious beliefs. The service may well be highly structured and quite formal. Hymns may be sung and prayers held. The emphasis tends to be on the communal aspect rather than on the individual's process of exploration. These are groups who are serious about their faith; this is demonstrated in the way it is often referred to as 'the work'. The psychoactive is truly used as a sacrament, fully incorporated into the ceremony.

Santo Daime

The Santo Daime Church, founded in Brazil but now spreading all over the world, is best known for its use of the psychoactive plant drug ayahuasca. The mix used by the Santo Daime consists of the bark of a vine, *Banisteriopsis caapi*, which contains harmine, and leaves of a plant called *Psychotria viridis* which contains dimethyltryptamine (DMT). Also known as yage, 'vine of the soul' and caapi, ayahuasca can produce visions and insights, and in Santo Daime services these are integrated into a collective religious experience. The doctrine of the Santo Daime includes beliefs from both Christianity and nature religions, and the services, at least in Brazil, are strongly community affairs.

The vision overwhelms me. 'I' disappear and merge with my environment, with the large wooden, hexagonal church in the middle of the Amazon rainforest. I become part of the surrounding jungle, part of the starry firmament above, part of the energy happening of the Daime ritual – no, not a part, I am all that, it has sucked me in, dragged me along in the universal flow of the universal longing which is the soul of our living globe.

The Daime vision transforms my perception, or is it refinement? Complex, geometrical patterns are superimposed on my vision, reminiscent of aboriginal tattoo patterns or those found on traditional weavings – living, four-dimensional ornaments, which tend to densify in some places to draw me into other spaces, into other, parallel, worlds. The room, meanwhile, is filled with a thundering roar coming out of multiple dimensions. It feels as if thousands of gigantic ventilators are blowing a mighty storm on and through us, carrying me away in a cosmic flight. And then the hymn sung by hundreds of throats draws me back down here, to the 'trabalho', the ritual work, to the precise rhythmical and vocal performance of this 114th hymn out of the 129 hymns of Master Irineu's hymnal. It is like meditation, back to the Self, to the mantra, to the here and now, in spite of the astral vision which wants to carry me away, out of my body – back here to the steps of the dance, the strokes of the marac, the lines of the hymn.

Often, when the Daime unfolds its full force in me, I have to sit down, just before my legs give way under me. Some participants just collapse and are carried away by the helpers, the 'fiscals', to a space behind the lines of dancers. Overwhelmed by the inner vision I then sometimes stretch out and let the spirit of the Daime do its healing work, while 'I' step aside and let go completely, in an attitude of 'Thy Will be done'. The Daime spiritually impregnates each and all fibres of my being, of my consciousness. My body, jerking and twitching, remembers the passage in the birth channel, then, total let go, I am Mother, Father, Son, Holy Ghost in the intra-uterine, pre-worldly paradise, merged into the 'sap' of the universe, where every ending is a beginning and where all beginning ends, where all is simultaneous, good and bad, strong and weak, right and wrong, birth and death, where everything has its own value and its proper truth, where all roads lead to everywhere...

(Dieter, aged 28, Germany)

How it began

The Santo Daime Church was founded in 1930 by Raimundo Irineu Serra. Irineu, born in Brazil in 1902, reached adulthood at the time of the great Brazilian rubber boom. He migrated in 1922, along with many other young Brazilians, from the north-eastern drought-ridden region of Brazil to the Amazonian rainforest where the rubber trade was thriving. He spent six years in the new town of Xapuri, in Acre, working as a rubber-tapper.

2

While learning the rubber trade, he was also serving a spiritual apprenticeship with the Peruvian Indians with whom he worked. Irineu had been brought up a Catholic, but he now came into contact with spiritism (religion based on the spirits of plants and animals) and native Indian beliefs. He tried the sacred ayahuasca tea and was shown the correct way to prepare it. He was taught methods for journeying into ecstatic states, and learned how to integrate the visions and knowledge he brought back from those journeys.

Irineu's first significant vision was of a divine lady, sitting in the moon, who told him he must retreat into the forest for eight days with only ayahuasca to drink and only macacheira (boiled manioc) to eat. During this retreat Irineu had visions of the 'Forest Queen' who told him that he must start a new faith in which the ayahuasca drink (to be called 'daime', meaning 'give me' in Portuguese) would be central. She would show him how the daime was to be used as a sacrament and guide him through the initial hostilities he and his followers would face.

Irineu started his new church in Rio Branco, the capital of Acre, in 1930. He was still receiving visions from the Forest Queen and he also channelled hymns. Collections of these hymns became the Church's principal guide.

Irineu died in 1971, but his work was continued by one of his key followers, Sebastiao Mota de Melo (who became known as Padrinho Sebastiao). He held Daime works ('services') with his family and friends until his death in 1990. Leadership passed to his son, Padrinho Alfredo Gregorio de Melo, who remains President of the organisation and its main spiritual leader.

> The first glass was strong enough to give interesting hallucinations, the second glass, as always accompanied by Santa Maria (pure cannabis), was quite strong. I could not stop yawning. At the same time I had feelings of complete unity. I was experiencing an all-embracing feeling of unity, of love and of wisdom. I caught out my own petty-mindedness. Why did I have all

these prejudices against Christianity, prejudices I don't have against other religions? Under the influence of Santo Daime and Santa Maria I could get rid of any prejudice, in fact I got rid of any judgement. I saw the ritual as something that passes by, as something not so important in comparison with what I was experiencing. I was communicating with an all-enfolding unity, a very great and high female spirit. I was weeping for a long time during the ritual, weeping for the love, wisdom and unity I was experiencing.

(Arno, aged 38, Holland)

Beliefs

The basis of the Santo Daime belief system is Christian, and the hundred or so hymns which Irineu received in his lifetime are considered to be a Third Testament of the Gospel of Christ. Santo Daime theology is, however, highly syncretic and includes beliefs from other religions in Brazil. The members feel a strong connection with the rainforest. Nature in general is revered, and is personified by the Forest Queen, or Virgin Mary.

The spirit of the ayahuasca vine is the teacher. The vine gives 'strength' and the leaf gives 'light', or the capacity for visions. These notions are often evident in the words of Irineu's hymns: 'daime forca, daime amor, daime luz' ('give me strength, give me love, give me light'). The Church believes that the visions produced by the Daime are not 'hallucinations' which have nothing to do with reality but are, in fact, the truest guide to reality. The tea is also seen as perfectly balanced, with the vine representing masculinity and the leaf signifying the feminine. The importance of the Daime to the doctrine of the Church cannot be overemphasised. A Santo Daime leader, Alex Polari de Alverga, states that 'the Santo Daime Doctrine evolved directly out of communion with this living sacrament'.[1] The Church itself describes its doctrine as being centred on the consecration of the Daime 'within the context of the Christian culture and symbolism and taking advantage of the American Indian, Brazilian, African and eastern transcendental wisdom'.[2]

Each Santo Daime community is headed by a padrinho or madrinha who acts as a guide to initiates. They stress, however, that the primary spiritual relationship is with the Daime and that it is Daime that should act as the main guide and teacher. When initiates encounter problems they should work directly on these themselves with the knowledge given to them by the Daime, although they can also consult their padrinho.

Initiates are members who have participated in a number of Santo Daime works and are ready to affirm that Daime is their sacrament, guide and master and that it has helped them to get in touch with their own 'divine light'. The initiate becomes part of the community of the Santo Daime.

2

> In a previous ritual I had the choice of a 'double consciousness': I could experience my visionary state and at the same time realise my existence in daily reality. Now something completely different was going on: it was impossible to experience daily reality, the only option I had was the visionary state, and that state was frightening.
>
> It had all changed 180 degrees: I wanted to be back on earth, but I could not get there. Every time I closed my eyes I left earth behind me, and I could not keep my eyes open and stay in the normal world...I told myself to be relaxed. It was just half an hour after I took my third glass of ayahuasca and I knew the effects would last for some time to come. I tried to calm down. 'Don't worry, life goes on,' I said to myself. It didn't work. I was convinced it all would end in a miserable way, I would never return to earth.
>
> **(Arno, aged 38, Holland)**

Community

By 1975 the Church had grown so much that a spiritual community composed of forty-five families was set up on the outskirts of Rio Branco. The aim was to achieve deeper harmony and union among Daime members through living and working together. The community found it increasingly difficult to survive as rubber-tappers due to the destruction of the rainforest around them, and Padrinho Sebastiao began to have visions in which the rainforest called to them to leave the city and move back to the forest. Eventually, in 1981, they settled in Ceu de Mapia (Heaven of Mapia), where they still live today. The community's home was safeguarded in 1989 by a decision by the Brazilian government to create a National Forest in the rainforest surrounding Ceu de Mapia, and they form the centre of a half-million-acre protected reserve. There are now about 700 people there, living an ecologically aware lifestyle. The strong sense of community and history among Santo Daime worshippers in Brazil shows that a *collective* religious experience occurs in the services, rather than an isolated individual journey. The Santo Daime also creates a strong form of community in other parts of the world. People may not necessarily live together as in Mapia, but the regular meetings enhance a bond between members. The madrinha or padrinho has an obligation to give advice and care for the members of the Church. This is done from a sense of calling rather than for financial gain. Members do contribute financially, to support not only their own group, but also the leaders, members and the Church in Brazil. Leaders from Brazil regularly visit churches in other places. In this way a sense of worldwide community is fostered.

> I was somewhere else, far, far away. I was not in this life any more. I was playing a game, I was in different lives, and every life was a game. I saw an opportunity in the game, and took my chances. I was horrified to discover where I ended: in this body in a Santo Daime ritual in March 1996. I could not have been more shocked if I had ended up as a purple worm on the planet Mars, 8,000 years ago. Did I really have to live this life? In this body? What a disappointment! I completely understood the illusionary nature of daily reality. Why did I have to go through this again? I did not want to go back to earth. I did not want to go back to this life.
>
> **(Arno, aged 38, Holland)**

Legal status

In Brazil, CONFEN (the Federal Drug Council) studied the Santo Daime, following long-running stories in Brazil's populist press claiming that the Church brainwashed followers, exploited the doctrine for touristic purposes and exported ayahuasca illegally.

An inquiry in 1987 concluded that Daime had a positive influence on the community and encouraged social harmony and integration. The report warned against looking at the pharmacological aspect of the Church in isolation and without its religious, social and cultural context. In June 1992 CONFEN stated definitively that the use of the ayahuasca drink was legal. CONFEN representatives had visited Ceu de Mapia and taken part in rituals. They found no evidence of harmful effects or potential for abuse of ayahuasca.

So far no country other than Brazil has officially permitted the use of ayahuasca for religious purposes and DMT is prohibited all over the world apart from those exceptions in Brazil. This has caused remarkably few problems, although in Holland the police did raid a service and take away a sample. But instead of the charge being possession of an illicit drug, prosecution was brought under the Public Health Act because the tea contained too many bacteria! In Italy, Germany and Japan the police have also taken samples for analysis but no charges have been brought. Followers have said that this is because they are 'protected', but an alternative explanation could be that the tea contains too little DMT to show up in the tests: psychoactive effects can be produced by harmine alone, although the visual effects are not strong.

2

Anja's account

I had read and heard about ayahuasca and was interested but apprehensive until a Dutch friend of mine told me about her experiences. She had felt a connection with her mother, and all mothers and spiritual teachers, but what convinced me most of all was her liveliness the next day. She was open and gentle and, with a glint in her eyes, said she would never be the same again.

We borrowed the required white clothes and rode on the back carriers of our friends' bikes to the venue, where we had to be vetted by the head of the Amsterdam church. When I arrived in the room, not having eaten for some time as was prescribed, I felt rather strange and sceptical at the sight of all these women with their dark blue pleated skirts and white shirts, while the men wore dark ties and a brass star that resembled that of a sheriff. This was not my style at all. The room had striplights, a table in the middle with images of Mary and Christ, and I thought: well, we'll see, but I'm not going to be converted here! However when I met the madrinha, the woman leader of the church, I was amazed at her bright eyes, vigour, open-heartedness and warmth. She also seemed very down to earth. I knew it would be OK and could trust the ceremony. I still felt uncomfortable, though, having to sit with my chair exactly in line with the others. The woman next to me did not seem to want to share her booklet of songs, so I humbly sat listening to all these Dutch people who were singing their hearts out in Portuguese. I had no idea what it was all about, but it sounded quite jolly. Occasionally there were Our Fathers and Hail Marys in Dutch. This triggered all sorts of feelings, because I knew them well from my childhood. What a strange experience to be back here in my home town Amsterdam, where one of the biggest Santo Daime communities in Europe is based, amongst all these Dutch people deeply involved in a Brazilian church, singing in Portuguese with a Dutch accent.

It was time for the 'tea'... We were directed to get up in a line and follow a precise route to a side table with a Brazilian elder behind it, just like going up to the altar to receive Holy Communion. When it came to my turn, I was brave. The taste was truly disgusting.

We went back to our designated places and I closed my eyes. I waited expectantly and some moving geometric shapes in electric colours appeared. I felt myself travelling in a bigger space. I also began to feel nauseous. 'Where is the little white bucket? Ah, thank God, it's near'. I took it and felt like I could really throw it up, but that would certainly make quite a noise as it hit the plastic bottom. I had not heard anyone making this sound and was not sure if it was the appropriate thing, so I held back and let out a little bit. Later I realised that was a shame, because it blocked me somewhat from then on and it would have been fine to let it all out. What really moved me was the woman who took my bucket and replaced it with a new one. She then disappeared quietly to clean up my vomit, leaving me with an incredible sense of humility. I got an image of a kind of bowl, a holding vessel and a ball, floating, searching for a fitting place. The ball slotted into the bowl and came to rest. The image was simple, but the insight I got was about conception: the place of rest being the beginning of life. This was not a thought process in words so much as the sort of sensation one can get when being absorbed by a film.

After some more singing and praying, we were called to have some more Daime. The Padrinho enthusiastically called 'Daime! Dai - me!' Many people joined in, eager to get further into it and have some more 'tea'. If the taste the first time was bad, the second time was definitely worse, probably because I anticipated that it would make me feel sick. However, in the hour that followed I realised that I could actually control my nausea. Once we had settled back in our places, the announcement was made: 'Santa Maria!' and the helpers immediately passed round joints. A neighbour told me to inhale three times: for the sun, the moon and the stars. So I did.

Then I found myself in a world between this life and the next. I had seen my hands turning blue, then white and waxy, the fingers curling up like dead hands. It did not disturb me in the slightest. I looked at my hands and thought: yes, that is what they look like when they're dead. In this in-between world, I had a choice either to go to the light, which I knew would be the best thing to do, or to go back to the earthly world I came from, back in my body, back to the people and situations that had been part of my life. When I was moving back into my body, I felt sick and nauseous, but if I concentrated fully and precisely, I could move out of it into another vibration, which would lead me to the light. My focus needed to be one hundred per cent though. As soon as I connected with my body, or the material world, it was as if I 'fell' back into it and my stomach started turning over again.

2

I was aware that I had a yes/no choice all the time. On the one hand it was obvious that I did want to go to the light and not feel sick, but I was surprised how difficult it was to keep full concentration and how strong the attraction of my body was, even though it made me feel horrible. Many pictures of situations and people in my life flashed past. It was as if I sat at a computer and clicked quick yes/no choices on each of them. I could go into any if I wished. It went so quickly that I cannot remember all the images, but one I do remember, which was a picture of my ex-husband. In a flash I could see all his pain and suffering and I felt a compassion for him which I had not felt since we separated.

The service ended with lots of songs. I had to stand during the singing, which I found quite difficult. I desperately wanted to lie down but that was clearly not an option. In fact there were no options: we all had to sing, stand and sit down together in a way that strongly resembled a Christian church service. At first I felt resentment for this restraint since I held the belief that psychedelics were to do with letting go and exploring. On reflection later, however, I saw how this could be of value in focusing each person's experience on the common aim of the ritual. The discipline provided a secure setting in which to allow the congregation to go deeply into the religious experience, while discouraging individuals from flying off into other realms.

By the time we finished, I was quite awake, bright and grounded.

I had been absorbed in my own world; it had been a very mental world, with little feeling. It took me a little while before I could make sense of it. It's not every day I practise dying.

John's account

I am an academic, specialising in one of the 'hard' sciences, male, late fifties, married but with no children.

For much of my adult life I have suffered from chronic depression at a sub-critical level – what I once heard R.D. Laing describe as being in a continuous state of 'driving with the brakes on'. I was brought up in Roman Catholicism and didn't finally move away from it (to whatever extent I have done so) until my late thirties.

But for an encounter with some 'new' therapies in my early forties I suspect that I would now have been swallowed up by depression. Instead I still keep walking the road. Two influences were instrumental in directing my footsteps towards the Santo Daime ritual – extended experience of Stan Grof's 'holotropic breathwork'* (a therapeutic tool which emerged from Grof's earlier pioneering work with LSD) and my own brief encounter in the late 1980s with Ecstasy and LSD under psychotherapeutic conditions. Both of these cemented my interest in the healing potential of altered states and reinforced a long-held conviction that my depression was, at its core, a spiritual crisis – the sickness of a soul which could not find God. Hence I have never seen any distinction – for myself, at least – between psychotherapeutic healing and spiritual healing.

About four years ago two close and trusted Dutch friends began to tell me about the Santo Daime church in Amsterdam which they had been attending regularly for some time, describing the Daime ritual as one of the most powerful exercises in 'letting go' that they had ever encountered. As someone who is a past master in not letting go (and, as it happens, is particularly phobic about vomiting – which I knew to be characteristic of ayahuasca rituals) I was deeply attracted by the notion of trying to surrender to the Santo Daime in a religious context, supported by a community all of whom were facing the same struggle. And underneath all this – but even more important – there was, of course, the faint hope of experiencing a long-sought touch of the divine.

The ritual began with prayers in Dutch, among which I was able to recognise the Our Father and Hail Mary. Vigorous hymn-singing in Portuguese followed but I rapidly lost my place in my hymnal and just hummed along with the melodies. Quite soon – far too soon for me – everyone stood up and began to move in line, women and men separately, towards a table at the rear of the room to receive the Daime. All that I had read about ayahuasca rituals had emphasised the absolutely revolting taste of the liquid. To my immense

*A method of breathing that enables an altered state of consciousness.

surprise it wasn't even remotely as bad as I had expected – not unlike tomato juice but with an unpleasant acrid after-taste.

I returned to my seat quite elated, hoping – since the taste of the Daime was tolerable – that the rest of the experience might not be so bad either. Soon I noticed that the spatial relationships between everything in my field of vision had begun to take on a strangeness and subtle sense of significance. Then my body began to feel strange too. Looking across the altar table at two of the female initiates I saw patterns of broad black lines – which, I was certain, were tribal markings – on their faces. This was a deeply moving moment for me – a powerful reassurance that I had not merely joined a group of middle-class Dutch people to experiment with psychotropics. Instead it seemed a witness, a sign, that there was something present among us which was power-fully connected with the culture and spirituality from which the Daime originated. Now the visual effects began to get more dramatic. My ability to judge distances became distorted and I began to see the edges of everything I looked at outlined by tiny rainbows or little coloured fluorescent lights.

2

My body began to shake and my face to contort. Initially I tried hard to remain in my seat at the altar, close to the focus of the ritual – but the shaking got progressively worse so I went to lie down on one of the gym mats which were provided at the periphery of the room. A helper laid a blanket over me with what seemed an infinite tenderness, which I found extremely moving. I thought: Now I can just let the shaking happen. But it wasn't so simple. I dis-covered that I had – so it seemed – to float up from some calm motionless place and make the shaking happen. And it came to me that the shaking, contortions and all, although they seemed involuntary, were actually manifestations of a struggle to avoid the calm place – and also, for some reason, to give me an excuse for not going back to my place at the altar. In a fashion that is all too characteristic of my normal behaviour pattern, I received this important reve-lation but put it to one side and went ahead to 'make' the shaking and contortions continue.

Another thing that I remember from this period is feeling – because I had left the central group – that I was one of the failures, one of the fallen ones, the ones that couldn't keep faith. I found myself wondering whether there was a place in the scheme of things for us weak ones, fallen ones. And then I suddenly thought: this is supposed to be a religious ritual, this is supposed to be a going to God, and I badly wanted reassurance that there was indeed a God to go to. The answer was instantaneous: what a silly question – of course there is! Now, I would have expected this experience to be one of intense emotion. On the contrary, it was just an utterly matter-of-fact realisation that God is, and God is in me and God is in everything, not concentrated as a God 'out there', but God none the less. No doubt my lack of emotional response reflected the fact that I had secretly ached for contact with a manifestation of a personal God.

So I lay on the mat and I shook and felt very nauseated. Eventually one of the initiates came and tapped me on the shoulder and asked me quietly if I would like to go for some more Daime? I felt reluctant but got to my feet and stood there, feeling my whole body shaking, almost falling over. Reassuring myself, 'Well this is what is, this is what is. This just is', I put my hands in a gesture of openness and staggered forward, somehow following the line. After drinking, I made my way back to the mattress and lay down. Again I began to shake, and from this point onwards my memory has a different quality as if the observer has departed, leaving only the experience itself.

From the beginning I had had an ambiguous reaction to the hymn tunes. Now, with the second dose of the Daime beginning to take effect, the singing began to sound monotonous and relentless, like a machine which would go on and on and grind over me like a steamroller. In this mood, for the first time, I began to feel somewhat alienated from the ritual.

But now the Daime really began to open me up and it seemed as if my ability to control the amount of sensory input to my mind/brain had been completely removed. All I could do was lie there with, as it were, the top of my skull removed – being flooded by horrible images, most of which I can no longer remember clearly. At one point I know that there was a lot of sado-masochistic stuff – cartoon-like people in black leather, very evil. Curiously, neither then nor later did I feel personally identified with the content of the images – it was more like watching a particularly repulsive movie, though none the less horrifying for that. Far more terrifying than the images themselves was my feeling of utter powerlessness in face of the mental bombardment and overload which now intensified as the images became even more horrible.

I tried to switch off my mind, but failed. I had an image of myself as a soldier in a huge besieged concrete bunker, running around in terror, closing steel window-shutters one after the other in an utterly futile attempt to keep the enemy out. Up until then I had, despite everything, managed to keep in contact with the ritual to some degree. Now I started to withdraw, and in a paranoid frenzy began to feel that the Santo Daime ritual itself and the initiates were inexpressibly evil and horrible, that I must have been mad to get involved and that never, ever again would I allow any psychotropic substance into my body.

In desperation I called the nearest initiate and told him that I was absolutely terrified, going crazy, couldn't take any more, absolutely must *stop*. He just touched me gently and said: 'There is nothing to be frightened of. There is nothing to be frightened of. Just lie down, just relax. There is nothing to be frightened of; this will pass.'

In my pleading for help I was aware of something strange which only made its way into my conscious mind with full clarity on the following day. In some way my cries for help and expressions of desperation were a lie, a front, an act. In some part of my being, behind the screen of terror, I was quite aware that, truly, there was nothing to be afraid of in the same way that I was aware – earlier in the ritual – of a calm place behind the shakings and contortions of my body. Yet I remained in the grip of nausea and overwhelming dread.

And then – without warning – the terror passed, my head felt clear and my visual field was a merciful featureless grey. My body relaxed and I felt good. With the passing of the terror, my perception of the hymns also changed. Now the singing appeared light, dancing and supportive, with some beautiful harmonies, and again I began to join in. (Since the hymns are actually sung in unison the 'harmonies' that I heard were clearly part of the Daime experience.)

There was a tap on my shoulder and I opened my eyes. It was very bright, and looking down at me was what I took to be an old man with an elaborately tattooed face, remarkably like the Maori chief pictured on the cover of the Penguin edition of Frazier's *Golden Bough*. Once again I felt a very strong connection with the tribal origins of the Santo Daime ritual – and then I saw that the man simply had a very lined face. He said, 'These are the last songs, and it will be very beautiful; will you join?' As I returned to my place around the central altar everybody stood up and began singing again. I raised my arms and swayed with the singing, humming along with it as much as I could, feeling good, light, and happy.

How do I evaluate my encounter with the Daime ritual? To begin with, what I witnessed and experienced leaves me in no doubt whatever that the Santo Daime celebrants in whose company I spent that extraordinary six hours are authentic seekers after the spirit and that the ritual is indeed a genuine and profound religious event. As for myself – I know that when I set off for Amsterdam I secretly hoped that the experience would change my life. An unrealistic hope, of course, particularly since fifteen years of various kinds of therapy have taught me that I have an infuriating ability to go deeply into powerful experiences – only to walk away afterwards seemingly unaffected, as if what I had been through had happened to someone else. It has not been greatly different with the Santo Daime. In the course of the ritual I had many powerful insights – the reality of God (albeit in a form that touches my heart not at all), the perception that my suffering and pain may actually be a defence against peace and calm, the recognition of the appalling level of terror that I carry inside me. Not to mention the ironic fact that my phobia about vomiting – which, paradoxically, drew me to the Daime in the first place – vanished completely, reappearing only whenever my commitment to the ritual wavered. I wish I could say that I have usefully integrated all of this – but the truth is that I have not done so. At best I make an act of faith that every experience changes me at some level, whether I am consciously aware of it or not. And I also feel a strong call to encounter the Daime again and feel sure that I will return. But, if it took some courage to go the first time, the next visit will require a great deal more.

Barquinha

Barquinha is an offshoot of the Santo Daime Church and the smallest of the three churches in Brazil which use ayahuasca. The name 'Barquinha' means 'boat', and their main church is on a riverboat in Amazonia.

As with Santo Daime, Barquinha incorporates beliefs from Christianity, spiritism, and native Brazilian rainforest religions, but it also includes elements of African Umbanda* spirituality. Ancestors may be contacted, as well as African deities known as orixas. Singing and dancing are important features of the ceremony.

*For instance, people reach trance states to commune with the spirits.

Uniao do Vegetal

Another church which uses the sacrament of ayahuasca is the Uniao do Vegetal (UDV). It also has its roots in Brazil and its members claim that their religion dates back to the tenth century before Christ and that, due to humanity's insufficient spiritual evolution, the UDV lay dormant before reappearing in the fourth and fifth centuries BCE, in the Inca civilisation in Peru. What we consider now to be the UDV Church was founded on 22 July 1961 in Porto Velho Rondonia, Brazil by José Gabriel da Costa (Mestre Gabriel).

2

Mestre Gabriel was born in 1922 in Coracao de Maria, a town near Feira de Santana. He received minimal education and, at the age of 20, he left Salvador to become a rubber-tapper in the Amazon region. Working in the rubber camps, he came into contact with the native Indians of Bolivia, and first experienced the effects of ayahuasca. The visions, spiritual revelations and sense of personal mission he discovered came together in a coherent belief-system and he began to gather a group of followers. As the religion spread throughout the Brazilian Amazon and the urban south of the country it also formed a clear organisational structure which continued to develop after Mestre Gabriel's death in 1971.

Structure

The administrative structure is hierarchical and has a sophisticated bureau-cracy with technical and judicial departments, by-laws and statutes. The UDV has sixty-six centres divided among eleven regions throughout Brazil. There are an estimated 6,000 members in Brazil, and the UDV is beginning to open centres in other countries. Each centre is a local congregation, or *nucleo*, where ayahuasca is ritually consumed in ceremonies presided over by a local 'mestre'.

Beliefs and practices

The ritual ceremonies are less 'active' than those of the Santo Daime and are more like a Quaker meeting. Long periods of silence are included in the service, where members seek self-knowledge through mental concentration. The 'vegetal' (ayahuasca tea) facilitates this and is described as being the 'key' to the process. There is space for people to share the teaching they received from the vegetal or to ask the 'mestre' (who leads the ceremony) questions. The members of the UDV emphasise the oral tradition in their doctrine and in the rituals the teachings of Mestre Gabriel are spoken, chamadas (similar to mantras) are chanted and hymns are sung. They believe that this simplicity reflects the life of their founder and that one of their roles is to 'worship and preserve his peasant roots, which translates the purity of his teachings; keeping alive the memory of the fact that one's degree of spiritual evolution is not dependent upon erudition or academic titles'.[3]

The teachings of the UDV are Christian-based but believers also stress the role of nature, describing the UDV as 'a religion based on the superior Christian values of love and fraternity among men, in full communion with Nature through the tea Hoasca, a vehicle synchronising it with the Divinity...ecology and spirituality are indivisible'.[4]

The Hoasca Project

The Hoasca Project is a thorough investigation of the effects of hoasca (ayahuasca). A multidisciplinary, collaborative, biomedical research project, it is led by Charles Grob, Dennis McKenna and Jace Callaway.[5]

As part of this study, fifteen long-term members of the UDV were assessed psychologically along with fifteen matched controls who had no history of ayahuasca consumption. The tests included structured psychiatric diagnostic interviews, personality testing and neuropsychological evaluation.

The preliminary results suggest that the apparent impact of ayahuasca on the subjects in the study appears to be positive and therapeutic, in both self-reported and objective testing. The psychiatric diagnostic assessments of the ayahuasca-using subjects showed that a large proportion had alcohol, depressive or anxiety disorders prior to their initiation into the UDV but that 'all disorders had remitted without recurrence after entry into the UDV'.[6] Eleven of the subjects had either heavy or moderate patterns of alcohol consumption before joining the UDV but achieved complete abstinence shortly after affiliating. The members were also

> quite emphatic that they had undergone radical transformations of their
> behaviour, attitudes toward others and outlook on life. They are convinced
> that they had been able to eliminate their chronic anger, resentment,
> aggression and alienation, as well as acquire greater self control,
> responsibility to family and community and personal fulfilment through
> their participation in the hoasca ceremonies of the UDV.[7]

The ayahuasca-using group scored higher on the neuropsychological testing than the controls and themselves claimed that they felt the ayahuasca had significantly improved their powers of memory and concentration. Without retrospective data this cannot be definitively substantiated, but 'indications are...that the long-term consumption of hoasca within the structured UDV ceremonial setting does not appear to exert a deleterious effect on neurophysical function'.[8]

2

Nicholas's account

I was expecting the Vegetal service to be much like the Santo Daime, but I was wrong.

Their church building relies on sheer simplicity and quality of craftsmanship for its elegance and beauty: a tall conical thatched roof with white walls and not a single icon or decoration. The centre has no altar but a plain oblong wooden table with jugs of water, glasses and a large glass dispenser for the ayahuasca, surrounded by the congregation sitting on reclining 'garden' chairs facing inwards. There was a light-hearted, almost casual, air – in fact we were given no instruction at all – yet we felt welcomed and well looked after without being told what to do or fussed over. The church was part of a well-kept complex of buildings including adequate WCs, a crèche and a hall with kitchen, quite extravagantly designed by an architect member and well built. It struck me that this showed signs of a religion that had recently become established: it had the feeling of self-confidence without the wild enthusiasm of the newly converted, yet it was still free of the heaviness and dogma of the older religions.

The ritual began with each person making their way to queue anticlockwise around the central table where an elder served the sacrament. He looked each person in the eye as they approached and then dispensed an appropriate quantity of ayahuasca into a glass, which we took back to our seats. Once everyone was seated, we all drank together. Water was offered to clear the taste and many people went out to spit or to the WCs before returning, settling back comfortably in their seats and closing their eyes. I relaxed into it too, and perhaps I shivered, as a poncho was gently laid over my knees.

I had strong visions which were different to previously: no brightly coloured geometric swirls this time. Instead, I became enveloped inside a warm and shady world, a forest scene, where trees and plants all had personalities which were clearly visible. They were all somehow vibrant and buzzing, and some morphed into faces as I watched. Some looked like flowers with hundreds of little tiny petals opening and closing like firework stars, but much softer and slower. I realised that I was being given a revelation of the spirits or life energy in everything: it was as though the spirits were showing me what was always there but I had not noticed, and I felt privileged. At the same time my internal dialogue carried on, describing the experience for the observer in me.

Later, perhaps when the effect had become weaker, I had a series of rather superficial visions, like dreams. I felt that I could steer these whichever way I wanted, including going deeper, yet I was aware that I chose not to through fear of what I might be faced with. While we were each meditating, an elder spoke monotonously and I was surprised to pick out enough words to hear that he was reciting a legal document, which I later learned was the Church's Articles of Inauguration. Later on there was a short but exquisite blast of violin music. Then people got up to speak, one at a time, like in a Quaker meeting, and somehow I felt that I could follow what was said in mood if not words.

After about three hours the service ended and we moved to another building decked out with food and (non-alcoholic) drinks, presumably brought by the congregation, for another three-hour social. The people were from various backgrounds and age groups; they were open, sincere and yet light-hearted. The few who spoke English came up to us: doctors, a pilot, a pop singer and the owner of a small engineering firm. It was a big family and I felt very welcome. I looked around and was struck by the gentleness of the men. The women were sparkling. They brought life and joy to the whole place. Their eyes were so bright and full of fire!

Gnostisismo Revolutionario de la Concienca de Krishna

Like the Santo Daime in Mapia, Brazil, Gnostisismo Revolutionario de la Concienca de Krishna is an example of a spiritual community based around the use of a psychoactive sacrament as an inspiration and teacher. Combining beliefs from various cultures, Gnostisismo Revolutionario de la Concienca de Krishna is a growing shamanic community which began fifteen years ago in the Putamayo and Caquetá regions of the Colombian jungle.

The name, 'Gnostisismo' relates to the group's association with the Gnostic movement. 'Revolutionario' refers to a (non-violent) 'revolution in consciousness as a means of changing the world to a place where the people live in equality and freedom as brothers and sisters'. 'De la concienca de Krishna' comes from the affinity of the community with the spiritual traditions of India and Krishna. The group is very ecologically and politically motivated, campaigning for the human rights of the *campesinos* who live in the jungle, and initiating ecological projects. Ayahuasca (known as yajé) is drunk in twice-weekly ceremonies. It is revered as a teacher and spirit guide and seen as a spiritual path which can be followed to gain access to the realms of healing, divination and inner knowledge, as well as for maintaining an intimacy with the immediate environment and the planet. The community is led by a shaman named Vasudev who has been living in the jungle for seventeen years, studying with indigenous shamans from Caquetá and Putamayo.

2

Those who live in the community follow a number of disciplines such as preparation through diet and the practice of tantra in their relationships. The children in the community participate in the ceremonies but menstruating and pregnant women are not permitted to drink yajé. Menstruation is seen as a sacred time for inner quiet, rest, purification and artistic expression. The women spend this time away from the rest of the group, in a 'women's hut' (*ranchito*).

Members of the community undergo an initiation when they feel ready to accept the Way of Yajé as their spiritual path. The initiate's head is shaved and he or she is given a spiritual name in a ceremony in front of the yajé altar. The ritual signifies the commitment of the initiate to yajé as their spiritual teacher.

A number of British people have visited this group and are now setting up a project with the aim of studying and making available information on the shamanic wisdom of Colombia and raising awareness about ecological and social issues arising from the abuse of nature and the worldwide oppression and exploitation of people, their land, communities and cultures by the prevailing capitalist and imperialist forces. They also aim to promote awareness of the use of sacred plants for healing and spiritual purposes and initiate a cultural exchange between people in Britain and the community. They plan to give more people access to the experience of yajé by organising group journeys to Colombia.

Robert Maclaine is one of the founders of this project. After two visits to the community he became an initiate and committed himself to working with the medicine on a long-term basis. Here is his account of his first yajé ceremony with the group:

On the day of my first ceremony we had a herbal purification wash and had fasted since breakfast in order to prepare our minds and bodies for the ritual. After dark everyone changed into their white ceremonial clothing and gathered upstairs in Vasudev's house. Some of the women gathered coca leaves from the bushes outside and placed them in baskets on the floor for everyone to help themselves; chewing the leaves of the coca bush gives a gentle clarity of mind and strengthens the body in readiness for yajé.

After a while Vasudev went to the altar to begin the ritual. A bowl of burning Paulo Santo (an incense for purification) was brought into the room and we all stood to pray for protection and guidance in the ritual.

After drinking we chew some more coca and then lie down on blankets which have been laid out on the floor.

I begin to feel an energy moving in my body. It feels as if some giant being is waking up and filling the house...Something is happening, I see shapes in my mind's eye, swirling patterns, colours, and then I am by the river near to the house. I am trying to cross it – I see Vasudev's brother, Marcello. His voice is in my mind: 'So you want to be an Indian?' I feel the presence of the other men and I feel like a frightened little boy. There are more voices and intense images crowding in on me, challenging me, laughing at me and all of a sudden I don't want to be here, I am panicking inside, I don't feel I'm up to this, I must have been stupid to think I was. But it doesn't end, it only gets more intense. I see little devils appearing and disappearing, taunting me, jumping in and out of my vision, there are doorways, stairs, different levels.

By this time the others have started chanting again but I am unable to move, paralysed by fear, so I listen and the chanting seems to help me focus. I feel stronger and slowly I raise myself to a sitting position. I look in the direction of Vasudev just as the chanting is stopping and I see him presiding over a portal, a kind of window into other worlds. Then, to my surprise, he turns and looks directly at me: 'There are many forces,' he says.

Someone puts some music on, Sufi chanting, and I shut my eyes in meditation. There is a beautiful light everywhere. I sit watching this beautiful expanding light flowing everywhere. I breathe it in and listen to the music feeling like I've just woken up in an entirely different, and yet somehow familiar, world. I see a huge sun slowly rising, Sufis facing it in deep prayer. Then, I am above the earth. I can see it spinning. The sun travels across it. I glide down over the Amazon and see Indians in a clearing dancing to the sun as it sets.

2

I am feeling quite nauseous and dizzy by now until eventually I have to get up to go and vomit. I make it outside just in time as streams of liquid come shooting out of my mouth and nostrils and my stomach retches violently. I look up and the plants are surrounded with colours, vibrating with life and, what's more, I can sense their consciousness. They seem curious as if they know that I am new to this place. I look down at the plant nearest to me, a very delicate looking herb which grows close to the ground. I can see it growing, stretching its leaves toward the sky. I look closer and I can see hundreds of little silver and violet lights moving all around the leaves and along the stems busy building – I can see them building the form of the plant. At this moment I see the lights as little beings, and the plant as their palace/temple. I look upon this scene with astonishment, feeling deep in my heart the miracle of life. For a while I gawp at everything. It seems that I have returned to the state of innocent wonder which I felt as a young child.

My experience continued for hours after this with many more visions and insights, not to mention a good deal of time spent crouched over a hole emptying my bowels. Eventually I went back inside the house feeling like I was returning from a long voyage. The atmosphere inside was relaxed, peaceful and focused, the people talking quietly in the candlelight and music playing in the background. I spent the rest of the night listening to and talking to the people. Later guitars and drums were brought out and we played and danced until the dawn light in joyous celebration.

Bwiti

In Gabon, use of the root bark of the shrub *Tabernanthe iboga*, known as iboga or eboka, is widespread. Iboga contains the alkaloid ibogaine, which has stimulating properties at moderate doses and produces a trance state in larger quantities. Iboga is used in both the traditional religion of the Pygmy tribes living in the equatorial forest and also as part of a more recent syncretic religion – Bwiti.

The Bwiti religion is a mix of traditional iboga religion and Christianity, and emerged over the last 150 years as a result of the attempts by Catholic missionaries to convert the indigenous populations of Apindji, Mitsogho and Fang. Bwiti embraces various sects. The main difference between them is generally how far they have absorbed Christian rites and symbols into their ceremonies. Each community head will also introduce certain changes in the ceremonies so that they reflect his personal interpretation of the religion. Both the traditional and Bwiti iboga religion can be considered 'mystery religion', meaning that initiates undergo a deep revelatory experience and are forbidden to reveal certain details of the rite and their experience afterwards.

> I would say that the whole concept of stillness through the use of a plant is best embodied through the use of iboga. It is the most peaceful, beautiful, still, loving plant I have yet encountered and the experience was pure peace and love.
>
> My initiation was essentially the equivalent of a Freemason's introduction to the elemental beings. It was quite the most beautiful and loving embrace by these beings that you could imagine and I think that the Bwiti have evolved an intricate and specific ritual that perfectly complements the universe you access through iboga.
>
> It is perfectly structured, smoothly and proficiently conducted with an ease and simplicity that belies a profound experience.
>
> The whole experience is built around you the individual, and is formulated with your happiness in mind.
>
> **(Tony, from South Africa, a practitioner of Tibetan Buddhism)**

In Bwiti, there are two main rites in which iboga is taken. The first of these is the *ngoze* (Mass), celebrated over three nights, where all members of the community take a small dose of iboga and then sing and dance until dawn.

The second is *tobe si* – the initiation rite. This rite was performed for centuries by the Pygmies, and is celebrated in the Bwiti whenever a new member joins. The initiate eats massive quantities of iboga until they enter a 'coma'. In this state the initiate's soul journeys to the other world and is enlightened about the 'roots of life' by divine entities. A *tobe si* is an event for the whole community and involves both psychological and practical preparation. For the novice, preparation includes abstaining from sexual activity, wine and certain foods for a number of days, collecting together a variety of foods and objects which will be used in the ceremony, spending a period of time alone and in silence before the initiation and, finally, fasting (and, in some sects, undergoing a purification diet) from the day before the initiation. Preparation for the community involves cleaning and preparing the Bwiti temple and then, from the night before the *tobe si*, taking a small amount of iboga and continuing to take it until the last day of the initiation rite.

2

An initiation usually lasts from Wednesday until Sunday. On the first day the novice must explain their reasons for undergoing *tobe si*, and make full confession. They are then at the disposal of the community. At noon on Thursday the novice is placed in position in the temple and is fed spoonfuls of iboga. The novice is continually monitored, with checks on pupils, urine, temperature and vomit. In May 1993 Giorgio Samorini became the first white man to be initiated into the Ndea Narizanga sect of the Fang Bwiti. He describes the process:

> Each time I vomited, my initiation mother tasted a little vomit in order to understand how iboga was acting in the stomach. My vomits were a very important sign for the group, causing frequent discussions. The novice must vomit and it is a cause of great concern if there is a delay or it does not happen at all. Generally, it is thought that the lack of vomit is caused by the fact that the novice has concealed some serious sins during confession and he/she is urged to complete the confession. If the vomit takes too long it may be decided to immediately stop the iboga ingestion and the whole initiation rite. It is one of the cases acknowledged by Bwitists in which the novice would be at risk of death.[9]

As the iboga takes effect it slows down the heart rate and cools the body until the novice becomes stiff and unable to move and finally loses consciousness. At this point iboga ingestion may be close to a fatal dose. James W. Fernandez notes that in the last forty years a dozen charges of murder or manslaughter have been brought against Bwiti leaders who have lost initiates.[10] When the novice collapses, iboga ingestion stops and the novice is placed on the ground and moved at regular intervals to prevent too much stiffness and chilling. The collapse is seen as a sign that the novice's soul has departed and is now moving towards the 'other world'. Giorgio Samorini found that:

> The first psychic effects occur 30–60 minutes after the beginning of the iboga ingestion and they become stronger and stronger, taking the novice towards more and more modified states of consciousness. The Bwitists then reported to me that in my case the iboga ingestion lasted 12 hours. During this time I experienced a strong 'psychedelic trip', characterised by visual hallucinations and 'revealing' deductive routes, and I achieved moments of true 'illumination'... Yet, the true 'journey' was still to begin...
>
> The moment in which the novice loses consciousness corresponds to 'leaving the body': as far as I am concerned it was a typical out-of-body experience. After a long psychedelic trip which took place during the iboga ingestion, characterised by visual, sound and tactile hallucinations and by the appearance of paranormal phenomena such as complete field vision (360 degrees), I experienced the moment of loss of consciousness 'seeing' clearly 'from above' my body, around which the officiants bustled about, while they moved it carefully from the stool and set it on the ground. I observed this scene farther and farther from above, from a greater distance, until when, 'looking up' I felt myself 'swallowed up' by a vortex of light, a kind of luminous, very fast, almost instantaneous lift. From that moment, I had no more 'hallucinations', but a 'pure vision', whose memory is still well impressed on my mind. Bwitists maintain that the 'great vision' is not forgotten for the rest of one's life.[11]

Musical instruments are played to welcome back the novice soul from the 'other world' as the initiate slowly regains consciousness. Samorini points out that it took several hours before all his senses were completely reawakened, and a residual stiffness in his limbs lasted for at least another full day and night. The novice is now 'new-born' and baptism rites in the forest are undertaken. Finally, the novice is asked detailed questions by Bwiti officials and describes the visions s/he experienced. It is only after this talk, and with the agreement of the community members, that the novice can be proclaimed *bandzi*:

> At present Gabon is the most 'open' state in the world with respect to the use of a strong entheogenic substance. The use is not limited to a particular ethnic group, it is allowed for everybody who sincerely wishes to have this experience, joining a Bwitist community. However the initiation to

Bwiti is hard. It is a question of courage and will to go and 'see'...I had the courage and the will to go and 'see' and, notwithstanding the 500+ bites from tropical insects, burns intentionally inflicted to my body during the dancing with fire, or the five kilograms of weight lost during the rite, it was one of the most fascinating and constructive experiences in my life. The reader will understand if I take the liberty of stating that I am proud of being a *bandzi*, a 'living dead person'.[12]

2

Tony's account

I have had profound experiences of insight with psilocybin and the *Trichocereus* cactus on a couple of occasions, understandings of the essential emptiness that is our fundamental reality, the 'skylike' nature of mind. Essentially these states allowed me to perceive that the fabric of our reality is our imagination, and thus that anything, absolutely anything is possible in the universe (however, it is important that we realise that it is all a product of our imagination).

Iboga functions in a subtly different way from these other plants. In small amounts it seems to somehow slow the metabolism down, more so the more you take. Your entire being becomes still and, through the stillness, you begin to see. You begin to be aware of what is going on around you, as your intellectual mind is stilled and the mechanisms that cloud your mind with random thought are all put on slow, or pause. Other senses start coming alive, as the five senses mix synergistically. This is the case up until you take the barely sub-lethal doses they give you in an initiation. Then you really start to see! Somehow the iboga manages to change your vibration, slow you down to such an extent that you become super-aware on the physical plane of events occurring at other dimensional vibrations. Your body cools down, you no longer seem to even breathe and it would look to an outsider as if you were comatose. In fact, although your motor co-ordination is not functioning properly, your consciousness is now coming into its own.

Early on in the experience you are extremely ill, unpleasantly so. This is understood as the 'dying'. Once dead you experience the profundity of the plant. One experiences pretty much what death is like but on a smaller scale. This is a difficult phase to talk about because no words come even close to describing the intensity. It is the essence of the iboga experience.

Through the stillness that iboga allows you to enter, you find yourself understanding the concepts of equanimity. And through this majestic gift you realise that no matter how incredible the visions are, no matter how sacred and profound are the feelings we have in the company of such awesomely compassionate and loving beings as abound in the universe, we realise that there is only emptiness, and that nothing exists, and that *everything* we are seeing and feeling is just a product of the imagination, manufactured in the oneness of the universal mind. And again I come round to the idea of possibilities: with this understanding absolutely *anything* is possible and *absolute* nothingness is possible too. The fundamental understanding of Rigpa, the nature of mind, allows us to understand that we don't exist.

A Bwiti ceremony is a week-long procedure, when rushed for Europeans. Two days are spent cleansing (internal/external) and then imbibing one to two days afterwards, then three or more days needed for rest and recuperation. The process is understood as being first day dying, second day death, third day onwards rebirth. This is a *serious* plant – iboga is regarded as the ultimate sacrament. The ritual is not conducted by a single shaman. The entire village takes part, each individual having a specific role to play, instrument to play, part to sing, and they know the ceremony intimately. Having an entire village dedicate two solid days or more to helping you clearly see through the fabric of this reality in the most profound manner by singing, chanting, dancing is an incomparable experience that even now moves me deeply. There is such love emanating from these people. And it isn't your normal African percussive trance-inducing music ceremony – the chief instrument is the eight-string harp of David, the drums are brought out for only a couple of minutes in the whole ceremony. There are so many instruments played, and all of them have a spiritual significance. I think the drums are used as a last resort, for those who have 'blockages', as they referred to them. The music is of a light and angelic nature as opposed to a heavy trancelike beat. Trying to use words to describe the effect of the music is impossible. It was too beautiful for thoughts, let alone words. The fact that it is a combined effort by the whole village, and that you are the centre of focus, you are the *bandzi*, the neophyte, initiate, makes this a very powerful experience indeed.

Native American Church
History

The peyote cactus (*Lophophora williamsii*) has a long history of use as a medicinal and sacramental herb. Fossilised peyote buttons have been found that are 5,000 years old and prehistoric trade in, and knowledge of, the sacred cactus was apparently well established prior to the European conquest of Mexico.

2

Mexican peyotism is perhaps best typified by the traditional practices of the Huichol tribe of the Sierra Occidental, along the Pacific coast of Mexico. Annual pilgrimages to ritually hunt the sacred cactus are still a central part of tribal myth and ceremony. A group leader, or *mara a'kame*, leads seekers in their mythical quest 'to find our life', as it has been described. Only peyote gathered in this ceremonial manner is suitable for the spiritual requirements of the tribe. The Cora and Tarahumara are related groups of people who use peyote as a sacrament. Cora people are known to trade for, or purchase, peyote from their Huichol neighbours, as their own traditions do not require the desert pilgrimage to collect the cactus.

In the mid-1800s, increased contact between American and Mexican Indians helped to spread the religious use of peyote northward. The Apache and Tonkawas were two of the first tribes to use peyote and the ceremony they established formed the basis of the Native American Church. Around the turn of the century, the Comanche and Kiowa also engaged in the ritual. Soon afterwards over fifty different tribes began using peyote as a sacrament. The practices of the native Americans differed from the shamanistic rituals used by their Mexican counterparts. The American tribes blended in Christian theology, and emphasised a communal ceremony of chanting, meditation and prayer. Today the number of members of the Native American Church exceeds 250,000.

Beliefs and practices[13]

Most formal peyote ceremonies mix drumming, singing, prayer and stories as a means of offering thanks and as a way of sharing the blessing with the Creator and their fellow communicants.

> By taking these plants, I was able to return to the origin of my intention. I
> wanted to feel life in its abundance, feel the beauty of nature, feel the love

in my heart, feel the deep peace of the spirit... feel the Creator within me and all around me.

In having encountered this medicine, this tradition, I am probably most grateful for having recovered a sense of family with all of humankind, and with animals, plants, the earth, stars, sun...with the whole universe. I feel part of the whole.

(Josep, aged 40, from Spain)

The peyote ceremony which was introduced to the American Plains Indians is a formalised, all-night prayer meeting, usually held in a teepee, hogan, or peyote house especially set aside for that purpose. Christian elements are often significantly present, depending on the particular tribe or group leader. Most of North American peyotism can be properly identified with the Native American Church (NAC), a large group of mostly native believers. There are numerous divisions of the NAC (NAC of North America, NAC of Navajoland, NAC of South Arizona, etc.), with each division being composed of several local chapters, or moons. Each chapter normally has officers who are trained in distinct clerical functions of the Church. The leader of a peyote meeting is known as the Road Chief, or Road Man. This is the person who is charged with the responsibility of overseeing the main elements of the meeting and leading others on the Peyote Road, the way of learning to live life well. Other offices include Cedar Man, Fire Man, Drum Man, and often, Earth Mother. Though ceremonies among different chapters tend to vary slightly, common elements are present in most NAC ceremonies. An eagle bone whistle, various feather fans, water drum and prayer staff are a few of the ceremonial items necessary to conduct the prayer meeting. Central tenets of the NAC usually involve avoidance of alcohol, devotion to family, and right living in general.

Grandfather Peyote strips me naked, sometimes gently, sometimes forcefully. He leaves me standing there in my True Essence, for me to see myself, if I have the courage, for how I truly am and for where I am at. He shows me with his gentleness how to open my heart to Life, Spirit and my self.

(Alison, aged 31, from England)

Probably the most simple and historically primitive form of peyotism is the vision quest, alone in nature. Usually this involves fasting, solitude, and quiet but steady contemplation. Peyote is eaten or consumed as a tea and a vigil is kept until such time as the communicant comes to a sense of physical and spiritual completion.

Legal situation

2

In the United States, the use of peyote was prohibited by the 1970 Controlled Substance Act. The Native American Church was exempted and the possession of peyote became subject to federal regulation. As a result, the legal situation varies from state to state. For instance, in Arizona and Oregon the exemption is based on religious sincerity, not race, denomination or physical boundaries and so non-Native American peyote organisations can exist. In contrast, in Texas a person wishing to use peyote for religious purposes must be not only a member of the Native American Church but of at least twenty-five per cent Native American descent in order to be immune to prosecution.[14]

Peyote Way Church

The Peyote Way Church was established by the Reverend Immanuel Pardeahtan Trujillo. He had joined the NAC in 1948 but objected to the race requirements and left in 1966. He founded the Peyote Way Church in 1977, on the Peaceful Valley Ranch in the isolated Aravaipa Valley in south-eastern Arizona for the specific purpose of 'stewarding, ingesting, distributing and growing the holy sacrament Peyote as the essential and inseparable part' of the members' religious beliefs.

The Peyote Way Church draws on Mormonism for its dietary regulations which prohibit alcohol, tobacco, caffeine, and foods containing white sugar or white flour.

The Peyote Way Church differs from the NAC in that it admits members of all races, and has replaced peyote meetings with the spirit walk, which involves solitude, fasting and quiet contemplation. It has 140 associate members and twelve clergy.

Leo Mercado's account: Wirikuta calling

Nearly a decade ago, I first journeyed to Wirikuta, the sacred land of peyote. The name Wirikuta has similar meaning for the Huichol people of Mexico as does our word heaven. Members of this tribe have been ceremonially re-enacting the peyote 'hunt' as far back as they can trace their origins. So it was that my interest in peyote and peyote people led me to this desolate but magical desert valley. Travelling to Mexico was definitely not in my plans that fall. Work, finances and family made it a pretty sure bet that any travelling I did would be done close to home. Enter Prem Das, an American married into the Huichol tribe, who at that time was based in Tepic, Nayarit. He had orig-inally contacted me by phone after reading an article in a popular magazine which I had provided information for. The article had been about peyote and its legal use in Arizona. Prem Das had been an avid student of peyote for several years. He let me know that if I shared his interest, I should make my way to the sacred valley of the Huichol as the next step in my own relationship with the sacrament. He listened patiently to all my reasons for staying home and being too busy to be bothered with spiritual travel adventures. One day, while visiting my home, Prem Das pulled an airline ticket out of his *bolsa* (shoulder bag). It was my ticket to Puerto Vallarta, flying with him and his wife to go visit their Huichol family. I was very happily surprised, but also disappointed with myself for knowing that I couldn't just pack up and hop on a plane within forty-eight hours, no matter how much I might like to. Life was way too complicated, and I was too previously occupied for that. I politely declined his generous offer.

That night we attended a peyote ceremony co-hosted by myself and members of a local artisan community. Prem Das was the Road Man for the evening. I mentioned to my artist acquaintances the airline ticket and my inabil-ity to accept it. Out of friendship and the concern for Prem Das's wasted purchase, I asked my artist friend, Sharon, to travel to Mexico in my place. Somewhat hesitantly she agreed after hearing out my situation. I had not, however, counted on the working of the spirit of peyote...

The medicine was very strong that night. During the peak of the ceremony, while my body sat apparently content, my inner being was in great turmoil. I sensed my life as I knew it had reached its natural conclusion. All my roads were leading nowhere. Life, for me, had become a charade. The driving tone of the water drum and Prem Das's chanting, normally very comforting, now seemed to stir my pot of doubt and insecurity until I could feel my spirit boiling over and evaporating into emptiness. Nothing in the world could at that moment have quenched my thirst for meaning, my hunger for purpose. Nothing, that is, except the hand of God. In my mind's eye I saw a weeping child (me) surrounded by empty space. Into that loneliness, a white, silvery eagle suddenly appeared. It swept down towards my vacant self, coming in for the kill, I thought. After all, my life felt more corpse-like than alive. As the sharp talons opened to grab its human prey, I suddenly felt the lifting of my self-pity and perhaps even fear. I was glad just to be able to let go and die in peace. Unexpectedly, I began to feel the eagle warm and bless me rather than scattering my soul to the void. A physical and spiritual blessing radiated from the eagle into my body, beginning where its formerly frightening talons now gently touched my head. I felt the peace of heart and mind that only God's Spirit can bring. Instantly, I realised that it had been too many years since I had fully bathed in God's healing light, too long running on my own knowledge and neglecting the daily blessings of Spirit.

2

I awoke from my vision with tears streaming down my face. I looked across the fire as the drum beat on and saw my friend Sharon watching me, smiling. I spent the rest of the night in meditative prayer, thanking God for the simple miracles of life.

In the morning, everyone who had participated in the ceremony visited each other and shared some of their experience. I sought out Sharon to thank her for standing in for me and accepting Prem Das's gift. 'I want you to see what I drew last night around the fire,' she said. She opened up her sketchpad which she often carried, artist that she was. With an understanding smile she showed me a pencil drawing of a white eagle coming to rest on the shoulders of a kneeling man. 'That's what I saw when I looked at you last night, when you wept,' she said. 'I think you should go with Prem Das yourself.' Almost in shock, I agreed. That was when Wirikuta welcomed me into itself and began to shape a new creature from an old lump of clay.

Rastafarianism

Rastafarians are members of a Jamaican messianic movement dating back to the 1930s. Within Rastafarianism, marijuana, or ganja, is considered to be the 'holy herb'. Rastafarians identify it as the substance written of in Psalm 104:14 of the Bible: 'He causeth the grass to grow for the cattle, and herb for the service of man'.

Rastafarians believe that there was a golden age in which all black peoples lived peacefully in a united continent called Ethiopia. European colonisers, using military might, divided up the continent into different nations and constructed a new Babylon based on divide and rule principles. Rastafarians look to the future when Babylon will break down and a black Zion will once again come into being.

Originally, inspiration was drawn from the teachings of Marcus Garvey (1887–1940) who believed that all black people in the West should rightfully return to Africa, their homeland. Garvey allegedly prophesied, 'Look to Africa when a black king shall be crowned for the day of deliverance is near', and the coronation in 1930 of Ras Tafari Makonnen as the Emperor of Ethiopia, Haile Selassie I was seen by many as the fulfilment of this prophecy. (Garvey himself never acknowledged Ras Tafari as redeemer.)

Rastafarianism started to spread outside Jamaica in the 1960s. To begin with, Rastafari ideas reached other islands with the return of students who had studied at the main campus of the University of the West Indies in Jamaica, and also via the inter-island contact that the fleet of federal boats facilitated. Then with the migration of Jamaicans Rastafarianism spread beyond the Caribbean. A further important factor in the growth of Rastafarianism throughout the world has been the internationalisation of reggae music and, in particular, the music of Bob Marley. Marley came to symbolise Rastafarian beliefs and values, writing and singing of Ras Tafari, Jah, Babylon, and the return to Africa. Through his music the Rastafarian message reached the United States as well as Japan and Australasia in the east, and he became a personal focus for many Rastafarians.

Beliefs and practices

Rastafarianism does not have a clearly defined orthodoxy but many believe that an underlying tenet of Rastafarian thought is that all are equal in 'human truths and rights' and this is symbolised in the use of the expression 'I and I', frequently heard in reasonings, rather than the dualistic 'you and I'. Integrity and straightforwardness are the principles by which life should be guided, and this comes under the philosophy of *ital livity*. *Ital livity* rejects modern Western consumerism and emphasises the value of more natural ways of living. Herbal remedies are preferred, as is organic food, and no meat or shellfish should be eaten. The characteristic dreadlocks of Rastafarians stem from Leviticus 21:5 'they shall not make baldness upon their head'.

Ganja, used as a sacrament by Rastafarians, is likened to the communion wine of the Christian churches. It was brought to Jamaica by Indian labourers in the nineteenth century and became rooted in folk beliefs as a panacea. Rastafarians adapted the Indian method of smoking it to form their own ritual. The chillum pipe is called a 'chalice'. To 'lick the chalice' is to partake in a communal sharing of ideas, as the chalice passes from hand to hand. This sacred ritual is called a 'reasoning'.

In Jamaica a ritual, called a *nyabinghi* or *binghi*, takes place several times a year on occasions such as the anniverary of Haile Selassie's coronation. There are reasonings throughout the day and chanting and drumming at night. Group rituals are less formalised outside Jamaica.

Temple of the True Inner Light

The Temple of the True Inner Light was formed in 1980, by Alan Birnbaum, as an offshoot of the New York City branch of the Native American Church. The Temple uses dipropyltyramine (DPT) as its sacrament and Temple followers regard it as the actual manifestation of God, rather than a means to access God. DPT is a short-acting tryptamine, inducing psychedelic experiences which last for about three and half hours and often end abruptly.

Beliefs and practices

DPT ingestion, according to the Temple, allows direct communication with spirit forms and this communication provides the source of their theology. The Temple theology has been described as 'eclectic drug-based Christian revisionism',[15] and the Temple itself states that:

> If you do not belong to Christ (our temple), you cannot receive the
> Salvation of Yahweh, the Psychedelic. They have told us clearly, and many
> times, that Christ (King Moses, David, Elijah, Jesus, Vishnu, Gautama,
> Mohammed, Mani, Quetzalcoatl), is alive again physically, and that the
> crucifixion has happened again...the mystery has been revealed.
>
> Anyone who enters into Their (the Psychedelic's), Presence without
> belonging to Christ's Body is an alien and a foreign visitor to Them. We are

Their Children and citizens of Their Realm.

Whoever does not belong to Christ, belongs to anti-Christ. As King Jesus said, 'whoever is not with me is against (anti) me'.

If anyone hears the Holy Spirit, which is Yahweh's, the Psychedelic's, Testimony that we (our temple), are the true Body of Christ, before having joined with us, they can no longer join us in this physical life.[17]

Sections of the Old and New Testament are re-examined and found to contain many references to psychedelics. A Temple member, Michael Hoana, says

this religion, the true religion, is not something that started in the '60s. If you look at the scriptures, the Bible, there are certain things like oil and unctions, that teach people, that teach directly. What can that possibly be? If it is an oil that is teaching you something then we are obviously talking about something that was extracted from a plant...there is the presence bread. Why would somebody call something 'presence' bread? They mention a living spirit in it and that is obviously not wheat. And to actually say that this is food from heaven, they can only be talking about a psychedelic'.[17]

All serious applicants are screened first via a personal interview. All sessions are conducted in the temple, semi-privately, and involve listening to tapes (which include readings of biblical texts) after ingesting DPT. According to Lyttle: 'the goal here is a particular gnosis and re-examination of inspired literature via DPT'.[18]

Peter Gorman, Executive Editor of *High Times*, visited the Temple in 1989[19]

Droning music plays on an old boom box. Over it, dubbed on to the tape, someone reads scripture. Michael, just 22 or 23, with straight brown hair nearly down to his waist, lights the raspberry leaves he's put in the hookah bowl, I suck the white-smoke sacrament and put the mouthpiece down.

I have no idea how high I will get and worry about that. I worry, too, because I am with a stranger and have no idea whether or not this is the right stranger to be getting high with. The whole scene is a little shaky; I'm in a New York City tenement, sitting on the floor beneath a loft bed, smoking a bowl of raspberry leaves which are covered in a psychotropic substance I've never heard of, listening to religious scripture with an avowed apostle of the Lord, one who has explained to me that I am a sinner for not accepting Jesus as my saviour, and the white smoke as Jesus. It's not the most conducive setting in which to experiment with the stability of my mind. Still, here I am, holding on to that smoke until I know nothing will escape when I open my mouth and gulp a fresh lungful of air.

The high is instant and hard. No warning, no intimation, just swallow and peak. Suddenly, my worries disappear and I'm warm and sitting in West Virginia and it is 1971...

2

I'd just returned to the East Coast from months of hitchhiking out West, to Norman's house in Sugar Grove, and it was Ellen's birthday and the three of us had planned on tripping together and when Ellen decided she didn't want to and walked off into the woods to make love with Norman I ate all three hits of windowpane and for the first time ever it was a large enough dose of acid to turn me inside out. Up on the ridge the trees started dancing and I felt them moving inside me. I felt the ground breathing with my breath. I spoke – in a way I couldn't identify – with the insects, warning them off with reminders that I was their brother.

The rain pounded, drumming in my blood, and I was Earth and Air and Goodness and Light and everything made sense in a way I'd never dreamed it could. I glimpsed the holistic system of things and communed with divinity and understood the life force and how it was in all things, even in those things which we don't think have it, like rocks – oh, how they were filled with life! – and when the rain told me to get in out of it, that it was about to let loose a violent storm, full of lightning and thunder, that's what I did, and there, on cue, in the main room of the little farmhouse someone had put Richard Alpert's *Be Here Now* right out in the middle of things and I read and understood and knew what being here – here in the minute, in the page, in the letters, in all things at all times, in history and in stone and in the lightning banging at the house – knew what that meant and that it was a truth I'd keep for ever.

The walls and I breathed together all that afternoon – their rhythm was fantastic and musical! – and when Norman and Ellen returned and saw that I'd eaten all the acid they asked whether I was all right and I assured them that not only was I all right, I was divine. They nodded. They knew the secret, too...

'Are you all right?' Michael asks gently.

'I'm fine. I'm thinking about something wonderful.'

'Do you want to share it?'

I think about that for a minute before answering. And when I answer I say no, it is too personal. Perhaps I think I can't express it well enough, or that if I do I would be putting water into the cup and diluting my moments, moments I haven't really thought about since the day they happened, nearly twenty years ago.

I have another toke from the raspberry bowl and think about the funny route things take sometimes, about how it happens that in 1989 I should be in a church which uses a potent psychedelic as its sacrament and seems to live according to what I know as Catholic dogma – reinterpreted through that psychedelic. This particular church, the Temple of the True Inner Light, views Christ in quite a literal biblical sense: Christ said he was in the Light; Temple members have recognised the psychedelics as Light, and therefore Christ is the psychedelic. When you eat the body of Christ – smoke the psychedelic – you can get high enough to see beings, and those beings are seen as the angels of the Lord, the messengers of God.

Operating out of Manhattan's Lower East Side, the Temple practises a revisionist Christianity and its members see themselves as apostles of a very real Jesus, a Jesus baptised by modern-day John the Baptist Timothy Leary, the man who spread the Word about the coming of Christ, the arrival of psychedelics. Inspired by visions in which members realised that the psychedelic was the Light, the Temple evolved its theology beginning with the revised story of the Garden of Eden. In their visions, they saw that what the biblical Serpent actually offered Eve was the psychedelic – intimate knowledge of God – a knowledge which both she and Adam accepted but which a morally corrupt mankind could not. The Temple's mission is to spread what they consider to be the true and inspired Word of God.

3

Psychoactives in World Religions

The most beautiful and deepest experience a man can have is the sense of the mysterious. It is the underlying principle of religion as well as all serious endeavour in art and science.

Albert Einstein

Ask yourself this:
'Are you a human being
having a spiritual
experience,
or a spiritual being
having a human
experience?'

Wayne Dyer

At first glance, all the world religions agree – drugs have no role to play in religious practice. On closer examination the situation is less clear-cut. The traditions vary in the strength of their views on the subject and within each faith there are also maverick voices speaking out for a more open outlook on the issue.

For the believer, psychoactives may act as an awakening vehicle, resulting in conversion to a major religion. Some followers also choose to continue to use drugs as an aid to their spiritual life while remaining within a mainstream religion. But the taboo on drug use, both in a societal and a religious context, means that most do so silently and at risk of losing much if discovered.

Attitudes towards drugs in mainstream religion

In the mainstream religions, while such mind-altering exercises as meditation, fasting or even flagellation may be encouraged, introducing certain psychoactive substances into the body is considered unacceptable.

The exception is alcohol. In Christianity, wine is a sanctified intoxicant with a purely symbolic function. It is canon law that fermented wine be used for Mass, rather than a substitute such as grape juice, but the levels are not such as to produce an altered state. The imagery of intoxication is used, though; an example is one of the early Latin hymns for the daily office, from the fourth century, which talks of the 'sober drunkenness' of the spirit. In Judaism, alcohol plays a key social role, especially during Passover.

Within Hinduism all psychoactives (incuding alcohol) are prohibited and in some sects, such as the Krishna Consciousness movement, even stimulants such as caffeine and nicotine are forbidden.

Islam also has strict views on the use of drugs. The Muslim College of London, for instance, told us that: 'The use of drugs that affect human perception and consciousness is totally prohibited by Islam. The only Muslim community who reportedly made use of drugs were the Hasheesn who used to persuade their disciples through the use of hasheesh to murder their enemies and who gave us the word assassin. They are regarded as heretics.' (There is more information about the exploits of the cannabis-consuming Order of the Assassins later in this chapter.)

Buddhist teachers argue that insights derived from drugs may be illusory, and a spiritual experience on drugs can hide the depth of change needed to transform oneself. Drugs reinforce the belief that external help is necessary to reach a certain state of mind, when in fact one should be seeking that state from within. The guidelines in Theravada Buddhism for dealing with intoxicants are included in the five basic precepts for living a wise life and require one to abstain from using intoxicants to the point of loss of awareness. Responsibility is thus placed on the individual to recognise the varying degrees of psychoactivity.

The first and perhaps most obvious reason for the discouragement of drug use by religious groups is the illegality of drugs. As in the rest of society, misinformation from media and governments can also lead to a knee-jerk reaction against all drugs. However, the reasons for prohibiting drugs in world religions depend to some extent on the beliefs of each religion.

3

Hindu teachers regard drug-induced experiences as dangerous as they are believed to cloud one's vision, thus compounding the illusory state (Maya) from which humans should be seeking to liberate themselves.

Evangelical Christians regard most drugs which alter one's perception (whether illegal or not) as sinful. Drugs are generally seen as unnatural,[1] leaving one out of control and in a state of openness to the devil. Drug use is seen as a substitute for authentic spiritual life rather than as a means of accessing spirituality, a point made by the Board of Social Responsibility of the Church of England: 'Drug use reflects an inner spiritual emptiness, and the search for a rich and fulfilling life.'[2]

Ironically, many of the early therapeutic LSD trips were taken by Anglican clergy under the psychiatric supervision of Dr Frank Lake, an Anglican clergyman who founded a school called Clinical Theology. Lake did not see LSD as simply a therapeutic tool. He practised therapy within a theological and mystical framework and used LSD in that context.

A deeper reason for the reluctance of mainstream religions to acknowledge that psychoactives may have a role to play in spiritual life could lie in the question of control. The word 'religion' itself comes from the Latin to bind (*religare*, to bind back), whereas drugs are often seen as a vehicle of release. Mystical experiences on drugs tend to be very private, personal affairs. It is generally a solitary path. While there are some churches that use a drug as a sacrament in a communal setting, such as the Santo Daime in Brazil, even then when an individual is in the depths of their experience they are completely alone. This has implications for religions where the priest or teacher has a mediating role. If a follower is able to experience a direct, personal relationship with the divine, the need for an intermediate authority may be reduced.

This point also applies to the wider issue of how the mainstream religions view the role of the mystical experience within their faith. Throughout history there has been a tension between the mystical and mainstream wings of certain of the world religions. Meister Eckhart, the German Dominican mystic of the thirteenth to fourteenth centuries, for instance, was denounced as a heretic by the Catholic Church because of his teachings.

Historical use

Looking to history, however, there are examples where the boundaries between religious drug use and the mainstream faiths have been less fixed.

Soma

Soma is a substance written about in the Vedas, a group of sacred texts which were used in 2000 BCE in the area known today as Afghanistan, Pakistan and northern India.

A collection of hymns – the Rig-Veda – is the earliest of the Vedic texts. Among the thousand hymns in the Rig-Veda, many portray soma variously as a god, a sacred plant, and a celestial drink transporting those who drink it into ecstatic, transcendental realms. The Vedic texts are obscure on the identity of this plant drug and give no explicit descriptions, but the methods of preparation of soma, and some of its uses, can be inferred. It is clear that it was a plant found near mountains, which was gathered by moonlight, then crushed to produce a golden liquid. Soma was used in a fire ritual in which three gods were celebrated: Agni (fire), Indra (god of the sky) and Soma (a god considered to be the divine personification of the soma liquid, and also the moon). Although the fire ritual continued to be observed after the Vedic period, the use of soma waned, perhaps due to supply difficulties, and soma instead became a philosophical concept, coming to mean any offering burnt on the ritual fire, the contents of the material world, or the 'life force'.

While Sanskrit scholars have shown little interest in the identity of the soma plant, the subject has been much debated among entheogenic explorers in the West. In 1971 Gordon Wasson published *Soma: Divine Mushroom of Immortality*,[3] setting out his theory that soma is the *Amanita muscaria* mushroom:

What is *Amanita muscaria*?

Amanita muscaria is a bright red mushroom, speckled with white, known also as the 'Fly Agaric' (said to derive from the belief that flies can be killed by it). Many people will recognise it as the 'fairy toadstool' often seen in fairy tale illustrations, suggesting ancient magical use of the mushroom.

The best-known ritual use of this plant is by shamanic tribes to induce religious trance. In some tribes only the shaman would eat the mushrooms, while in others all the men of the tribe would partake, but in all tribes where it was used it was central to their religious practices.

The mushrooms were usually dried, increasing their psychoactivity fivefold, and then chewed. The principal psychoactive ingredients in *Amanita muscaria* are ibotenic acid and muscimole, an alkaloid which remains active even when passed through kidneys. The psychoactive constituents remain present in the urine of a person who has eaten the mushroom, leading to the practice of 'recycling' the effects of the mushroom through urine-drinking.

3

Wasson suggests that soma is a mushroom because in the Rig-Veda no mention is made of leaves, roots or branches in relation to the plant, and it is referred to as 'the Not-Born Single Foot' which fits with the way mushrooms spring up suddenly and without seed, while 'single-foot' and 'one-legged' are widespread euphemisms for mushrooms. To support his argument that soma is the species of mushroom *Amanita muscaria*, he points to passages in the Rig-Veda which allude to urination, given the practice of recycling the urine of one who has consumed *Amanita muscaria* amongst Siberian tribes. He points to one in particular: 'Those charged with office, richly gifted, do full homage to Soma. The swollen men piss the flowing [soma].' This, however, does not actually link soma and urine drinking. Other criticisms of Wasson's theory relate to the geographical availability of soma.

The true identity of soma continues to be debated but it is clear that it was a psychoactive substance and that it was used as part of a religious rite.

The Order of the Assassins

It has been claimed that hashish played a leading role in the Ismaili sect of Islam, the 'Order of the Assasins'.[4] Founded by Hasan I Sabbah in eleventh-century Afghanistan, its followers were completely unafraid of death. They were certain that they would, on death, be entering a wonderful heavenly realm, and they *knew* it would be wonderful because they had already experienced it, through the 'magic' of their leader.

Robert Anton Wilson explains:

> The secret of Hasan's power – the trip to paradise given to all his followers – rested upon the powerful combination of hashish and some talented young ladies...Filled with hashish-stuffed food, the candidate for initiation was ushered into a certain Garden of Delights in Hasan's fortress temple of Alamout, high in the mountains of Afghanistan. There, the ladies, pretending to be the supernatural houris described by Mohammed in his vision of heaven, performed in such a manner that the men came out of their hashish trance with very clear memories of 'divine' sexual experiences and other earthly delights. None ever doubted that they had been in heaven...[5]

The sacred mushroom and the Cross

Rather more idiosyncratic speculation comes from a theory about the true origins of the Christian Church. In *The Sacred Mushroom and the Cross* John Allegro puts forward the theory that the Christian Church stemmed from an ancient fertility cult centred around the *Amanita muscaria* mushroom cult.[6] Biblical stories of Jesus are to be seen as mushroom myths, a cover story, written in a secret code during a time when the cult was under threat. The cult eventually perished but the stories became an historical basis on which a new cult – Christianity – was founded. This theory is very controversial and has not received much support from other scholars of religion.

Shifting perceptions?

In contemporary society the established religions, while holding the view that the use of psychoactive substances is wrong, are unable to ignore the issue of the impact of drugs on society. Since the 1960s the world religions have had to respond to major changes in society and the emergence of a new youth culture in which drugs and drug imagery play a major role.

The use of drugs by young people who have grown up within the faith is a particular dilemma for religious leaders. In 1995 the Evangelical Alliance commissioned a survey of the use of drugs amongst young British Christians. In the 17–30 age group it was found that 46.1 per cent had been offered drugs and 23.3 per cent had tried them, broadly similar to the figures found in general surveys of young people.

Mainstream religions often have to tackle drug use in society in ways which other groups do not. With the rise in the use of heroin and crack cocaine in recent years, inner city ministries, in particular, have been on the front line through their pastoral work in helping drug casualties. Their experience of the problems that drugs can cause may well lead to a further hardening of the attitude that all drug use is, or leads to, abuse and is therefore dangerous. But such work can also lead to a greater understanding of the complexity of the drug scene (or scenes).

3

There are individuals within the established faiths who believe that psychoactives may have a role to play in spiritual practice, albeit in a limited way. Their potential role is as a starting point in a spiritual journey. Drugs may have a place in establishing an initial spiritual connection which can be developed through more accepted practices and structures.

The spiritual teacher Ram Dass, formerly known as Richard Alpert, was a lecturer in psychology at Harvard University when his explorations into human consciousness led him to conduct intensive research with LSD and other psychedelics. The controversy this caused resulted in his dismissal from Harvard (along with Timothy Leary) and he travelled to India where he met his spiritual teacher Neem Karoli Baba and received his new name. His book *Be Here Now* has become a classic spiritual guide. In an interview in a Buddhist magazine he commented: 'I don't see psychedelics as an enlightening vehicle, but I do see them as an awakening vehicle. I see them as beginning a process that awakens you to the possibility...'[7]

Reverend Dr Kenneth Leech is a community theologian working in the East End of London. He has wide experience of drug work, having been a curate in London throughout the 1960s and 1970s. He was a founder of the Soho Drugs Group and of Centrepoint, an all-night shelter for homeless young people. In *Drugs and Pastoral Care* he says,'I have never understood why, in principle at least, mind-altering chemicals should not be used in the context of the spiritual journey'.[8] Intrigued by this, we interviewed him and asked him to expand on this point:

> I've seen people whose consciousness of reality is one-dimensional and very, very rigid and they regard the whole area of the transcendent and the whole imaginative world as a lot of nonsense. Then they take a psychedelic drug and their whole way of looking at the world changes. That may or may not be a positive thing but in many cases it has been.
>
> I think the people I've seen where that has been a positive development are people who haven't gone on to use drugs on a very regular basis. They haven't become anti-drug either, they've simply said, 'This has helped us, this has taken us part of the way, we now need something else to take us further.'
>
> These were the people Allen Cohen termed the meta-hippies – people who had initially started to take an interest in spiritual paths because of their drug experience and might never have done so had they not taken drugs.
>
> It seems to me that there is no basic difference between getting absorbed in drug highs and getting absorbed in any other kind of high. There's a whole range of aids to spiritual experience which have been used and can also be misused. There's nothing special about drugs.
>
> I think the question about drugs is whether they can have a place within a framework of creating a 'healthy ecology of the spirit'. I would say, in principle, yes. But I think we need to move on and say what kind of place and in what conditions and with whom. I wouldn't say that any use of anything is necessarily right for everybody.
>
> It's curious that Christians should use the *problems* of drug use as an argument as there is a long tradition in the Church that the abuse of something does not alter its legitimate use. This is a basic teaching of moral theology since the time of Thomas Aquinas onwards, but people seem to forget it when they're talking about drugs.

Kenneth Leech has been criticised by both politicians and others within the Church for his views, but there does seem to be a growing recognition that young people, in particular, are seeking a sense of transcendence in places other than churches, synagogues and mosques.

One attempt to address this problem was the introduction of rave-style services in the 1980s with the Nine O'Clock Service in Sheffield, England. There is more on this phenomenon in the chapter, 'Rave Spirituality'.

A rabbi, albeit one with unconventional views, spoke to Nicholas on this issue facing the traditional religions:

> Nowadays, young people are more likely to have a spiritual experience at a rave than in a church or synagogue. The feeling of oneness and seeing life from a new aspect is an equally valuable experience for ravers. Priests who want to understand young people should take Ecstasy for themselves, both in order to understand them, and to see the validity of spiritual experiences produced by drugs.

3

Conversion

One of the ways in which the alliance of drugs and spirituality has most strongly challenged the mainstream faiths is through people who convert as a result of their drug experiences. This has been more of an issue for some religions than for others.

In January 1996 the Buddhist magazine *Tricycle* published a special issue called 'Psychedelics: Help or Hindrance?' In a survey included in the magazine over 40 per cent of readers said that their interest in Buddhism was sparked off by psychedelics; 59 per cent thought that psychedelics and Buddhism do mix, while 41 per cent disagreed; 71 per cent believed that 'psychedelics are not a path, but can provide a glimpse of the reality to which Buddhist practice points'. The age of the respondents was significant, with more using psychedelics over 50 or under 30 than those aged between 30 and 50, the latter category being the most against the use of drugs.

Hinduism has also attracted many followers as a result of drug experiences. In the 1960s and 1970s ISKCON (International Society for Krishna Consciousness), in particular, benefited from the growing interest in both Eastern religions and psychoactive drugs. A follower in the London temple said that anybody who came to them after a drug-induced experience would be treated in the same way as any other seeker. Their experience would be examined to see how far it matched what the scriptures say, they would be warned that drug-induced visions are likely to be illusory, and they would be encouraged to follow the devotional path of chanting, reading the scriptures, and purifying their material existence.

The Eastern religions certainly benefited disproportionately in the 1960s from an influx of converts who were seeking answers to spiritual questions following drug experiences. Since most Hindu teachings, particularly, are quite strict on the use of mind-altering substances, it might seem unusual that they attracted such a number of these seekers. However, awareness of the Eastern mystical traditions was very high at the time. The hippie era popularised Eastern-style clothes, music and religion. Writers such as Ram Dass and Alan Watts, an ex-Anglican priest turned Zen Buddhist, were influential. Timothy Leary, the high priest of the LSD movement, wrote (along with Ralph Metzner and Richard Alpert/Ram Dass) a manual for psychedelic use based on *The Tibetan Book of the Dead*. The arrival of cheap, mass air travel meant that seekers could quite easily go to India to find out for themselves about yoga, meditation and chanting. In addition, during that period the Christian Church was at the peak of its liberal phase, and much more concerned with wider social issues than with mysticism or contemplation. For those who had had a great mystical feeling of unity on LSD or mescalin it seemed completely natural to turn eastwards. The nature of the experiences themselves also has to be considered. It has been argued that where there are no strong pre-existing beliefs or leanings, a spiritual experience on psychoactives will tend to turn one towards pantheistic faiths.

Questions raised by a drug experience can spark off a spiritual quest which leads the seeker to explore a variety of paths to find that which best matches their values, beliefs and background. In this way John, an Englishman, became a Quaker after an LSD trip.

> Before I had the experience (on LSD), I was in a really negative state of mind. I was suffering from clinical depression, and I was prescribed various antidepressants. There were many factors contributing to my depression, one major factor being an incredible, and often overwhelming, fear of death. This often resulted in quite severe panic attacks. I think this is because I had always taken a highly logical/scientific view of things. Death, for me, was a biological process...All brain activity would cease and I would stop thinking. I guess I didn't ever want to stop thinking. These thoughts

occupied my mind far too much of the time, leaving daily life somewhat difficult to cope with.

The experience itself is very difficult to describe. I was having intense feelings of infinite knowledge...It was as if I had discovered the true nature of the universe. There was a great sense of unity. I knew that I had died, or at least that I was no longer human, but that brought with it some kind of ecstatic freedom. It was as if I was one with the universe, or one with God (personally, I don't differentiate between the two).

The trip did turn sour though. I think it was because it had been challenging all my previous thoughts about spirituality, and maybe as I was coming down, my rational mind was taking over again. I had some really frightening hallucinations...I heard voices shouting at me. Sometimes I felt that the voices were punishing me. I could feel entities trying to take away my life energy. I saw visions of myself as an old man, lying dead on the floor. I looked in the mirror and saw my face as if I were a hundred years old.

3

I have tried to interpret this experience many times, and failed to draw any satisfactory conclusions. What it did do, was to give me a new perspective on my own spirituality. It gave me confidence that there is, or at least there might be, something out there. That something is binding us, and our universe together that defies the laws of science. Maybe not God in the biblical sense, but I suppose God is as good a word as any. It was this that prompted me to become a Quaker.

The Religious Society of Friends (Quakers), unlike many other religons, have no set laws or beliefs. Most of us are Christians, but this is by no means mandatory. In Quaker meeting, we sit for the majority of the time in silent contemplation. If someone feels moved to speak, they may do so. People say anything, from a short story, to something that happened to them on their way to work. In this way, we can help guide each other's thoughts, or we can choose not to be guided if we so desire. Afterwards most of us stay and talk. It's a great opportunity to learn from each other, and share thoughts.

My experience was the first step in helping me form my own spiritual beliefs. I became a Quaker because I wanted to share my thoughts and meditation with others, and yet my spiritual beliefs did not conform to those outlined by other religions.

Conversion can also be a very sudden event where an individual is called to a particular faith through a vision, or voices, in a drug-induced experience. This was the case with 'Jill' and 'Edward' to whose story Ian Cotton devotes a whole chapter in his book on the revival of evangelical and charismatic Christianity, *The Hallelujah Revolution*. After taking two 'soft green tablets' (sold to them as Ecstasy) in a club off the Charing Cross Road, they experienced terrifying visions of pain, death, evil and the devil. After many hours the experience suddenly changed and they saw visions of the Cross. They began to pray and repent and finally 'that all-pervasive sense of wickedness was gradually replaced by the most profound joy either Edward or Jill had ever known. More, the voice of God himself was in the flat there talking to them...'

Cotton concludes that 'to Edward and Jill, their conversion experience, far from being less real (because drug-induced) than the rest of their lives, was a thousand times more real than anything they had ever known. So it is quite natural that their commitment, so deeply embedded in their conscious-ness, was so passionate and strong.'

Continued use

Once someone has converted to a world religion following a drug experience they may face a dilemma. While some will view their drug-use as an awakening vehicle which has served its purpose, others will wish to continue to use psy-choactives as a sacrament within a traditional belief system. In most cases this is not a decision which is taken lightly. Individuals who choose this path risk the opprobrium of their fellow believers if they are open about their activi-ties, and in a close-knit religious community may also face losing their jobs, friends and entire social support structure. If use is covert then they may have to face feelings of fear and guilt which could colour their experience. Yet, as demonstrated in the account below, the value of using psychoactives may be judged to be worth the risks involved.

Lee, a social worker from the American Midwest, became a Christian sixteen years ago, and he attributes much of his spiritual growth to his experiences with LSD at the time of his conversion. In his account here he focuses on his struggle to reconcile his inner need to explore entheogen use and mysticism with the strict views of his conservative evangelical church:

When I was 21 years old, I became a Christian after spending most of my teenage years avoiding the sermons and influences of pious relatives. I had come to the end of my ability to tolerate the bitter, self-absorbed young man I had become, and my conversion marked a significant point of development for me in my spiritual growth. This, and even the mental conception of my life as having a spiritual dimension, was dramatically influenced by a series of experiences I had a year earlier involving the use of LSD. In my view, none of my subsequent religious commitments would have happened if not for the opening to the spirit that this substance facilitated.

My experience as a Christian has almost entirely been in the context of conservative evangelicalism, a way of belief that is notoriously mistrustful of most forms of mysticism, especially those that involve drugs or trance states. For most of the past fifteen years, I publicly subscribed to the Church's view that psychoactive drugs were taboo unless prescribed by a doctor, and that intentionally seeking an altered state of consciousness in order to make spiritual discoveries was opening the door to deviant and deceptive forms of spirituality. To challenge these opinions would open me up to scrutiny and potential confrontation with those who saw themselves as guardians of the faith. Even though I could look back on my own drug use and glean from those experiences some powerfully transforming insights (as well as many happy personal memories), I also saw how obsessed I became with LSD after my first few eye-opening trips. I knew from personal experience how aimless and wasteful a drug-centred existence could become after several years of living that way.

After my conversion, the changes in my personal habits, my appreciation of life's simpler pleasures, and my increased sense of being able to 'fit in' all registered as notable improvements on the years prior to embracing Jesus as my saviour. It was not too difficult for me to adopt the view that God had graciously redeemed me from a path that was certain to lead to further dissipation and spiritual blindness. I heard confident confirmations from many enthusiastic Christians, who had once seemed so strange to me but were now my brothers and sisters in the Lord, that a fulfilling and happy life was best found without the corrupting influence of drugs.

However, despite my honest agreement with many who saw drugs as a scourge, I knew, and kept private, that I certainly would not have given any religious ideas much consideration if I had not seen my life from the 'eternal perspective' that LSD made possible. The use of drugs had now been confined to my pre-Christian era: I was taught that no respectable believers would ever set themselves up for temptation by taking drugs intentionally to see what it was like from a Christian vantage point. Most importantly, I was now in a new community, soon to be married and had no drug connections, so I could not seriously resolve my questions, other than by reading what others had to say. Among my Christian friends were several people who had used different kinds of drugs before their conversion. Within this peer group, a form of status-seeking was practised which involved taking the most militant, uncompromising stand against any religious idea that seemed to lower our regard for the Bible as God's Word or the Gospel as God's only way of salvation. The prospects were slim for reasoned, level-headed, informed debate on the nature or value of drug-induced (or other) forms of altered consciousness.

The preceding paragraph covers the first decade and a half of my Christian life. Over those years, I veered back and forth internally, doing a lot of reading, praying and reflecting on the various implications of living as a spiritually maturing Christian man. I look back now and see how the outer expectations of a largely conformist, conservative Christian subculture conflicted with my inner inclinations toward more tolerant, mystical concepts of faith and relationship to God. A kind of spiritual personality split finally broke out into the open during the summer and fall of 1997. I had made numerous efforts to find the evangelical perspective on life more convincing. I took on the role of deacon in our Calvinistic Presbyterian congregation, teaching children's and adult Sunday School. I read many sophisticated arguments defending the biblical worldview from classical as well as contemporary sources. I listened intently to the sermons, taking notes and analysing the cases that were made, almost all aimed at pointing out the fundamental errors and deliberate suppressions of God's truth in modern culture. I kept at arm's length the siren songs of liberalism, evolutionism, globalism, secular humanism and all the other -isms that I'd been warned were the wiles of Satan trying to rob me of God's blessings, and even my very salvation. At Bible studies I met kind, generous, concerned individuals who combined personal integrity with a sincere concern for the lost (those who didn't have a personal relationship with Jesus Christ.)

But in all of that, there was still something missing...something really big, really real, that I had once known and was now wondering how or if I might ever find again. That something was the intimate, soul-grabbing tenderness of the presence of God, not some kind of intellectual, aesthetic comprehension, but a vivid and unmistakable manner that didn't leave me feeling as if I'd been talked into it. It was the sort of life-transforming vision that I read about in the Christian mystics, like Thomas Merton, Meister Eckhart, John of the Cross, Teresa of Avila. I sought freedom and intense genuineness of spiritual experience, not the taut, rationalistic, scholastically defended apologetics of evangelical theologians, or the militant, pious imagery of the leading preachers and devotional writers widely represented in our church library. It is not an easy thing to reconsider one's course in midstream, and much more difficult to actively redirect it. Indeed, I would not recommend such a change to any person unless they have the most compelling crisis of conscience to motivate them. I just couldn't remain a part of this movement, because it wound up rubbing too strongly against the grain of my basic personality.

3

After about a year or two of struggling significantly with this inner conflict between my conservative public persona and my hippie-mystic within, I began studying in earnest the literature of mysticism. About this time I was getting around to finishing up my Bachelor's degree, doing a lot of reading and writing in the liberal arts. I was learning how to use the Internet, I was doing professional social work with emotionally impaired teenagers and I was going through all of the mundane but mind-blowing changes of life. A young acquaintance of mine was getting involved with the use of drugs, specifically marijuana and LSD, at about the same age that I was when I started doing that stuff. I shared with him my longtime interest in the subject of psychedelics, and we talked about our experiences. The rapport that we were able to establish made me revisit some of the journals and papers I had written during those years and rekindled my desire once more to actively participate in the psychedelic experience.

However, LSD's illegality remained worrying to me. I had no desire to put my family or myself at risk of trouble with the law, even though the ideals I pursued were of high importance to me. Plus there was the not-so-trivial matter of my wife's fervent opposition to the use of drugs. So it was quite clear that, much as I desired another LSD trip, there was no chance of it becoming a part of my lifestyle. I kept this interest to myself. A couple of months of reflection passed, where I analysed the records of my own and others' experiences, read more about it from medical and intellectual perspectives, and had some email dialogue with trippers I'd found on the Internet. Then I came upon a substance that seemed to offer me an easy passport into the psychedelic realms: DXM (dextromethorphan), a cough suppressant that was in the process of being popularised for a new generation of teenagers looking for a cheap buzz. I read up on the drug at a few different websites dedicated to passing on reliable, factual knowledge of how it could be used to achieve enhanced psychoactive states of consciousness. I became proficient at navigating my way through some very remarkable, low-level trips in the comfort of my own home, undetected by my family, gradually growing in confidence that I was doing a worthwhile thing. I saw the effect that it was having on my personal creativity and my rejuvenation from the spiritual weariness that I was feeling as a result of my increasing dissatisfaction with the teachings and rigid perspective of our Church. DXM seemed to come along at a time when I needed reassurance that daily life was something more than just a holding pattern until we arrive at the Last Judgment. Simple things like conversations with my family and co-workers, the textures of nature and humanity's bumbling attempts to improve upon it, and the patterns of our ideas and mental life all took on new, fascinating qualities. These insights remained with me for a long time after the drug wore off, and conveyed to me again that sense of life as joyous possibility that everyday pressures are so adept at squelching. And of course, I saw music, movies and other creative artefacts more vividly as expressions of the deep magnificence of being. All this, as well as the growing network of new relationships that I was developing over the Internet, had quite a stimulating effect on me.

But I still felt an unfortunate need to maintain secrecy, which put a damper on things. I knew that I could not go on for long concealing this new interest from my wife. One night I told her about it, tentatively hoping that the easy availability and legality of the substance might at least convince her to let me use it more openly, and perhaps try it herself so that she could have a mystical experience of her own. My hopes were deeply disappointed (in order to be fair, I must add, so were her hopes for me). She reacted with the outraged incredulity that I probably should have expected.

I've recently stopped attending my conservative Church and I'm looking at more inclusive, less authoritarian expressions of Christianity. The use of entheogens is way outside the parameters of our Church's teaching and practice, and this interest has probably hastened my withdrawal from the congregation and emboldened me to express my doctrinal disagreements. But I'm reluctant to concede that I've fallen away due to drugs. To me, this is a path that I've been on for a number of years, and drugs are just one small component of a larger vision I'm pursuing. In fact, I'm willingly giving up the use of DXM and other psychoactives while I work out some things in my marriage. I've made it clear to my wife that I'm not necessarily quitting this practice permanently, but I don't expect that I will use drugs more than a few times per year, and maybe even less frequently. My spiritual roadblock has been dismantled, and now my practice is to incorporate what I've learned into everyday life. In public I've not made it known that I'm in favour of tripping; much as I would like to, I still fear the potential social and economic repercussions (I don't want to get fired from my job over this!). I would like to get into a position where I can become more publicly involved as a responsible citizen—advocate for discerning, intentional and responsible use of entheogens on a clinical basis, and eventually within the tolerable limits of the wider culture.

3

I know that most people on either side of the issue regard drugs and Christianity as utterly opposed and incompatible, but despite this tension, there is a tremendous amount of creative potential when the two sources of insight are brought into contact. They both have an enormous power to shape the manner in which we interact with other people and our environment, and I believe that if we can get beyond the atmosphere of suspicion and hostility that each group holds toward the other, many good things will result. The Christian legacy of evocative symbols and compassionate ethics (when rightly applied) runs deep through Western consciousness and has much to offer to global society. Likewise, the psychedelic vision can have a profound effect in snapping the materialistic and egocentric straitjackets that have bound us to many destructive habits, as long as we are able to avoid abusing the substances.

In some ways, I feel like an isolated pioneer who knows that there's gold hidden in the hills, but I just haven't found the tools and people that will help me bring it out to the full light of day. I pray that more people will be drawn to join in this endeavour.

Nicholas interviewed two Buddhist monks, both of whom use Ecstasy, one in the Soto Zen tradition, and the other Rinzai Zen.

Otto first took LSD at university. In fact, he moved into a commune that took LSD at regular weekly rituals, but later this quest for knowledge led him away from drugs and to yoga, which he practised intensively for several years. He then travelled and got involved with Zen, living in a Soto Zen community for ten years, until he was ordained as a monk. He has since been made an abbot by his master, i.e. given the power to ordain new Zen monks. He divides his time between Buddhism and social/ecological activism. Over the previous five years, Otto had taken Ecstasy about fifteen times, usually alone or with his wife or intimate friends. It provided him with great clarity and calmness, as after a week-long sitting, when everything became more clear, more awake. Although Eastern teachings are usually strongly anti-drug, his particular tradition was an exception to the rule, and his teacher in Japan had used peyote, LSD and Ecstasy.

Otto has used Ecstasy for teaching with a few students, including one who has since been ordained a monk. This was a man who was extremely keen, and put tremendous effort into trying to succeed in meditation. Ecstasy helped him to see that trying itself was his main obstacle. Another student was a very successful and hard-driving businessman. Ecstasy simply stopped him – he made a dramatic change into a warm contented person who just wanted to sit quietly in the zendo. When I asked if success through the use of Ecstasy was as valid as without, he replied: 'It is the experience that matters, not how you get there. Look back at the history of the major religions. Many of their founders and saints had their mystical unions during wound fever, during which, as we know today, the body produces psychedelic substances. A good example would be Ignatius de Loyola, the founder of the Jesuit order.'

I asked if Otto thought there might be types of people who would not benefit from Ecstasy, or who might be misled by it. 'It could be a problem for those who are not sufficiently well grounded, those who have a tendency to float into other worlds rather easily anyway. However, most of us are too earthbound, too stuck in this particular reality, and a little help from a friend can be of great value. Unlike LSD and other drugs, Ecstasy works in terms of relationships – with oneself, God, nature. It even opens up a common ground with other people whom one does not yet know.'

I asked Otto whether there was any point in using Ecstasy once enlightenment had been achieved. 'Enlightenment is a transitory experience for most of us, and it's seldom achieved. After a while, the true experience becomes replaced by a memory of it. We need direct experience to refresh us from time to time.'

But, I asked, is the drug-induced experience really the same? After some hesitation Otto replied, 'Yes, the state of mind is identical, yet there is a subtle difference, perhaps due to the drug's physical effects on the body. Without the drug, there is one less factor. This is simpler, and perhaps this implies it is better. The value of the state is the same: to be able to look back and see one's "normal" state of mind with a clear but different perspective.'

3

I asked what the ideal situation is for a beginner. 'A trusted, more experienced friend is highly recommended. You must create an environment that you find conducive. Do whatever spiritual practice you have. For some this may be singing, praying, painting, meditating or sitting in a cathedral; for others walking alone in the mountains. You must be prepared to accept that not every attempt is positive. The spiritual path is like a climber walking in the mountains who is lost in the fog and unable to see the peak he has set out to climb. All of a sudden the fog clears and he experiences the reality of the peak, and gains a sense of direction. Even though the fog moves in again, and it's still a long, hard climb, this glimpse of the goal and direction is usually an enormous help and encouragement. And Ecstasy can provide that glimpse.'

I was also visited by Werner, a Zen Buddhist monk and teacher of meditation in his early seventies. Werner has taken Ecstasy about twenty-five times over ten years. He has found it most effective on the second day of a seven-day meditation. The first day is spent in preparation for the meditative state, so that he is already fully focused on the task by the time he actually takes the drug, which makes it easier for him to go deeply into the meditative state. He feels that the experience would be of great value to some of his devout but stiff fellow Zen monks, but there is only one who shares his secret.

Werner's story

All my life I have been searching for spiritual values, the meaning of life...While living in the States I was introduced to marijuana and used it for recreational purpose, without any significant experience. Later on I experimented once with mescalin with equally disappointing results. However, two nights later I awoke during the night with a jolt, presumably from a dream. Anyway, I sat straight up in bed and 'saw' everything as if through a microscope. Furniture and walls were no longer solid as we see them normally. I saw empty space between particles on the one hand and on the other hand I saw everything interconnected with everything else. There was no longer any 'separateness' of things.

This vision was overwhelming and I fell back on the pillow and back to sleep again. The next day my life was changed and 'the hunt was on'! I could no longer continue with the conventional life and decided on concrete steps which eventually brought me to become a Zen monk and study Buddhism. After some years of intensive training I experimented with MDMA, with astonishing results. Primarily the effects were the opening of my heart, feeling loving in a way that I had never before experienced. In addition to it I saw things in a totally new way and felt the need to put it in writing which, however, turned out poorly due to the fact that I never was good at using words.

On later occasions using MDMA, or what was supposed to be it, the effects were more mental. I could focus on a subject and stay with it for extended periods, lasting for hours and even days. I would say that the emphasis lay in intuitive perception rather than intellectual activity. It has to be remembered, that at that time my thinking, or better my consciousness, was preoccupied with grasping the absolute reality, spending all my time with meditation and Zen practice. With the aid of MDMA I could spend extended periods focusing my attention on subjects that I could not have done to that extent without it.

I came to the conclusion that certain psychedelics (I never have used LSD) could be beneficial in the spiritual quest as a starter, an occasional support, or a deepening agent. However, I'm convinced that one must have an inclination in that direction to start with. I believe firmly that psychedelics will only bring to the surface what lies dormant. If there is confusion, fear and guilt, you'll experience the proverbial 'bum trip'.

Within Sufism there is anecdotal evidence of cannabis use, although many orthodox Sufis reject the use of drugs completely as not the way of a true mystic. Peter Lamborn Wilson travelled in the East for a number of years and made these observations:

> I met many thousands of gurus, mursheds, fakirs and full-time dervishes.
> Among the most impressive were several devoted cannabis users...I have
> heard some Sufis claim spiritual benefits from opium, usually on the
> grounds that by releasing them from tension and sadness it allows them to
> concentrate on spiritual matters.[9]

Mention should also be made of the *nagas-babbas*, wandering Hindu holy
men, who are also known for their use of cannabis.

A means to an end

3

Finding either lay members or those with leadership responsibilities in the
mainstream faiths who are willing to talk openly about positive aspects of drug
use is difficult. If anything, it is more difficult now than in the 1960s when
greater numbers of people moved towards world religions as a result of their
drug experiences.

Yet it is clear from the accounts and interviews in this chapter that psychoactives *can* have a role to play in the spiritual life of those in mainstream
religions. It is also clear that those who do use them in this way do so with an
awareness of their potential for spiritual growth, but also of their limitations.
These accounts show psychoactives used with respect and care. Preoccupation
with their use is discouraged, as is confusing the messenger with the message.

4

Contemporary Shamanism for Westerners

It's not what we learn about plants

that is important, but what they can

teach us about themselves that is.

Jason Volpe

We must beware of committing the fatally common fallacy of assuming that all we see is all there is to see.

C.W. Leadbeater

Contemporary shamanism for Westerners – is this not a con-
tradiction in terms?[1] If we look at the traditional indigenous
village and the role of the shaman therein, certainly. It is not
difficult to give a romantic account that would fit an entheo-
tourist brochure: 'We entered a remote village in the middle of the Amazonian
jungle and saw a circle of natives gathered for ceremony. They drank a brew
made of divine plants, which gave them beautiful visions, taught them about
healing and allowed them to communicate with the spirits.'

This is what many hope for when they venture out into the mysterious
jungles, deserts and mountains, looking for a special adventure. However, naively,
it overlooks the complex social structures and spiritual belief systems which
govern these so-called primitive cultures. For Westerners it would require years
of study and experience of the culture to understand the way that native people
use psychoactives. It is only given to a few to explore fully the shamanic way.

Having said that, there is a growing interest in shamanic practices, even
though they may be watered down from their origins. Maybe it is our search
for new forms of spirituality or the quest for forgotten knowledge that drives
the Westerner to take his pick from shamanic practices. And who is to say that
this cannot be fruitful? It could be that the pick and mix method is the only
accessible way to use and integrate shamanic wisdom in an industrialised
society.

The accounts in this chapter are not from indigenous people themselves,
but from visitors or people who have adopted some of the indigenous ways to
give structure and depth to the ceremonies or workshops in which psychoactives are used with spiritual intent. This is the context in which we look at
contemporary shamanism for Westerners.

How indigenous people use medicine

In indigenous cultures psychoactives have always played an important role. In
the absence of chemical industries in these societies, the traditional shamanic
use of psychoactives is plant based, such as ayahuasca for the Cashinahua,
mushrooms for the Mazatecs, peyote for the Huichols, or San Pedro for the
Andean Indians.

Sometimes ingestion is confined to the shaman, who is at once priest and healer. The concepts of spirit and health are completely interwoven in traditional societies. When someone is physically ill, it is most often seen as an illness of the spirit and therefore healing is not restricted to the body. The 'medicine', as the psychoactive is called in this context, is used to cure physically (for example as a purgative), and at the same time spiritually, as in the case of soul retrieval. This is where the psychoactive component of the medicine becomes very important. Through the psychoactive, the healer/shaman gets to see beyond ordinary vision and uses the spirit of the plant to help him diagnose the illness. In this way he can get information about what damages his patient emotionally or see if other spirits have attacked his soul. The plant spirit indicates what his patient needs in order to come back to balance again – a very holistic form of healing. The shaman is often an archetypal wounded healer. He (or she) has gone through a severe illness, even a near-death experience, before becoming the village 'medicine man'. He is therefore qualified to travel to the 'world beyond' and speak with the plant-spirits.

4

In other tribes, all the adults will take the medicine and a form of self-healing takes place through the insights the plant-spirit offers. In a group, people can make their own individual journeys, but within a clear ceremonial context. Depending on the tradition, this can take the form of praying to the earth spirits or the ancestors; or the elaborate construction of an altar. It may be that the ceremony is preceded by a period of fasting, dieting or solitude. Meditation of various kinds, dances, special music, ceremonial gestures and clothing may also accompany the taking of the medicine. This is not so different from some of the more 'new age' workshops that are occurring in the Western world.

Medicines are considered sacred and there is always a purpose to taking them: for healing, divination, gaining insight or receiving information from the spirit world. Since the spirit world is so much part of the day-to-day touchable world in these cultures, it is not considered so extraordinary to communicate with plant-spirits.

All shamans speak of talking to plants as a matter of course. Enriques Gonzales Rubio visited the Mazatec shamans. They spoke of the mushroom spirits which live amongst them and as far as they are concerned have always been around to help them. One of the shamans, Don Pablo, says:

> The mushrooms are something wonderful. You can see very deep to resolve problems. When someone gets sick, their spirit ends up lost somewhere out there. With the mushroom, you can find their spirit, in the mountains, the gorges, the basements, the woods, the bottom of the sea. Even in other planets or the Great Beyond. The practice of eating the mushroom is very old, very ancient. Before the Spaniards came, the Mazatecos already had this tradition. I inherited my knowledge from my dead mother. She was a good healer.[2]

The plant medicines are tied up with a whole cosmology. Most indigenous tribes using visionary plants will tell stories of how the plants showed them their origin and the creation of the world.

Red Eagle is a native American shaman. She gives a picture of the world as she came to know it through the plant-spirit of cannabis:

> The whole system is crossed by a huge labyrinth system of tunnels. A shaman enters these tunnels for journeys. Some are guarded, however, and plants such as cannabis are powerful keepers of tunnel entrances. You have to 'friend' the spirit of the drug, so it will allow you to pass. Via that tunnel you may then enter secret worlds of perception, and access the knowledge taken to these chambers by travellers who came before. In the case of cannabis the treasure trove is huge, since it is one of the most ancient companions of mankind.

While someone from an indigenous tribe and someone from the industrialised world might find they have a similar individual response to a psychoactive, different social structures mean that the psychoactive plays a very different role in collective social life. Pedro Fernandes Leite da Luz visited the Hupda people in the northwestern Amazonian region and looked at the important role that psychoactive plants play in the social life of the Hupda men:

> The Hupda are skilled hunters and specialists in the collection and cultivation of psychoactive and poisonous plants used not only by themselves but also by other neighbouring groups with whom they interact.
>
> *Patu Erythroxylum coca var. ipadu* is known by the Hupda as 'patu' and is used daily. Starting around 4.30 p.m. the sound of the wooden mortar and pestle that prepares the leaves can be heard in almost all of the

households. Then till about ten at night the men eat patu and talk about the trails used in hunting, discuss problems affecting the group, or organise a party. As such patu has an important role in the socialisation of the Hupda men.

Another plant is 'xenhet', a red powder made from trees of the genus *Virola*. Xenhet is at the same time a tree, a powder made from the tree, and an 'enchanted being'. This being, the 'Xenhet', is considered to be a man about eight centimetres tall who, when the shaman inhales the powder for the first time, starts living in the shaman's ear. Here he teaches the shaman about the visions and knowledge which come from 'caapi' (a psychoactive vine) consumption. Extremely valued by the Hupda, the use of xenhet is fundamental for those who want to be a shaman.

In taking caapi the Hupda see 'how the world moves', as they say, which means the reason for the creation of the world, how it was done, and the laws which govern its workings. To obtain knowledge, to be intelligent and have good vision and discernment, it is necessary to take caapi and to learn from it the true form and meaning of all things. In spite of being the same plant, *Banisteriopsis caapi*, the Hupda distinguish seven different types of caapi in accord with the maturity of the plant, the part used and the general appearance of the vine. To ingest caapi with the goal of having good visions, one must observe certain procedures. For some days beforehand one cannot eat anything roasted, salted, warm, or prepared by a menstruating woman. It is necessary to clean the body repeatedly by taking an emetic drink, as well as by maintaining sexual abstinence. Both the preparation and the ingestion of caapi take place far from the eyes of women and children, otherwise the drinker may get sick. Caapi is used in fertility rites and by the shaman to heal and for its capacity to show sickness and its causes. Those who want to be good hunters also drink caapi, which will show where to find game and how not to be perceived by it. Therefore, the caapi plays an important role in Hupda society as the principal medicine and also the primary conduit for all tribal knowledge...[3]

4

Entheotourism, a new industry?

'What will you do for your holidays this year?'

Looking in the holiday sections of new age magazines one can find some alluring advertisements for jungle tours offering psychoactive substances:

three all night ayahuasca ceremonies per week

gliding down the river

desert vision quests

motorised canoes

rites of passage with plant-spirit guides

meet the master shaman

laundry service

sacred journey

gourmet meals

indigenous style living in the wilderness

chanting beneath the tall trees
that are the abode of the healing spirits of the forest

Sounds great! An exotic adventure: native ceremonies, real shamans, spirit encounters, a journey of a lifetime and many stories to tell your friends afterwards...But is this the whole story? It is very easy to idealise these trips sitting comfortably at home... The reality can be quite different.

Traditional cultures don't use these plants for a quick high, but as guides. They know that the lessons are not necessarily pleasant ones. In order to receive these teachings one may have to persevere for a long time and endure a lot of physical discomfort.

The shaman Don Pablo explains it to Enriques Gonzales Rubio in this way:

'In order to acquire those powers, it is necessary to understand the Path of your trip. You have to have courage and you have to stand whatever your trip shows you. You can see many things without knowing what they are. Those who take the mushroom for the first time suffer greatly. It is natural, just as it should be. All the pain from the past crowds the mind. But once you get over it, you are totally at peace. Many things become clear. You no longer have this angst. I have always been able to confirm that the mushroom is something wonderful. It takes you to the bottom of things. My forefathers, they were great priests. My mother was one.'

'What prayer do you say?'

'Once you smoke the mushroom over the copal*, you bless them seven times with the sign of the Cross. You ask the spirits to make the mushroom talk. If you are caught somewhere, in a bewitched place, the mushroom goes to pick you up and bring you home. Home is your body. That is why you have to invoke the Mountains, the Wind, Water and Fire, our gods. With their help, you can heal the sick. But to do this, you have to be clean and pure.'

'What happens when the healer is not?'

'He is not a healer.'

'Then it must be very difficult to be a healer?'

'It is.'

The journey may turn out to be less comfortable than the advertisements promise and the shaman may not be the one who can save one's life. There is an old saying: 'When the student is ready the teacher will appear.' The great shaman, who has the glossiest brochure and the best facilities to receive tourists eager to experience a touch of the divine, may not be the best teacher for the individual. The best healers are often simple, unassuming people, who are easily overlooked. As the anthropologist Gordon Wasson, who researched extensively the ritual use of psilocybin mushrooms amongst the Mazatec Indians said:

4

> Perhaps you will learn the names of a number of renowned curanderos, and your emissaries will even promise to deliver them to you, but then you wait and wait and they never come. You will brush past them in the market place and they will know you but you will not know them. The judge in the town hall may be the very man you are seeking and you may pass the time of day with him, yet never know that he is your curandero.

People look for shamans now in the way they looked for gurus in the Sixties, but in the shamanic tradition the plant itself is seen as the teacher, with the shaman being only the guide. It is, however, possible to stumble upon someone by accident who subsequently turns out to be a great teacher. This is what happened to Alan Shoemaker, who now leads tours himself:

> I explained to the schoolteacher that I had come looking for a shaman. As always, I felt silly using the vernacular, shaman, but curandero, the correct

*Incense used to cleanse sacred space.

term for the healers in South America, is way too confusing for the normal gringo.

The schoolteacher reached into his back pocket, pulling a business card from his billfold. It was the complicated, colour calling card of Dr Valentin Hampjes – Psychiatrist, Scientific Investigator of Medicinal Plants, and Neuro-Medicine.

'Must be a subtle way of saying he's a shaman,' I joked.

Dr Valentin Hampjes's business card somehow managed to remain with me for two weeks, so I decided to phone him. He invited us to his home in Tumbaco, a small community twenty miles outside of Quito. We knocked on the door and were greeted by a man of about 55 years with silver hair, beard, and laughing, mischievous eyes. He invited us in.

On the north wall inside his home was an altar covered with fresh and dried flowers with every deity imaginable represented by statuettes, photos and postcards. He even had a living enlightened master, Si Baba, resting there in a framed photograph. To the right of the altar, above the door to his private medicinal and massage room, was a poster of the Virgin Maria in a blissful repose. From the look of all these icons, it was clear Valentin was not the type of curandero to leave anything to chance.

He spoke to me of activating the 'healer within' by the use of the sacred power plants. If there are specific psychological or spiritual maladies, the patient can be shown, through visions while under the influence of one of the sacred power plants, when and where the errors were made. In many cases the manifestation of an illness, i.e. tumour, arthritis, etc. is based in unhealed traumas to the soul. These lead to psychological imbalances as well as physical manifestations. If we can allow the plants to show us why the disturbances exist (where they came from) we can begin to heal ourselves.

He invited us to return the next day, Saturday, at noon for a San Pedro ceremony. His pre-ceremonial dietary instructions were to fast upon awakening Saturday morning. He gave us a long list of herbs we were to purchase in the Quito market as well as to bring fresh cut flowers for the altar.

Candles were burning on the altar and the smell of incense filled his living room.

We found a comfortable seat against the walls of the room and Valentin instructed us on the proper behaviour to maintain during the ceremony.

'When you begin to feel the medicine you must not try and keep your rational mind in focus. This only makes it more difficult. Relax and allow the medicine to move through your body. Ego has no place here. The more you try and hold on to it the more the medicine will fight you. Get out of its way as quickly as possible. You may see images presented as if on a television screen. Try and not think on them tonight. You will have ample time for that in your reflections tomorrow. If you see something from your past or present, even your future, and it is sad, you may cry if you wish. But do not allow yourself to become too entrenched in it. Do not wallow in it. Allow it to pass. And the same if you see things that make you laugh. Validate it, but do not try and maintain it. Remember, "Yea, though I walk through the valley of the shadow of death, I will fear no evil, for thou art with me." However, if there come images you feel you cannot deal with, simply call me, my assistants Mohita or Muridunga, and we will come to sweep them away.'

'Please do not converse here in this room, it disturbs not only the others, who may be deeply involved with their personal work, but you must realise it prevents you from getting the information you need also. Conversation is of this waking reality and works on a different part of the brain. It will distract you from whatever messages you might receive. If you feel you must talk please go outside.'

'Should we be thinking of anything, or have some kind of focus as the San Pedro is taking effect?' someone asked.

Valentin said, '*Bueno*. It is sometimes good to focus your thoughts on something you want, for to empty your mind of all thoughts is a difficult task to master. And so, no matter how you prefer to approach your ecstatic state, remember: There is an old American song that goes something like, "you may not get what you want, but you get what you need",' and he laughed that big, semi-hysterical, head-tilted-back laugh that I have become accustomed to love.

Valentin changed into white clothing and began praying, standing in the centre of the room and then kneeling on the floor in front of the altar. He blew smoke from his pipe on the floor in front of the altar, crossing himself before each exhale, and then to the north, south, east, and west. He continued his prayers for several hours.

'When is he going to give us the San Pedro?' whispered one of the guests. It was becoming obvious to me that the natives were becoming restless.

'Soon,' I said. Surely five hours of praying meant it couldn't be much longer.

His two apprentices rose and together with Valentin blew tobacco smoke into the bottle of San Pedro, the glass it would be poured into, and another bottle of very dark liquid.

'Drink this, Alan,' and Valentin handed me the glass.

'Tobacco juice? But won't this make me throw up?' I questioned.

'We hope so.' He smiled. 'It will clean out your stomach and act as a catalyst for the San Pedro.'

Half an hour later our stomachs settled and we were given an equal amount of San Pedro. The flavour was just as wicked. We waited. He had cooked it the entire day with no additives, just pure, unadulterated San Pedro cactus; the entire plant. One dose was the length of your arm, from the elbow to the knuckles of your closed fist.

Almost an hour had passed since we drank the medicine. I felt a heat spreading through my system and my palms were starting to sweat. Having had experiences with mushrooms and LSD, I measured their strength from the character of the scenery. But here, feeling the medicine in my system without the benefit of any light source, there was no measuring stick.

I decided to move outside. Standing there in Valentin's front yard I needed to step closely by and pass another man. As I did this, I not only felt but also glimpsed my aura pass through him and re-enter me on the other side, sharing for a second or two the same space as his aura. I felt like I had been washed by a rainbow. He looked back at me with one of those 'My God!' type of expressions and before I could finish saying, 'Did you feel that?' he was already responding, 'Whoa!' I knew then the medicine truly had its hand on me.

Occasionally, Valentin would call one of his patients to sit on a tree stump placed in front of his altar for a curing. He took a set of palm leaves (*suriponga* in Quichua, *schacapa* in the Incan language) from the side of the altar and began by blowing (*soplar*) *mapacho* tobacco smoke into them for purification of any possible negative energies. This was followed by a misting of *agua florida* (Florida water) by Valentin first sipping the liquid and then pressure-spraying it from his mouth on to the leaves, himself, and the client. Valentin began singing an *icaro* (a power song) as he swept the client with the *suriponga* from their head to their waist. His apprentice/assistant, Marcelo, rang tiny bells near and far from their ears to realign possible misaligned audio-neural pathways. When he was finished he flipped the palm broom *suriponga* toward the altar to safely discard any energies it had attracted during the cleansing.

After having witnessed this very important aspect of healings during numerous ceremonies, we began to call this portion of the ritual 'soul dusting'. Over the last seven years as I became more adept at it, I began noticing an interesting phenomenon: when I place the *suriponga* on the crown of the client's head to begin the cleaning, I sometimes see dark splotches or what the curanderos call *manchas*, attached to the soul-body. They look like they're hanging on to the aura. I focus on sweeping them away with the *suriponga*. I have learned that there are also other astral or spiritual parasites that the mestizo curanderos refer to as *biches*, but in seven years of apprenticing I have yet to see them. I have no doubt that they exist as too many other superstitious, mystical, and mythical things have stunningly proved themselves to be true.

4

My apprenticing has been a constant deciphering of myth and acknowledgement of the miraculous. I have a difficult time accepting things just because I am told they are true. Normally, I believe if a divine mystery is not gifted, first hand by the spirit world, then I should remain sceptical. For this, my growth as a *curandero* has been slow and steady, but sure. That first ceremonial night with the medicine was absolutely magical. From all of the praying and singing combined with the effect of the medicine, I felt more spiritually connected than I have in my life.

Some people have been fortunate enough to come across great shamans or shamanas, such as the well-known Maria Sabina, a Mazatec shaman, who lives in Huantla de Jimenez in Mexico. She introduced the anthropologist Gordon Wasson to the spirituality of the mushroom. Wasson has written extensively about her work. Maria was both Mazatec and Catholic (she belonged to the sisterhood of the Sacred Heart of Jesus), and the 'saint children' (psilocybin mushrooms) were the body and blood of Christ.

Enriques Gonzales Rubio was also lucky enough to work with her personally. This is his account of their first meeting:[4]

An old woman, white hair with grey patches, thin, not very tall, brown, Indian appearance. She was the famous Maria Sabina.

Around nine o'clock, we went into the central room of the house. Maria Sabina ordered the figures on her altar: a figure of Jesus Christ, one of

Saint Anthony, flowers, candles, and a brazier for the copal.

From a bag she took out several mushrooms. She gave me six and took six for herself. She rubbed ground tobacco on my arms, lit the copal and passed the mushrooms several times over the smoky aroma while praying in a low voice. I felt filled with mystery and expectation; something solemn and sacred was about to happen.

Within thirty minutes I was feeling dizzy and I told her so.

Maria Sabina began to pray very low in Mazateco. She asked me my name and I told her.

I saw many coloured lights which changed in brightness and intensity with the tone of her singing. The singing was rhythmic and hypnotic. It was a shamanic chant, sacred, ancient. I felt her singing gently rocking me and transporting me to faraway worlds.

Not once did I see any terrible visions nor sense any other negative vibration. Instead I experienced infinite peace, the sensation of flying in a spiral of colour. In the centre of the room next to the wall, I saw a white light of great intensity. Maria continued to pray. Suddenly I heard someone say 'Saint Peter, Saint Paul, Lord Jesus Christ, Enrique, Enrique, Enrique, holy, holy, holy...'

These words touched me very deeply and I felt like Jesus on the Cross. I could feel the Crown of Thorns, I could feel the blood dripping from my forehead. The Light became visible again.

I felt a great fear and the need to pray for protection...

I turned my face to heaven and saw the millions of stars and galaxies. I repeated the Lord's Prayer. I recited the prayer with my eyes closed, and miraculously, the fear passed. I learned that the words to the Lord's Prayer hold a great power that puts the supplicant in touch with the Sacred Being.

I opened my eyes and looked at the sky. In the sky, the stars made the shape of a face. A timeless visage, as of an old man with a long flowing beard and white long hair. I felt that this was the face of God in a human form so I could relate to Him.

My body shook in ecstasies as I prayed for forgiveness of all my sins. I saw my life and my death pale in importance compared to the greatness that I was witnessing. A great interior peace took over me, and I had the sensation of power and balance, beauty and harmony.

We remained sitting there quietly, with only a candle to light the room.

And she began to sing in a low voice again.

She stopped her song suddenly, and she smiled at me with a great goodness. I was totally impressed by the personality of this woman and her ceremony.

It is not easy to find a genuine shaman or shamana as they often live deep in the mountains, jungles or deserts. If one does manage to find them it may be difficult to connect with them because the social values in their society may be very different, especially for women. This became clear one day when we visited a remote village to take part in a ceremony and Anja started to unpack her rucksack:

> As I settled into my little corner of the hut about fifteen women and children were watching. We did not speak any common language, but their body language expressed clearly that they were curious. As I took my belongings out, I became more and more embarrassed: everything I had brought seemed so useless! Lots of clothes: no one around me was wearing any. A couple of bras: all the women watching me were bare breasted. Books: the people here did not read or write. Toiletries, hair gel, moisturiser, mascara, they all seemed ridiculous. Did I have any beads? No: my rings, necklace and earrings were all too precious to me to give away. Any antibiotics? No I didn't have any. Anything for a headache? Yes, I said, relieved, I had some lavender oil. The bottle was gone quickly and I even worried about ever getting it back. I felt ashamed of myself. These people were so beautiful and what did I have to offer them?

4

Before even trying to find a shaman it is good to consider some questions: Do these people want to be bothered by outside visitors? What possible environmental damage could be caused? Will tourists affect their cultural heritage in a negative way? How are the indigenous people themselves benefiting from the visitors?

During our field research we were privileged to be able to participate in a variety of ceremonies with local people. This was exciting, but also awkward at times when we were unfamiliar with the language or the customs. For indigenous people, 'medicines' are intrinsically connected with their culture and we felt a need to familiarise ourselves with this, but this was not always possible in the limited time we had. It brought up the issue of exploitation: is it all right to consume people's products, in this case their medicines, without regard for their culture and giving something in return?

Full moon ceremony: Nicholas's account

We were invited to attend a full moon ceremony in a remote Penare village in Venezuela. For the past ten years, two remarkable men have been quietly collaborating on projects to preserve the traditional pre-Colombian spiritual and religious practices of the Aboriginal peoples of the Americas. One is an initiated medicine man and ceremonialist who has been learning shamanic divination and healing from traditional elders of tribes throughout Central and South America for over twenty-five years, while the other is a philanthropist who has devoted his life to the spiritual welfare of others.

Their method is to catalyse ceremonial gatherings among native people by bringing together shamans, traditional healers, and native ceremonialists from different tribes. These gatherings last from one to five days and involve the use of visionary plants, purification rituals, songs, dances and prayers to heal individuals and communities, and to empower the people to face and resist the forces of personal and cultural destruction in their lives.

Missionaries have been responsible for much of the damage. They teach that traditional beliefs are wrong, then demonstrate the superiority of antibiotics over the plant medicines used by shamans. This opens the way to persuading people to reject their shamanic culture. Missionaries then teach that traditional spiritual practices are evil, and frequently go on to attack other aspects of traditional culture as being contrary to the Ten Commandments.

This is how many missionaries worldwide have spread their message, and some have even done so with sincerity and compassion. The result has been to make people reject their own culture even when they have nothing else. Once their pride and self-confidence have been demolished, tribal people are far more easily exploited by governments, loggers and oil companies. This is not a thing of the past: we learned that the impending millennium has provided a goal for some missions to convert with increased zeal.

In this particular village, the local missionaries are the 'New Tribes Mission' whose stated aim is 'To bring the Gospel to every tribe'. In doing so they had eradicated much of the Penare culture, including their traditional songs, dances and shamanic rituals, although the villagers still wore loincloths with breasts covered only by strings of white beads. Meanwhile other missionaries had persuaded villagers in a nearby village to dress 'decently' (in jeans and T-shirts), but had tolerated their songs and dances. These two groups were brought together along with several shamans from more isolated villages. The event was wildly successful and we witnessed spontaneous sessions where people from one village taught songs and dances, while the others tried on loincloths. The three-night festival may have undone several decades of missionary activity.

The shamans did not use ayahuasca in this region, but another two-part psychoactive called yopo (*Anadenanthera peregrina*). The first part, containing inhibitors, is the root of the same vine that ayahuasca is made from, which is chewed beforehand. The psychoactive component consists of the seeds of a common tree containing DMT, which are dried, ground to a powder and snorted. The components are equivalent to those used in ayahuasca, but instead of a gradual build-up the effect is sudden and intense.

4

We did not know the shamans or speak their language. We had been told to trust them. After about half an hour of searching for a suitable place we ended up in our own hut. We just waited to see what was going to happen and so did half the village, who gradually dropped in with great curiosity to see how these white people would handle the medicine.

The shaman opened a box, sprinkled some greenish-brown powder on a piece of wood and ground it with a pestle. Then, without further ritual, he demonstrated that we should snort the powder up both nostrils simultaneously using a forked tube.

It felt like splinters of glass hitting the back of my mouth, but I dutifully followed the mimed instructions to massage it into my nostrils and snort some more. Then I sat with my back leaning against a pole, took some deep breaths and waited...

I saw the shaman and his friend having a conversation on their own, but also noticed that everyone's bodies were offset at about waist level. I was not aware of being under the influence of any drug; it was simply that their top halves were all shifted a bit to one side. That's odd, I thought, and closed my eyes. That was a shock. What I saw was the same whether my eyes were open or closed! Next I heard a male voice speaking to me in English. He was speaking clearly and softly right into my left ear and seemed absolutely real. What's more, he was giving me an important personal message, although later I was unable to recall any of it.

I was no longer able to be the observer, and had no way of telling what was 'real'. My 'normal' state of reference had been undermined and this made me feel panicky...I had been prepared to 'face my deepest fears', but not this! However, any fear quickly dissolved into sheer amazement. This probably lasted for some time, although I cannot remember the content, as I eventually regained enough consciousness to find my mouth hanging wide open and completely dried up inside.

With my consciousness back in control, I decided to explore where I was going, and to steer the course into introspection. There was no story line that I could follow. I shook myself and tried again, but the experience was all too fast and fragmented for me to get a handle on.

After some time it felt right to go out to see the dances of the Indians, which we could hear in the background. The moon and the stars were incredibly bright and a gentle peacefulness surrounded the village.

Mestizo shamans

In many places the shamans are mestizos, a mix of indigenous and white people. They speak European languages and are influenced by Christianity. Their rituals often take place in the towns and suburbs and their altars may contain crosses and statues of the Virgin Mary, as well as foetuses of llamas (which are meant to be very lucky), copal incense or traditional power objects.

Some are genuine with real knowledge and experience passed on through generations; others do whatever they think will sell their 'product'.

Iquitos in Peru is one of the centres where you can find mestizo-shamans who will be happy to serve a visitor from the West as shown in Nicholas's account below:

We arrived in the jungle city of Iquitos after twenty-eight hours of travel, and straight away were taken to visit a shaman.

He was drunk, but pleased to see us and keen to answer questions. He explained that there were two types of shaman in the Amazon, curanderos and *brujos*. *Brujos* learned the same skills but they concentrated on magic and curses rather than healing like curanderos. But *brujos* can also heal, and curanderos also have a bad side: good and evil are opposites, but also reflections of each other. Later we learnt that the term 'shaman' came from Siberia and that 'brujo' was used historically without negative connotation. Locally the word 'curandero' was used, with the term 'banco' used for experienced elders.

This curandero was very keen to give us a session (for $50 each), and showed us his 'temple'. It was a back shed separated from his house by a small yard occupied by a pig and the outside WC. Inside it was very dark with a low roof, and had a kind of altar with a crucifix, some kitsch 'holy pictures' and various morbid things including a human skull and a crocodile skull. I did not like the feel of it at all, and refused his invitation although we had been told that his ayahuasca was excellent.

Later my intuition was confirmed when we interviewed a local woman of about 30 who had attended one of his sessions. When the ayahuasca took effect, she became aware that evil spirits were trying to enter her vagina, attempting to psychically rape her, and was grateful that she had worn black to protect herself. She knew that the curandero was aware, if not the cause, of what she felt and was trying to seduce her. The only other participant went outside to the WC and did not come back, afterwards telling her that he felt unable to do so; meanwhile she felt scared but unable to leave. She spent the session fighting off the sexual invasion, and when it ended the curandero scolded her for wearing black, at the same time congratulating her on being so strong.

4

We heard many more stories of corrupt curanderos taking advantage of people, particularly white women. Local people did not regard curanderos as holy men. They were simply people who had learned some skills, and that included how to enter the spirit world. Like present-day vicars, many of them make their living through providing services but without having spiritual powers. Those curanderos who have the powers are not always good: they may use their powers to harm or heal, according to what they are paid to do. The reality is a far cry from the myth of uncorrupted curanderos who do not accept money: these healers are either inaccessible or don't welcome visitors.

It is important to realise that accepted local values may contrast with our own. Many people go for instant reward regardless of the consequences: cheating someone who has more than they have is acceptable. We met someone who had employed a team of men to look after valuable animals, only to find them butchered for meat as soon as he turned his back: the men chose to make some quick cash even though it meant losing long-term jobs.

The next thing to realise is that the Peruvians (or Ecuadorians or Brazilians) who deal with tourists are sophisticated people. They are well aware of the *Celestine Prophecy* syndrome – that people may be on the lookout for a signal from a stranger to lead them to a shaman – and will try to fulfil hopes. However, their choice is likely to be a relative or whoever gives them the most commission, since their motivation is no more noble than if they were helping you find someone to have sex with. In spite of this, many punters are satisfied simply because they have no other entheogenic experience to compare it with.

Finally, there are some cultural differences that apply specifically to shamanism. Local people regard curanderos like the witches of medieval Europe: they respect their supernatural powers, but not their integrity. Then there is a very different attitude to illness. Curanderos see illness as the result of a spell put on the victim and any cure involves removing that spell. The strength of the spell depends on the power of the person who cast it, and to remove it requires more power. A very persistent disease, therefore, can only be cured by a very powerful curandero.

The easiest option for many tourists are tour operators who hire shamans and facilities, then put together a package in much the same way that others arrange skiing holidays. The result may be more palatable to people who are sympathetic to new age ideals, are worried about disease and don't like mosquitoes. There are several reasonably comfortable facilities which can be hired, from riverboats to cabins in the jungle, all equipped with mosquito nets and cooks who know what foreigners like to eat. Advertised tours may lack romance, but they do provide most seekers with what they really want: to have the opportunity of a spiritual experience in reasonable comfort without being robbed or abused. It is much more likely that tourists will be satisfied by people organising such tours from their own culture who can identify with their needs. We spoke to a number of participants from several different organisations who were still satisfied when we followed them up months later.

However, an independent traveller determined to seek out an alternative should be able to find a ceremony if he or she is prepared to make time to gain the trust of local people, through talking to them and being sensitive to the local culture, and is prepared to use his or her own judgement. Making contact with gringos who have chosen to live in the area can also be useful.

Within Iquitos there are various curanderos who hold ayahuasca sessions every Friday night for local people. We attended one in the suburbs. The session, called La Purga (purge), was attended by people with a physical illness and although the curandero sang *icaros* (power songs of the shamans) they were uninspiring: still, it provides an experience more genuine than many tourists would find by asking a taxi driver.

A Mestizo curandero

Anja writes:

> This ritual was at the house of a curandero, a healer. We visited in the morning to meet him. His house was made of wood and had about three dark rooms on two levels. We talked on the veranda, which looked out over the dusty paths and the scattered wooden houses of the neighbours. He had a fascinating collection of wallhangings: a picture of the football team, plenty of 'curandero certificates', a picture of Jesus and a pin-up of a nude blonde. We decided he was all right because his eyes were soft and open and he spoke and moved in an unassuming, gentle way.
>
> We asked him a few questions. Where was the ritual to be held? Apparently in the kitchen, with the back of the garden as the purging place. Did he cook his own ayahuasca? Oh yes! This was very important. He was a renowned healer, as were his father and grandfather, and he pointed to his certificates on the wall, one of which was granted to him by the university, no less. He obviously felt he had to impress us, but it was really more the 'feel' of him and the calm in the place that convinced us he was OK. When would he conduct the session? Every day he held a 'surgery' for healing and herbal remedies, but on Friday nights the ayahuasca sessions took place. He told us that many locals came to drink weekly. That was a good sign. How much would the session be? Fifty dollars per person for us. An average for gringos (as Western travellers are called), although his prices for locals were much lower. He did not overcharge and he did not give any false promises: The sign on the wall just gave prices for (1) Consultation, (2) Stomach purge. We were going for the stomach purge. Knowing the workings of ayahuasca, I was sure he could provide that!
>
> We arrived at nine in the evening after our taxi had struggled up the sandy track. The house was lit with only a few kerosene lamps. We went to the kitchen area and I made myself comfortable on the floor, but most

4

people were sitting on wooden benches. Four gringos and about six locals, plus two curanderos. The tea was blessed with tobacco smoke, as is the custom in Peru, and we all drank our little bowl in turn.

The kerosene lamps were blown out and the darkness was very suggestive, but no clear images presented themselves. I closed my eyes. Then some visions of animals appeared: lots of catlike creatures, some with jaws and sharp teeth. The animals were rotating in three dimensions and I could see their fur as if in close-up. I was aware that although some of the animals looked quite strange, I did not have any sense of danger or fear. From time to time my stomach would feel a little uncomfortable, but I would direct the energy down, as I wanted to let the ayahuasca go through my body before throwing up. I did have a shit, though. It was nice to be outside. I was very aware of the different parts of nature and myself, the tree-trunks, the leaf that dropped on me, the stars bright and numerous. I felt grateful to the earth for taking my shit and as soon as I thought that, it was as if the earth said thank you in return. I realised that's what good relationships are about: it is not a matter of giving or receiving. In a balanced relationship there is mutual benefit. It really made sense to me. That is how nature works! I took my time before returning and felt fine, although a little floaty. I took a breath before going inside. Then as soon as I had two feet in the door, it was as if an energy hit me. Even before I could sit down a gulp of vomit came up and I had to return outside immediately. I threw up clear liquid without effort and got rid of whatever it was easily. Now I felt as clear and awake as anything. No effects of ayahuasca remained.

One of the other gringos suggested that I ask for a little more to get back into it. So I did. More tobacco was blown in the bottle and I was told to just take a swig straight out of it. I knew it wasn't the thing to bring up matters of hygiene, so I put the bottle to my lips. The curandero then asked me to sit next to him and blew smoke on my head, spine, front and hands. Then he asked me to smoke some myself. I knew the smoke was to drive unwanted forces away, so I smoked a little and blew out forcefully to the door. That seemed to meet with some approval. At least I had understood the idea, which was a relief, because I wasn't sure of what was going on most of the time, since my Spanish is pretty hopeless. Then I was told to concentrate on the light. I asked to be shown what I needed to see and I saw a picture of abstract swirling lines. I directed my energy up to the highest point of light I could get in touch with and this made the swirling lines look brighter. It was an invisible connection from inside my own head to this bright light that changed my perception of everything around me and made it look brighter. When I lost the connection people and things would return to normal. This became an exercise for me to practise. I did not come out of this session with a great revelation, but I still practise the exercise in my meditations.

In the jungle

The following ceremony was held in Brazil and led by French people, who had been studying for a long time with respected Peruvian shamans. The setting was one of the most authentic we experienced. We were led to the middle of the jungle by boat. This gave us time to acclimatise ourselves, both going there and on the way back. The style was typically Peruvian: in the dark and with no other sounds than those of nature, the *chakapa* (leaf rattle) and the singing of the *icaros* (the power songs of the shaman). The shamans showed great integrity and the participants were not just excited tourists but serious seekers. Anja writes:

4

> We moved down the river, calm, gliding. Jungle around us. It got dark and we landed. We walked into the wooden hut. Lanterns, torches, candles, ropes, organising, bustle. I try to fit in, centre myself, bring in the four directions (north, east, south, west), the ancestors, protection and all that. They tell us: 'Let it flow, don't hold or push, stay moveable and don't forget the joy.' One by one we drink...three sips...tastes, oh well, not too bad. I want to take it in – let it in – penetrate me. The candles are blown out. Darkness. I sit and wait. The shamans start singing. Little visions of Indian patterns like on wrapping paper. Foggy, sleepy, try to stay awake. Not sure anything is happening, the bowl is there reassuringly. 'Are you all right? – dizzy?' No I am nothing, it's not working, I think. I get into a dozy sleepy state. Waking up – I have given up the idea that anything is going to happen, but I'd like to stay open. I must have been here for hours. Do I want to go out? Seems a lot of effort. I drift off...
>
> 'Anja, would you like a second go?' 'Yes, please.' The taste is putrid, sour, like vomit. I feel drowsy, misty, I am a bit bored, and decide to have a look outside. I stand up and am surprised how wobbly I feel – something must be going on! Outside. It is open and calm and real. I like being there. I

empty, a great gush of liquid out of my bum. I feel good about it, light.

I come back – I breathe through my empty spaces, the nausea comes back, I'd better have the bowl, I make the movement one-two-three times, vomit gushes out, to my surprise. I let it come from deep in my stomach, more and more again, I want to let it out from the very depth of me. Now I feel open, I feel as if I am the bamboo flute, the channel, as if I give birth, let it out top and bottom, all through me an open channel, pour it through. Yes I give up, I surrender. Nothing outer matters, I am blowing through, being blown through. I breathe right down to my anus. I feel reborn.

One of the shamans comes, sits in front of me and sings and rattles the leaves all around me. His voice is so pure, so resonant, so flowing, I feel like a baby drinking it in and letting it through, right to the bottom and out. His voice is so melodious, it's like a lullaby, just for me, I feel so supported, so grateful, so privileged, so safe to let go and be, so acknowledged, like a reward for my letting go. I am really moved – I'm so happy – there is help. My emotions fill me. I start crying, deep cries. What do I cry for? Am I sad? No. Do I feel sadness? Yes. I cry for the old part, the frightened part, the part that struggled so hard, I feel for her, I pity her, I cry for her suffering. It is as if I can see me from the side of the spirit-guides. All guides, beings, energies are with me – and what's more, I am with them. I cry and cry and laugh and feel the immense relief and breathe and laugh and take in more and let it flow right through. I feel alive and happy and I feel I belong. I feel a strong blow on my crown chakra; an icy flamey feeling and camphor runs over my head and down my face. Three times the shaman blows; it feels exhilarating! Then he blows forcefully down my front, my breasts are bare and I feel the camphorous air right down my belly. Then he blows three more times down my spine. Life, new life, is blown into me. He gently strokes my back a few times. He asks me for my hands. I give them eagerly. I feel like an initiate. He blows the camphor in my hands. My face is dripping – my body tingling. I let it all be and feel an enormous strong awakening – 'whoosh' energy. I feel alive. I want to laugh, to really laugh, and run and open and dance and enjoy. Now I know the meaning of what the shaman said in the beginning: 'Don't forget the joy!' The joy, I feel so joyous, I am overflowing – I am flowing over and connecting with the whole space. Thank you. The songs continue. I flow into the song. My movement is one with the song, I almost know the words. I want to join in, I feel the dynamic, I know when it becomes faster, when it gets strong, when it finishes with the last blowy breath. I take part. I am part of the healing just by taking part, not by projecting, doing, just tuning into the air which is filled with vibration and motion. I go out. Another little shit – why not? I float on the singing, feel the leaves around me rattling, I do t'ai chi-like movements, my arms just floating. The shit around me is all part of it. I flow into the song again – the song flows through my body. I move into a large energy field. One woman throws up violently towards the end; she is helped afterwards. I understand: first we need to let go, help is at hand, but afterwards. The struggle to let go is a process to take on alone.

Years later, I still feel this has been my most profound spiritual experience with psychoactives.

Shamanic healing

4

One motivation for travelling to the jungle can be to find a cure for a physical or mental illness. When interviewing people who came for this reason, it was remarkable that they all agreed that the medicine had brought a spiritual aspect to their lives which allowed them to make profound changes. The psychoactive substance did not seem so much to provide a direct cure as to instigate a change in perspective, which allowed healing to take place. The following accounts are examples of physical and mental healing. Of course, healing is never guaranteed and there are also many people who return home disappointed.

Naomi was suffering from cancer when she ventured into the jungle:

When I went out there I had been told I was going to die. I had searched for alternative cures for the last two years. I had just undergone seven months of chemotherapy and they said that the only thing left for me was radiation and that might give me an extra year, or it might not, it might foul up my other organs. I said forget it, I'm going to the jungle. My friend warned me that the ceremony was called the Rope of Death and in the first ceremony I did indeed feel as if I was dying and I was asking myself – what am I doing here? I've come all this way, it's cost me all this money, I've been puking for seven months and now I've come to the jungle to do the same thing – this is crazy! And in between these thoughts I'm seeing all these images on the back of my eyelids.

I had to face something about myself which was awful and I had to face it now or die with it. When I realised this everything turned for me and I had a rush of memories. In ten minutes I had about a year's worth of therapy. Going there puts you in a state of openness to that. It has not ceased to keep working on me.

It has been a real gift. The biggest thing was that I thought I was going to die and then I just knew that I wasn't going to die from cancer. I got the cancer for a reason and it was to wake up. I knew this after the first session. The next day I had to walk somewhere – I could hardly make the walk into the jungle. A week later we had to go two and a half hours further in and I literally flew across, jumping from one root to another. I felt like a different person.

Two years later we contacted Naomi and she wrote:

Two weeks after returning, X-rays revealed NO sign of tumours! This information was withheld from me until six months later, when my oncologist was away and his replacement congratulated me. In the past two years I have had regular check-ups. Last month they did test my blood and the results proved no trace of cancer in my body. Ayahuasca has been my teacher and I am grateful.

Emotional healing came to Maya, a Swiss woman in her late seventies who had completed a three-week session with the aim of coming to terms with the death of her husband ten years before. She had previously tried various new age therapies including rebirthing, kinesiology and holotropic breathwork, and also group therapy using LSD, but none of these had been successful in easing her pain.

In the first session my aim was to be liberated from my grieving for the past ten years and from crying every day for seven years. The plant showed me wonderful flowers in all colours and in all forms, and afterwards it showed me children's playthings. I understood I have to be more joyful and it will come. After this vision I knew I would find the help I needed.

The fourth session was painful. My knee hurt and I could not walk without support. I felt terror. I was again in a cage but this time it was the kind you use for a big bird. I was in there, and there were overhanging branches and all the snakes you could imagine and they came near me, everywhere. It was frightening and I really gave up, I said 'I can't do this'.

The shaman felt my pain, he came and blew smoke at me and sang for me and then I said, 'Help me, I have to go out or else I die' so we went out. I was trembling and the shaman held me and at that time I felt an empathy clear and pure with this man who helps people through such difficult times. I was trembling like a leaf and I felt this love, this divine state of purity.

During the sessions I wore a handkerchief around my neck that used to belong to my husband. I opened it at the knot and placed it in the shaman's pocket. At that moment I felt able to vomit and litres of liquid came out. It was as if it was tearing me apart. But afterwards I felt good and I thought: 'I let go of my husband'. This was the liberating moment. I had closed myself off in this cage and all the snakes were all the fears and accusations, guilt and shame I torture myself with. All these negative thoughts were with me in this cage and this liberated me and I could vomit it out.

Stress-related illness prompted Sarah to travel to Peru:

4

While producing a horror film trailer at Saturday Night Live, in which a variety of fruits go wild and take over a household in the suburbs, I had an ischaemic attack. For half a minute my left arm became paralysed, my speech slurred and I had a droopy eyelid. Several months later after dealing with a nightmare of doctors, I had less money in the bank and no answers as to why it had occurred, except for my own term, BAFIS Syndrome – 'Blew A Fuse because of Intense Stress'. A month after this occurrence I was on a plane to Peru to investigate shamanism and continue my personal spiritual journey which I had left aside for some time and was now renewing. BAFIS had scared me into action. That trip to Peru renewed the side of me whose core yearns for a spiritual connection with all things.

The ayahuasca journey in Peru was profound and spiritual:

The glass poised before my lips, my thoughts racing, I attempted to calm my mind, to embrace what I was about to experience. I was sitting in a circle of nineteen people of whom I knew three. I was about to drink ayahuasca, the death vine, as a participant in a sacred ceremony.

I relaxed as the liquid gently slid into my stomach. I felt it move throughout my body with a numbing effect. I closed my eyes. There was light and colour on the left side behind my eyelids and it spread to fill the right. The visions were incredibly vivid, like a hologram. A voice, the spirit of the medicine, spoke to me. It took my hand and led me. I felt the pain of my childhood, the loneliness, the lack of life. Intense waves of nausea went through my body. I kept on thinking: control, power, wisdom. I felt all my senses, and every cell in my body, totally alive. Experiences bombarded me one after the other. I had always wanted to be more fully aware. I asked ayahuasca to stop. 'It's too painful,' I pleaded. The spirit retorted, gently chiding 'But this is what you have asked for.' 'Yes but I see that this is too open. I am feeling too much at the same moment.' He taught me how to protect myself and yet retain an openness.

The shaman, maestro of ayahuasca, played music and danced, keeping the energies moving in the room. I experienced the pain of people who are starving, the pain from acts of violence. My body became heavier. I saw myself leaning over, holding my head in my hands, so heavy with thoughts and choices it was impossible to hold. I felt intense pain and confusion. I felt it and then it was released.

It is with the ayahuasca that we remember spirit and all that is, with clarity and beauty. I accepted where I am in my life and became calm.

I travelled to other worlds, exquisite places with several moons and suns. Ayahuasca encouraged me. 'Let go,' he advised. 'You don't need to hold on to this pain. You can experience joy.' I experienced death, as spirit, floating among the stars. The shaman worked on my crown chakra and other energy centres. I sat up very straight and tall. My heart and throat chakras were energised; the visions and instruction continued to flow. I felt the blood flowing through my veins. I felt my heart and healed it. I experienced myself as a black panther and ran as a wildcat through the forest. I learned yes, and moved my head up and down, yes. I felt intense joy. I saw a fragment of the light of God, an illumination of enormous intensity.

On returning from Peru Sarah discovered a teacher, a shaman, and began working with her on a regular basis, using ayahuasca as a tool. She has found healing on physical, emotional and spiritual levels:

I have since met ayahuasca nine more times and each time has been a different experience. My self-esteem is stronger. I no longer need to hold my head in my hands in confusion. I keep the vision, my dream, in my mind to focus me. I have not solved all of my problems, but they have been peeling away in therapy sessions more easily, more quickly than before. It is very important to process all the information, all the gifts. The asthma I have suffered has become milder. I no longer use an inhaler. I am more aware in nature. A porcupine or a rabbit can teach me when I listen. This is one of the visionary drugs that can help to open the energy centres within us. There are the drugs, legal and illegal, that dull the senses to feeling, to life. We must all make the journey of bringing to consciousness the hidden pains and darkness within us. Whatever the path we choose – psychotherapy, regression therapy, bio-energetics, or any combination – we can free ourselves from being victims, to become more creative, joyful beings. I do not advocate ayahuasca for everyone but it is a rite for those who choose it.

Treatment of addiction

Plant medicines may also play an important role in overcoming addiction. Iboga and ayahuasca have been particularly successful in this way.

4

We spoke with Jacques Mabit, who is the founder of the Takiwasi centre in Peru. He works with drug addicts (mainly cocaine addicts) and sometimes organises seminars for people interested in the centre's work.

> I had had about ten sessions with ayahuasca when the spirit of the plant told me that I was to work with drug addicts. Before that I had never had any interest in that area at all...It was a total surprise and at that moment I had no idea what to do. But this ayahuasca revelation was so strong, it felt more real than ordinary reality. From 1986 to 1989 I didn't do anything about drug addiction and just carried on doing ayahuasca and diets and fasting, following the way of learning to cure myself.
>
> In 1989 I had another ayahuasca session when the ayahuasca spirit told me that it was time for me to begin. We went to Thailand to visit a Buddhist temple where they cure drug addicts with plants and include a strong spiritual dimension. I asked the monks to teach me 'through the dreams' and they agreed. I am still guided in the decisions I make through the ayahuasca and dreams. Sometimes in daily life there will be a sudden flash of insight – people tell you something and you know that it is not really these people speaking, but something else.

Spirituality is an important element in the treatment of drug addiction at Takiwasi and Jacques describes it as the highest of the three levels used in their programme:

For the first month we concentrate on the physical level when we just cure the physical body in order to be able to take the next step. The next level is the psychological/affective/emotional level. Patients connect with family, emotions, memories, sadness, their location in the context of humanity. The third step is the spiritual level. Their life has a meaning. Every patient has a very different connection with spirituality, but all of them ask for spiritual connection when they commit themselves to stay here.

Thiérry is a 30-year-old Frenchman who had just completed an eight-month-long treatment for cocaine addiction at the Takiwasi centre:

During the cleansing diet you don't eat salt or sugar and you take different kinds of plants during eight days that give you dreams and sometimes indications about yourself. You are in constant isolation in the forest, apart from once a day when you receive a short visit of a curandero who follows your development and helps you if you feel bad. You are in a process of evolution and when you take ayahuasca after your first diet you see that your level of perception is stronger, higher. After my first diet I met a new curandero and I had one of my strongest sessions. Normally the visions are for all the group, but this curandero had the power to make special visions with each person, controlling the effects. He confronted me with my death, because during my drug sessions I was looking to die. You want to die but you are just playing, you are playing with your addiction. During this ayahuasca session the death came to me. It appeared to me. I had heard that it was a woman: a lot of books talk about woman as the death but I never knew why. But I could see it was a woman who came to me, a beautiful woman, it was incredible. She was speaking to me: 'Hello Thiérry, here I am – you were looking for me so many times and now I am here and I am talking to you. Look at me. I am here. What do you want?' And I was looking and thinking: wow, it is so wonderful. And she was telling me, 'You think I am wonderful but look what you are really looking for', and her face changed and it was horrible, I couldn't see it any more. It was like a spectre, it was looking at me with red eyes and trying to enter into my face and trying to show me that really what I was looking for was dangerous. You can't play with death. You don't have the right to play with death. That was the lesson of that ayahuasca session. That I have to value my life. It was the most important thing I learnt. I was confronting my death and I say, 'Wow, this is strong.' Of course, in all the ayahuasca sessions you see a lot of beautiful things. You have access to all the spirit worlds. I can feel the whole world, all the beauty of what I have near.

You don't respect the rules when you are drugging yourself as the preparation of the drugs is done without any tradition. It's done by people who want to make business, not to cure people. You do it to relieve yourself or because you want to destroy yourself. The worlds you access through heroin are not the same worlds that you access through ayahuasca. Heroin alters your perception. It makes you think that everything is OK, it changes your perception of things. Sometimes you are dreaming or have thoughts and you access certain kinds of information, but you are not doing anything with that because you are drugging and destroying yourself: the drug is doing violence to you. So you can't use that kind of information. With ayahuasca, the plants change your perception, show you something which you can use in your own life to help you grow up and not destroy you.

4

I have recovered some of my sensitivity, my feelings. I accept the entirety of life more. Before, I thought I was right about everything. Now I've learned to try to achieve a balance, to see the good and the bad and not be so extreme in my ways. To find an equilibrium. I'm always trying to find a good way to integrate all these things. I had lost my spirituality but I have faith now. Ayahuasca taught me not to have any more doubts about spirits, plants, power, magic things. When you do the diet the spirit of the plant comes to you and teaches you. If you respect the spirit, if you prepare yourself, then you will be on your way and you will be strong. If you don't respect it then the spirit will go. At the beginning it seems a little strange, but it is true.

Importing shamanism

For some people, venturing out into the jungle is just what they need to open them up to an inner journey, while others find that the unfamiliarity of other cultures brings more fear to the experience. Staying at home and finding ways to incorporate some of the wisdom and ceremonial aspects of shamanism into our culture is another option. There are workshops which try to do just that so there is no need to travel abroad. It is certainly cheaper and it may be easier to integrate the experience into daily life. However, it doesn't sound quite so adventurous, and psychoactives, generally, are illegal in the West.

Peter, a 30-year-old British man, attended a medicine ceremony in Europe:

I first met Grandfather Peyote in a ceremony in the south of Spain. At that time I was living with my partner and daughter in a community in the Sierra Nevada in Granada – we lived close to the earth and spent many hours around the fire making music and singing chants. We would celebrate the solstices and equinoxes with an all-night fire, sometimes accompanied by magic mushrooms. We took the mushrooms with respect and they opened us up to some wonderful experiences of beauty and joy especially, for me, through singing in the circle.

So when a friend told us about a medicine ceremony with peyote that was happening nearby we felt strongly moved to take part. This friend had been in ceremonies in the north of Spain with some native American Indians – she had been so deeply touched that she had invited them to share this medicine with the people in the south.

We arrived at the site of the ceremony in late afternoon, in time to help prepare the space. The large stone-paved threshing mound where we were to sit throughout the night was cleared and a hole was dug in the earth a few yards outside the circle.

When everything was ready the medicine man was introduced and he told us something about the ceremony he was to lead us through. It was to be a ceremony for prayer and healing; we would connect with the fire, with the earth, with our hearts, with Great Spirit – and all this in a traditional manner, in a form that had been revealed to our ancestors and had been passed down from them to us. Now it was necessary for this tradition to be shared with people outside America, to help others remember their connection to spirit, to help restore unity and harmony to all corners of the earth.

After the talk we took our places in the circle. Normally there might have been a central fire, but it was summer and there was a strict ban on open fires in the area. Instead, embers were carried in from a fire inside the house and placed in the centre of the circle. Throughout the night, fresh embers were added.

The ceremony started when the friend who had asked for the ceremony lit a 'tobacco' – this had been prepared from a blend of tobacco and herbs and rolled up in a dried corn husk. It looked like a fat cigar. Using this tobacco to pray with, in much the same way I imagined one might use a

sacred pipe, she thanked the medicine man and his companions for
coming, along with others in the circle, and went on to explain the purpose
of this particular ceremony. Every gathering of this type has a purpose –
and on this occasion it was to ask for healing of the feminine side in all of
us. This was the first of four main tobaccos which marked the four parts,
the four rounds of the ceremony.

Following this, corn husks and bags of this 'sacred tobacco' were
passed around and we all had the chance to prepare our own tobacco and
say our own prayers out loud or in silence. I had never used tobacco in this
way before and I was used to praying but only in the set words of a
meditation – asking God for help like this was something I'd not done
since I was a child, so the whole procedure felt quite peculiar but certainly
positive. Many prayers were said for a friend who was dying of cancer,
others asked for healing of the earth, as well as the feminine side within us,
and many were prayers of thanks.

After we had all finished praying with these tobaccos, their remains
were collected and placed on a simple earth altar around the central fire.
Then the medicine, the peyote, was brought around the circle. The
medicine man came round with a bowl and offered four small spoons of
peyote paste (the dried plant mixed with water) to each one of us. As he
spoon-fed me he had a clear, serious but also generous and warm look in
his eyes, and I was soon to find that the medicine also bore these qualities.
Some sweetened peyote tea was also passed round – this helped to wash
down the bitter taste of the paste. By the time the tea reached us the
medicine was already having a powerful effect on us, so I only poured
myself half a cup. I was feeling strong waves of energy flowing through my
body, which was in some way pleasant but at the same time left me feeling
nauseous. It felt as if my illness came from specific points in my body which
were where the energy flow appeared blocked. As I focused within I could
feel the energy slowly moving through these blocks.

4

In the meantime some others were shifting their blocks by actually
throwing up. This was all dealt with in a very civilised manner – there were
people helping who brought round plastic bags, collected them once they
were filled up and carried them off to dispose of them in the hole which
had been dug beforehand. In this way, we were told, our illnesses were
offered back to Mother Earth for healing.

Also, a drum and a rattle were being passed around the circle. The drumbeat was meant to represent the heartbeat of the unborn baby and was always played in the same fast rhythm. Whoever held the rattle had the chance to sing if they felt like it. This was very different from the way I was used to singing in my community – there, drums would follow varied rhythms depending on the song and we'd usually sing together quite harmoniously. But here I felt the energy descending into chaos. Only a few people actually chose to sing. Those who had obviously been in other ceremonies sang songs I didn't know so I started to feel frustrated. I found myself judging the people leading the ceremony: Oh no, they really need to do something to shift the energy!!! I thought.

Around this time came the main tobacco of the ceremony. The medicine man presented this to our friend and after she had prayed with it she took it around the circle, just passing it to a few people, including my partner.

Dawn was breaking as this tobacco came to an end and I didn't know how it had happened but the heavy energy had moved into a lighter, open space.

In the final quarter of the ceremony some women carried in bowls of maize, meat and fruit, and a jug of water. A mother-to-be was presented with a final tobacco to bless the food. This, for me, was one of the most beautiful moments of the ceremony, indeed of my whole life. The woman praying over the food spoke with such beauty and such gratitude for the gifts of Mother Earth that I was moved to tears, along with most of the rest of the circle. The openness which the medicine and the ceremony had created in me allowed the meaning of these words, the love within these words, to touch my heart in a profound way.

The warm, sunny morning welcomed in a feeling of wholeness, heart-connection and clarity. When the man who had been looking after the drum prayed with his tobacco, he told us, 'This is not a religion, this is a way of life.' I understood why this was called a 'medicine ceremony' – the tobacco, the peyote, the form of the ceremony, all these were medicines which could help us to see our illness and move through it into a better way of being with ourselves and with all creation. I felt humbled and recognised all my judgements, all my doubts of the night before, for what they were – tricks of my mind, which were themselves part of my own illness, part of what was closing my heart and blocking a free connection with spirit.

By the end of the ceremony I was experiencing bliss like never before, which I could only describe as feeling as if a heart had been wrenched open with a crowbar! If the feminine side is the place of the heart, then my feminine side had certainly received a big healing. I recognised everyone in the circle as my family and myself and all things as part of the same vibrant energy. And this was more than just a passing feeling – I had been touched so deeply that the essential message, the healing, the love of this ceremony have never left me.

This was my first step on a path which has taken me up the Vision Quest mountain and to a firm commitment to working with the tobacco, the peyote, the many medicines in this tradition of the earth. It has led me to a place of greater respect for all life, a deeper sense of gratitude for the gifts we receive and more clarity about my own nature and path. When my partner and I split up, the ceremonies and the teachings they brought were invaluable in helping us work through these difficult times and in helping us heal our relationship with one another.

'Aho mitakuy oyasin' – 'to all our relations' – is what is said to close a prayer and it is not spoken in vain. I see it as a sincere wish for good health for all life and healing of our relationship with all things, with all beings.

Aho mitakuy oyasin

4

Some workshops do not adopt the setting of an indigenous culture. There are no teepees, no sweat lodges or vision quests; it is more the kind of environment one would expect in a self-development workshop. The following account describes a workshop we attended in a private house in America.

Anja's account

I had heard of Californian workshops involving ayahuasca for some years. Some, I was told, involved importing a genuine shaman from Peru for a session while others simply used shamanistic techniques or invented their own. Although this particular group leader was highly recommended, I imagined it could be advertised as 'all the wonders of working with a jungle shaman in the comfort of our luxury condominium'. We arrived at the venue at 9a.m. Our facilitators were both established and respected bodyworkers and had run many such entheogenic workshops before. They welcomed us warmly and made us some carrot and ginger soup which was not only meant to settle our stomachs, but 'just in case', our vomit would be less offensive for us and our neighbours. We were also offered ginkgo tablets which were supposed to help us to remember our experiences and thus make them easier to integrate afterwards. There were two other couples, making six in our group. All three couples had come from afar and had not taken part in such a workshop before although, like us, they had used various psychedelics. We sat around a low table which was used as an 'altar' where we could place any personal objects for the session. Then we were given a cup of ayahuasca and a cup of herb tea to wash it down with. I dread the taste, but this was not so bad, as it was thick and syrupy like treacle. We put on blindfolds and lay back.

We were treated throughout to beautiful music starting with didgeridoo which got me well grounded. I could feel the vibration in my body. Incense surrounded us. Bells and singing bowls kept our consciousness clear. Rattles dispersed our thought patterns. The medicine started to work slowly. I felt myself floating up in a world of pretty moving patterns. I felt invited to observe this world. It is not my world. There is something alien about it, but beyond it could be the world of spirits. I feel motivated to draw spirit down, rather than flying up to it. I ask how I can be a better channel for receiving Spirit. For some time music from the curanderos in Peru has been playing. I am transported back to my intense rebirth experience with them in Brazil. This time I have grown up a bit more. I know I have more responsibility now. I have to do more myself. A voice says, 'You know what to do – empty yourself, become this empty vessel again.' I feel slightly nauseous. I start singing softly, with small sounds, a song from elsewhere. I feel connected with my/a/the spirit part. Before I know it, I throw up. I let it out happily, knowing this is just what is needed. I am not bothered with tissues or comforting gestures. I want to clear out, fully – become this clear channel to pull Spirit down. Ronnie holds my hand. I hear other people throw up and – still blindfold – indicate gently that I am OK, so she can attend to them. She keeps holding my hand. I realise I find it quite hard to accept this full attention. I feel in debt to her. I realise this is how I behave in relationships. I don't want to fully receive, because then I have to fully give back. I like to build up 'credit' first – then I feel OK about receiving. I realise this holds me back from a fully committed relationship. I see what it is like to demand 100 per cent attention, like a baby does. I can suddenly appreciate the brilliance in this, whereas before this relentless demanding struck me as an enormous burden when I thought about the idea of having a child. I intend to ask for 100 per cent attention (I warned Nicholas later), but in the knowing that I will return the same. I feel this is an essential part of a committed relationship. My mind feels very clear throughout the whole session; there is hardly any fuzziness at all. I love the incense and the leaf rattles that pass by several times. My spirit/mind is playing with the rattle. I then see my neighbour's energy, which is very beautiful and full of love in pink/magenta, dark red and gold. I hear the rattle around her and tune into her beauty. This feels very good and it teaches me to appreciate other people's beauty more often, rather than acquiring more for myself. I come back to a gently meditative state. I reach out to connect with spirit. My world is bluish and soft; white/golden funnels of light are coming in. I am reminded of a gesture I have intuitively been doing for a while now after healing sessions or sometimes in gratitude. They are three hand gestures, one in front of my brow; one in front of my heart and one in front of my hara (abdomen). I can see clearly these gestures connecting to a symbol. It feels a good tool to have. The music changes to Tibetan flute and monks singing. This music brings me right home – right in the moment. Finally I come out. Half the group has gone out – some people are still in it. I dance on the music, allowing my body to just follow the energy. I am swirling for a long time seeing the carpet patterns turning but feeling hooked up by something above my head and not getting in the slightest bit dizzy. I feel well connected with myself – spirit and my surroundings.

4

Afterwards we were given a nice meal and shared our experiences. All the participants thought it was well worthwhile although it cost $325, and some had come a long way for it. Perhaps the most comic part was the option to wear adult nappies: one girl said, 'I came prepared for anything today, but never thought that I would be putting diapers on my boyfriend!'

Whereas in indigenous cultures the ceremonial aspect of ritual, the preparation of the place and the people, is taken care of through tradition, in modern societies this generally needs to be given extra attention if the medicine is to be experienced with the support of a shamanic structure.

Not all traditional settings are suitable for integration in our social structures, nor can success be guaranteed by travelling to unfamiliar cultures and experiencing their way of using psychoactives. The extent to which integration is possible depends on the flexibility of the individual as well as on the type of experience sought.

More information about the preparation and integration of a psychoactive journey can be found in the chapter 'Before, During and After'.

5

Home Users of Psychoactives

We shall not cease from exploration

And the end of all our exploring

Will be to arrive where we started

And know the place for the first time.

T.S. Eliot

*All understanding
begins with
not accepting
the world as
it appears.*

Alan C. Kay

So far we have been looking at people who use psychoactive substances within an existing framework. The framework can vary. It might be a church setting, like the Santo Daime, or a belief system like Buddhism. It can draw upon a tradition like shamanism or at least provide an accepted structure like an entheogenic workshop. The framework is there to support a spiritual experience. Some people would argue that it is dangerous to take psychoactives without such a framework, or might doubt the validity of a spiritual experience without the spiritual setting.

It is clear from our research that psychoactives are used spiritually at home, in a familiar setting, alone or with good friends. A survey aimed at 'people who have had a spiritual experience induced by a drug' was placed on two Internet sites. We wanted to know what people, who did not belong to a specific religion, defined as spiritual; which substances facilitated a spiritual experience; and in what circumstances the psychoactive was taken. We were also interested in what the experiences meant to our respondents afterwards and to what extent their lives have been changed. The survey was not intended to be methodologically rigorous but rather to be a device for research, to allow people to share their experiences, including the personal accounts in this chapter.

The survey included such questions as the following:

- 'Spiritual' can mean a variety of things. What do you mean?
- Which drugs have enabled you to have a spiritual experience?
- In what situations have you had a spiritual experience while using a drug?
- Do you feel that such experiences have been harmful or valuable to you and in what way?
- Have such experiences made you want to explore spirituality in other ways and, if so, in what ways?

Examples of how people answered the first question are given in the first chapter 'Drugs and Spirituality?' Here the focus is on the nature of the experience itself, and the value or harm of such an experience. The circumstances of each case vary. For instance, some people use psychoactives with the express purpose of accessing the divine, whereas others have such an experience out of the blue. The substances used are also diverse: respondents were not restricted in the type or number of drugs they could mention and some people listed as many as seven different psychoactives. The five drugs mentioned most often were: LSD, Ecstasy, cannabis, psilocybin mushrooms and DMT.

However, amongst all the diversity it is possible to see common threads and elements in what makes up a drug-induced spiritual experience. An overwhelmingly positive reaction to spiritual experiences on psychoactives came across strongly in our survey. Many people were unequivocal in their appreciation of the value of their experiences: 'they allow me to realise just how grand and wonderful life is' and 'they have brought me to peace with things'. These positive feelings can be grouped into four categories: unity and sense of place, feelings of overwhelming love, increased openness, and a changed view of death.

Unity and place

The most common theme running through the accounts of spiritual experience was of how feelings of transcendence of time and place produced an incredible sense of connectedness and oneness with all creation. This is demonstrated in the following account of an epic experience of this kind:

5

> Always on the lookout for new and effective ways to access God consciousness, I was looking forward to trying ibogaine. As we assembled, we discussed the preparation. We had all fasted for two days and spent the day before quietly reading, meditating and doing yoga to ensure the best possible experience. We disconnected the phone and put up a sign: 'Meditation in progress'. We each took a quantity of ibogaine hydrochloride – a chalky white powder with a bitter, earthy taste.
>
> We waited one, two, three hours and nothing happened. I had no desire to move. I was in a humming electric cocoon that gave me little funnybone shocks if I touched it. I was in the middle, centred between euphoria and depression. I felt balanced. My eyes focused in a different way, clear but taking everything in and then the room started to spin. The whirling increased and I felt like I was in the centre of a pinwheel. Faster and faster it spun and then I was rising like a projection through the roof, great chunks of wall and brick peeling back and falling away in slow motion. I shot up into the stars, a pair of disembodied eyes wandering, searching. I was an essence, a solo awareness flying though the universe, exploring, seeking.
>
> I continued on through the galaxies until I arrived above a whirling vortex that was coalescing into a solar system. I watched a planet form and

came closer to observe. I skimmed the planet, seeing and being everything I came across. As I watched I saw life appear. I observed spots of green forming along the seashores. The oceans seemed to be teeming with life and then the first buglike creatures started to crawl out on land. Slowly it dawned on me I was watching the history of the planet earth! Manlike creatures appeared, civilisations bloomed, I witnessed slaughter and mayhem. I was there, in it, feeling both the doer and the done to. For what seemed an interminably long time civilisations rose and fell in interfolding waves of creation, only to fall in smoking ruins followed by ages of darkness. As I lived through this flux and change, there arose in me an awareness of the noble and brave potential of humanity and its duty as the intelligent species to protect the life forms of the planet. I was experiencing a feeling of sacred unity with all life. I felt how all life was precious, interconnecting and supportive of all other life. I dedicated my spirit not to destroy any part of this puzzle of divine mystery that is the milk of creation. Throughout was this balance and acknowledgement of the intertwining of opposites, the negative and positive, the base and the noble. This feeling went through me as a dual aspect of one energy, total, deep and sweeping me away on this immense journey of life's history. It was like falling in love, so entrancing was this vision. Hours had gone by.

What I learned from this trip is that there is a new paradigm arising for man. Transcending mind, he finds spirit and soul.

(Nick, aged 40, from Canada.
This account was written in San Francisco county jail)

With the loss of ego and sense of self that comes with a powerful experience, the feeling of being part of something much bigger can involve an awareness of fluidity that is often described in terms of 'energy'.

Soon after taking the 2CB I closed my eyes and began to see some of the most beautiful patterns morph into living organism. I felt a rush of energy that went from my torso to my lower extremities and out of my body altogether. I felt unusually dichotomous – a part of everything and at the same time detached from everybody else. Besides all the physiological effects I was experiencing, my mind was on overdrive.

I began thinking about energy and how it can transform and carry on. I began to think of myself as energy and that when I die I too will transform and continue existing. This wasn't reincarnation but rather a transfer of sorts where my energy will continue on some physical level even if I'm not alive. I found great comfort in this thought and all of a sudden death did not worry me any more. I was living for a change!

I was on my back near a lake looking up at the sky. I felt a part of everything and it seemed that I could sense energy all around me. Trees, flowers, grass, the water – they all seemed to have an entity of their own. I kept thinking about a supreme being and the entire hierarchical nature of it all. All of a sudden I became filled with a sense of peace and had a realisation: God/dess is merely an energy that people can be a part of and become in tune with without the traditional 'I'm not worthy' worship mentality.

I think entheogens have already shown me the path and it is now up to me to follow it.

(A Hispanic American man, aged 23, working as a social studies teacher)

An increased sense of place in the world, a sense of belonging, was a positive feeling emphasised by many who had experienced an underlying oneness with the universe during a trip.

The first time I took LSD I did so with the intention of broadening my mind and having a new experience. The trip started out as fun: my friend Mandy and I watched *The Wizard of Oz* on video and thought it was sheer magic as we went into and flew over the rainbow. Then I had a sense of what I can only describe as timelessness; it was as though time as I knew it no longer existed and as this happened I felt that I became something else – my whole identity as a human being in a physical body on an everyday plane of existence began to evaporate, as though I had become energy or my consciousness had left my body. The room was flooded with bright white light and a feeling of serenity came over me, as though who 'I' was didn't matter any more.

5

Then I was filled with a sense of joy and amazement as I experienced cosmic consciousness: a sense of all things in the universe being interconnected. Everything felt so right, so perfect as I realised that the planet was alive and time and distance were irrelevant. I understood that no matter where we travel to on the earth, we are already spiritually connected to the entire universe – but our lives and society are constructed so that our attention is taken away from this feeling of belonging.

I was finally enlightened to the fact that although we spend our lives trying to achieve something – wealth, happiness, or to get somewhere – it is the journey itself that is important; in other words, life itself is the ultimate 'trip'.

(Julie, aged 33, from England)

The feelings of unity with the universe which some people experienced as a result of entheogens appeared to remain after the experience and to provide a sense of balance and perspective:

> I can put myself in a frame. I feel now that I am part of the One. I gained some stability from my experience which serves as a base upon which my entire life can be built up. It led me out of chaos. It gave me faith.
>
> **(experience on LSD)**

In one case a wider feeling of belonging led to better relationships on a smaller scale too:

> I have a much stronger idea of what it means to be human and where I 'fit' into the grand scheme of things. As a result of my entheogenic experiences, I have gradually moved from an atheistic perspective, feeling lost, being prone to frequent depressive episodes and suicidal tendencies, feeling disconnected from society, community and friends, to being a generally peaceful and optimistic person with a strong religious and spiritual bent, taking an active role in the unfolding of my life, and feeling connected to friends and community.
>
> **(experiences on LSD and DXM)**

The sense of unity can also occur on an individual rather than universal level:

> The best that I ever felt on Ecstasy was something that was not quite happiness or euphoria, but rather a profound and perfect sense of unity of mind, body, spirit and soul; and I understood in an instant exactly what happiness and being happy involved; and at the same time I was overwhelmed by a hope that I would some day get there. I realised that I was looking for something that few people understand or achieve; something that I understand but haven't achieved and cannot articulate. I am searching for a state of being in which mind, body, spirit and soul are fundamentally indivisible yet each feeds the understanding of the other – a feeling that all the words in the world can only understate. That night I almost found it. Some day I think I might.'

Overwhelming love

The comfort to be derived from having an increased feeling of security and belonging within the world may be heightened if the emotion frequently described by those who encounter it as a feeling of 'overwhelming love' is also encountered.

I consumed some LSD along with a quantity of mescalin sulphate and at the peak of the ensuing journey I had a totally paradigm-shattering experience...

I was lying on my bed, incense and ceremonial candles alight, meditating. The air seemed to grow somehow thick, as though pregnant with energy, like a thundercloud about to burst. My visual acuity seemed to sharpen at the same time, as I looked at my hand and began to be able to make out tiny iridescent curlicues that were superimposed as if upon a clear scrim on top of everything that I saw. Then automatically, as if by instinct, I began to manipulate my eye muscles in a manner very similar to the technique used to view those magic eye 3-D images, where you un-focus your eyes and attempt to look through the gibberish image to see the real picture. When I did this, the curlicues suddenly sprang into strong three-dimensional relief, and were revealed to be translucent, iridescent tentacles or tendrils of some sort that looked like they were formed out of ectoplasm. The room was electric with a sense of presence, and I followed the line of these tendrils away from my hand to their source. I was utterly unprepared for what I saw when I did so...

Floating in the corner of my room was an enormous, shimmering, translucent, opalescent, octopoid/jellyfish-like creature from which the tentacles protruded! My initial reaction was one of disbelief mixed with a substantial degree of fear. However, the thing immediately began to caress me with its tendrils as if to reassure me, and my apprehension completely melted away. Amazingly, I actually perceived a gentle, soothing pressure against my skin as it caressed me like a child! As it touched me I felt its consciousness partially merge with mine, and I was then flooded with a sense of love unlike anything I have ever experienced before or even imagined to be possible. Comparing any experience of transcendence that I had previously had to this is like trying to compare a candle to the sun. I had the sense that this was a guardian angel or something similar who was always with me, watching over me, and it was absolutely overjoyed that I could finally perceive and communicate with it directly. I was so moved by this that I wept openly with joy for a large portion of the time. I lay there soaking up its affection for nearly half an hour before it eventually vanished. The trip began to gradually, gently decline shortly afterwards.

I was, and remain, stunned and amazed by this.

5

(Rick, aged 24, from America)

Ecstasy and openness

A long-term benefit from these experiences, it emerges, is improved relation-ships with others. This seems to be particularly true of Ecstasy. A common thread in the responses of those who had had a spiritual experience on Ecstasy was a feeling of increased openness and positiveness towards other people. As one respondent described it:

> My Ecstasy breakthrough showed me many things...like the way humans can share energy, as well as steal energy from each other. I can now look to the future with hope rather than fear because I have realised that I *can* change the world in some sense by changing my own mind...changing the ways I deal with people...spreading love and joy instead of hate.

A man who took Ecstasy three times in a small-group situation gave this descrip-tion of the value of the experience:

> I take the liberty of saying that all of the members of the group have gained value from the experiences. We all dropped our inhibitions to just be. We ducked out from beneath societal pressures and returned to our true selves. We learned to be more understanding and less judgemental towards others. We saw different perspectives. We were free to tell each other all the things we had wanted to, to deal with the hurtful situations from the past (such as rape), for females to kiss females in the non-sexual human need for touch, for men to hug men, to breathe the air and be thankful for it, to smell with pure untouched senses, to taste the colours in popsicles, to feel each separate fibre in the carpet with our fingers, to be like the innocent, wondering children unscathed by society that we once were. It was clean, pure, safe and loving again. Long after the experimentation was over we learned to be more understanding, tolerant and less judgemental of those around us. To watch the sunset and truly experience the colours and sounds and smells it brings. To be grateful for the bright, clear blue sky, to give a compliment to another without a second thought.

As well as openness towards others, entheogenic experiences could encour-age openness towards more abstract notions – allowing a freedom to think the previously unthinkable:

> Drug experiences can inspire you with visions of euphoria and what could be, if you set your mind to it. Drugs have allowed me to open my mind and feel easy about some taboos and explore different ways of thinking.

Death

For some, their experience changed the way they viewed death. A different perspective on death was also a source of stronger feelings of stability and hope. One reply simply stated that 'I no longer fear death'. Another said that the

> profoundest benefit has been that through direct encounters with the spiritual Consciousness that lies behind 'reality' I now know, without a doubt, that the death of my body and my identity is not the same as the death of the spiritual force that animates them, for that force is part of that greater Consciousness. Although I don't feel that 'I' will live on after death, this is perfectly OK.

One respondent had a history of severe panic attacks, associated with thoughts of death, and would become overwhelmed with fear at the thought of death's finality. After his experience he said, 'I felt very different about the prospect of continued existence after death. It's as if it gave me an alternative to the idea that death was the end, and although I don't want to believe it, it has shown me that other possibilities may exist.'

Difficult trips

A common theme that emerged from the survey responses was that entheogenic experiences were valuable as new experiences offering huge potential for learning and personal growth: 'They have been valuable in letting me experience more than other people. I feel that when things happen in everyday life, I have a broader range of experiences from which to draw a response.' This is especially the case with difficult experiences: 'Learning to deal with the bummer psychedelic trip (which can be violently dark and terrifying) is a practice run for when this kind of shit really happens,' as one respondent put it.

Difficult trips were often valued for the insights they provided, even when those insights were not initially welcomed.

> Before I used entheogens I was depressed, alienated, nihilistic, very angry. I'm not giving all the credit to the chemicals, it took me much hard work to get where I am today, but they showed me that there was real beauty in the world, all around us, all the time. They stripped my soul bare and forced me to look at things I would rather have ignored.

Occasionally the process of extreme ego-loss encountered in a 'difficult' trip can have more harmful, long-term effects, highlighting the fact that psychoactives are powerful substances, as Jason describes in this account.

I'd been itching for some time to try a larger LSD dose (eight hits, each most likely of a pretty typical strength for the US) than I had in the past and a four-day weekend provided the opportunity.

Most of the trip went beautifully. On a walk in the woods, I experienced some profoundly transcendent moments. I felt as though I embodied a whole universe of pure consciousness, shaped into the particular experience of the trees, snow, rocks, and sky about me. I was thinking a lot about striving to achieve a unity between my thoughts, actions, perceptions, and language and this unity would be equivalent to allowing the divine to express itself most fully through my being. For quite some time, this unity seemed to be achieved.

Suddenly, I felt out of control and went to lie down on my bed in an effort to calm myself.

It seemed an increasing amount of 'J' was being replaced by this random stream of human consciousness. The process – which I felt then was divine, yet cruel and terrifying now – seemed to be attempting to dissolve me. I called to my friend, I tried to explain, but it was difficult to speak and to concentrate. There were quite a few moments when I was so absorbed in fighting the dissolution that I remained silent and still for what seemed like long periods of time.

As the dissolution continued, I felt as though my body was becoming possessed by random personalities that flowed in from the stream of core human consciousness. I remember looking at my friend with the consciousness of others, touching him as though he was some remarkable alien thing. The urging toward dissolution became so intense that I was sure that 'I' would not return from the trip. I was terrified – I didn't want to die. I thought I was literally losing my mind, and losing it permanently. I managed to express some of this to my friend; he held me while I moaned and cried in the grips of what I was sure was death and madness. Everything around me seemed utterly alien; once, when my friend tried to talk to me, I felt I had lost the ability to understand language.

My friend was eventually able to get through to me, to talk me back to a state of semi-sanity. It took a tremendous amount of will on my part to cling to his words and make sense of them and, as I did so, I felt I was the whole of the universe clawing its way out of darkness and madness toward a divine radiance and sense of health and salvation. This continued for some time; it was utterly exhausting, and I didn't know how long I would be able to bear it. The feeling of dissolution had taken on a physical character – a searing iciness seemed to be taking my body over. My friend continued to reassure me that I'd be OK. Eventually, I began to feel like it. I had made it 'to the Light', it seemed, and felt a peace return and saturate my being. Concentrating on the Light, I was able to manifest it in greater and greater degrees. It seemed I had turned my soul – which was also the soul of the universe – away from drowning in a river of fragments of human consciousness toward something that I could only call the genuinely divine.

The ego dissolution continued now, but peacefully. Whatever parts of me left were replaced by that divinity. Visions of joyously dissolving into the sun and the sky accompanied the experience and there was an unutterable feeling of the infinite and the sacred. I encountered the stream of human consciousness again, but this time I looked on it with what I felt to be the love of God. It was beautiful, touching, precious beyond all description. It had been nearly twelve hours since I'd dosed, and the effects were subsiding. I focused on reshaping my own self/ego in that divine image.

The profound and terrifying ego-loss experience induced by eight hits of LSD had unanticipated effects. Over the next several months I became increasingly 'religious', perfectly confident that my soul had literally touched the divine. Subsequent lower-dose experiments induced religious and mystical experiences that I would have thought inaccessible at all but the highest doses. While this appeared a positive and fortunate trend at first, the experiences soon became distinctly more serious and somehow 'darker'. For instance, near Christmas, I experienced a haunting vision of Christ as an inflamed and swollen sun rising above a lifeless desert. I understood the sun as a symbol of Christ's passion and, far from radiating a loving and forgiving warmth, the sun appeared agonised, enraged, harsh and cruel. Now the sun became a heart and the heart was split down the middle but continued beating, flooding the desert with the blood of Christ's passion. Inasmuch as the blood enriched the soil, making it fertile for life, the heart or Christ was in the unspeakable agony of crucifixion and it was this very agony that was the life within the blood. If becoming such a martyr is my spiritual destiny, I thought, I cannot bear it. I panicked, much as I had during my ego-loss experience, losing myself in a blind and icy fear

5

that seemed to pervade my whole being.

After a few more such experiences, I decided to stop using psychedelics for a while. I had, I felt, begun to lose touch with reality to a dangerous degree: I was growing increasingly paranoid and prone to increasingly severe panic attacks, a flood of long-buried memories, some traumatic, some trivial, occurred to me on an almost daily basis. I was haunted by strange and disturbing mental imagery (often bloody and violent) that I could make little sense of and that frequently seemed to contain powerful 'Jungian' overtones, and I even experienced a few genuine hallucinations – again, usually of rather disturbing content – while completely sober. The situation worsened to the degree that ego loss – which I interpreted as punishment from God for refusing to become a wandering homeless ascetic – almost always coincided, to some degree, with the panic attacks. As soon as I tried to find 'grounding' within myself to help me ride out the attack, all sense of personal identity would vanish, leaving nothing of me but raw panic and emotional agony. I was convinced I was becoming insane. This whole period culminated in a brief stay in a local mental hospital, I was put on antidepressant and anti-anxiety medication. Gradually, I started getting better.

That which had the most powerful healing effect, however, was the reading of certain post-Nietzschean philosophers (i.e. Martin Heidegger, M. Merleau-Ponty and Jacques Derrida) to whom I was introduced by a favourite teacher. As I made inroads into understanding some of the writings of these philosophers, I began to understand how the content of so many of my most powerful psychedelic experiences had been determined by certain Western philosophical presuppositions whose validity had been called into question literally centuries ago but which were nevertheless very much alive and influential among those people I'd encountered in various 'hippie' or 'alternative' subcultures. The capacity which I was developing to move my thinking away from the thinking determined by those presuppositions revealed to me that my entheogenic experiences had been not so much genuine revelations of the divine as intensely vivid experiences of both a collective and a personal mythology which I had discovered and developed over the past four or five years – a mythology which, because it was so pervasive among those with whom I associated, I had taken for truth unquestioningly. Realising that the content of my entheogenic experiences – including the prescriptive 'lessons' learned from those experiences — might have been radically different had my 'set and setting' been radically different allowed me to examine that content more rationally; in so doing, its grip on my psyche was loosened.

The healing process is far from over, but I no longer feel that I'm teetering on the brink of insanity at every waking moment – my psyche is gradually reconstructing itself and is thereby regaining a coherence, which I had, for a time, lost. Nevertheless, I still struggle, at least on occasion, with panic and periods of severe depression; flashbacks are not infrequent, and both my physical senses and my emotions frequently seem painfully overstimulated. Most disturbing is that I now often feel unfamiliar and alien to myself – as though much of 'who I am' was literally and permanently 'erased'. At the same time, I think that, if I manage eventually to regain a sense of being grounded within myself, I will have, in that process, 'lived' authentically and fully and to the depth of my being.

In summary, I would urge extreme caution in approaching entheogens for spiritual reasons. One's grasp of reality can slide away right beneath one's nose, without one ever realising it until it's far too late to recover. Always keep as clear a head as possible — and if anything threatens that clarity, heed it as a very serious and very dire warning.

(Jason, aged 28, from America)

5

Information on difficult trips is given in the chapter 'Before, During and After'.

Problems of integration

When a life-changing experience occurs suddenly, and possibly more so if it is one that occurs outside of consensus reality, it is not surprising that there should be some difficulties readjusting to life afterwards, even if the experience is seen to have beneficial effects overall. When those who had had a peak experience on a psychoactive were asked if the experience had been harmful in any way, the resultant change in perspective on the world was foremost in the responses. One man said that his experiences had been 'temporarily harmful in that they shattered the paradigms I'd used to relate to the world – an experience which is likely to be at least a little traumatic'. In the same vein an experience was 'harmful in the sense that one can no longer live with society's blinkers on' and another man said he felt that his LSD experiences had made it more difficult for him to function in the 'normal' world now that he had an awareness of a transcendent reality.

But even this aspect is not always seen as completely negative – one respondent wrote that 'the only way these experiences could be seen as harmful is that they have made it impossible for me to believe in, and difficult for me to participate in, our materialistic consumer-oriented culture'.

The sheer weirdness of some experiences can make it difficult to make sense of the world afterwards. For example:

I have finally succeeded in achieving the true, undeniable DMT space. It was easily the most bizarre and frightening experience I've ever had. I now understand the true meaning of shamanism – what is meant by walking the line between worlds, tapping into a completely alien source of knowledge. It isn't something that I think I care to repeat. It was simply too awesome.

Several things converged to finally make the experience possible. I had processed quite a large amount of M. hostilis rootbark, having had only very limited effects from past attempts using smaller quantities. I also used a tab of Moclobemide as the MAO inhibitor. I was very curious to see if it made a difference as opposed to using harmala extract, and I definitely think it did.

When the effects commenced some two hours after I drank the bitter sludge, they did not really creep in gradually as before. They hit fast in an accelerated rush, not unlike my first MDMA experience. I was standing up at the time, and had to go lie down as I thought I might faint on the spot.

For a minute it seemed pleasant enough, but then something happened that I am still attempting to sort out for myself. I have read with some degree of scepticism the many reports on DMT trips which talk about alien intelligence, alien presence, etc. and always thought that this was other people's interpretation of what was going on in their minds during their trip, and that my mind would not go there. I was wrong. To my utter disbelief, and even though I was fighting it at the time (and losing), I experienced what I can only call an alien presence. It felt like an invasive mental probing by an alien force. I did not want to believe in it, I was fighting it, but it was undeniable. As preposterous as the concept was, there it was, posing as truth, running my mind. At the peak of this section of the experience, I was having 'revelations' that were so outlandish that I realised I probably could not express them to my friends or anyone later on, because they just sounded too insane. They still do to me as well.

Principally, I had a sudden vision, or I should say a concept or a 'truth', that was so out there that it terrified me that I had gone so far as to think it, no matter what I was high on. I was 'told' that all human life on earth was merely a long-term genetic experiment by extraplanetary life forms alien to us. Our very existence was owed to them although it was in their programme not to have us realise this. I had been chosen to be allowed to know the incredible secret to human existence: that these aliens had taken their own genetic material and hybridised it with primates found on the planet at the time of their arrival millions of years ago (only a short time in their scale), resulting in us 'humans'. All human ideology about religion, God, self-determination, and most of all, our perception that 'we' are the only ones in control of what happens on this planet were shown to me to be a total joke, a delusion that we create ourselves. The tendency to see 'Gods' as essentially human models (Jesus, Buddha, Mohammed, etc.) was shown to me to be all part of their plan. The catch-22 was seamless and perfect – I had been shown the awesome truth, but of course I can never reveal it to the world because I will only sound insane to everyone. For a moment the Heaven's Gate* people seemed to be more sane than anyone. That's when I knew I was really out of it. It was scary that I would even think such a thing.

5

The experience I had was completely different than the one I have been chasing. I wanted a trip where incredible open-eye visuals dominate, taking the imagination for a ride, one that wrapped unreal visuals together in balance with awesome realisations. But there were really no visuals to speak of in this experience. There was some distortion but that was all. It was all an incredibly powerful mindfuck. I was having crying jags that were not connected to any thought or cause that I could see, they were just releases of raw emotion, as if I was a puppet being manipulated. I was alternately fighting it and trying to roll with it. I experienced time distortion on a scale that I hadn't thought possible. I was caught in a hellish loop that was timeless. I thought the effects would never end. I was listening to an album that I knew was only about 45 minutes long, but each time I would feel as if an eternity – hours, days, a lifetime – had passed,

*Religious group, the members of which committed suicide in 1997.

and surely the album had ended, I would open my eyes and focus on the music and realise that it had only been a minute or two! This was discomfiting because it made me feel that I had gone insane – permanently. I began to believe that I had ruined my life, finally toyed with entheogens enough to lose my mind. I began to have insidious suicidal thoughts. I had to say 'No, no, no!' out loud to push away the thoughts of getting up, getting a gun and shooting myself.

The news isn't all bad. I did have flashes of positive messages telling me that my own potential was limitless and that all the limitations that exist in my life are self-created, that my genetic material is far superior to that of the vast majority of human beings and has been chosen for the kind of knowledge that we appear to have been given. But in the end, even these good thoughts seemed delusional. In fact delusional doesn't even begin to describe the state I was in, despite the fact that at the very same time my rational mind was present and trying to process all of it.

Finally I threw up the purple muck and the ride was over. It had lasted from about 9:30 p.m. to about 12.30 a.m. What has been referred to as 'the Holy Grail' I now see as something more like 'the Evil Confuser'. It's going to take a while to integrate and understand what happened.

(Isomer, aged 35, software tester in America)

Psychedelic trips tend to be hard to describe afterwards, and more so when they have a transcendental dimension. The ineffability of certain experiences on drugs can make it difficult to share one's experience with others, leading to feelings of isolation. A spiritual experience in which one feels 'special' or 'chosen' can compound this problem. Spiritual experiences are not an everyday topic of conversation in our society, and a spiritual experience on a drug puts one doubly outside societal norms. Internet mailing lists and newsgroups can play a valuable role in allowing people to share their experiences in an open way with like-minded people.

While a feeling of increased sensitivity (to others, to the society one lives in) after a peak experience is frequently a key feature and is generally welcomed, over-sensitivity can become a problem. Ecstasy helped one respondent to 'feel' music more intensely, but this also led to depression because now he 'can also "feel" other people's emotions. I am strongly affected by the "vibe" or emotions people close to me emit.'

The sheer power of the experience may be overwhelming: 'It took me a long time to get my head together afterwards. It's as if the experience was so strong that it hardwired itself into my brain. It was about a year before I could finally look at the experience in a positive way.'

Another respondent to the survey pointed out that drugs can be an easy way to feel the best you have ever felt and can lead to a lack of motivation to achieve those feelings in other ways. However, this seemed not generally to be the case, judging from the responses to the question 'Have entheogenic experiences made you want to explore spirituality in other ways and, if so, in what ways?'

Further spiritual exploration

Psychedelic experience is only a glimpse of genuine mystical insight, but a glimpse which can be matured and deepened by the various ways of meditation in which drugs are no longer necessary or useful. When you get the message, hang up the phone. For psychedelic drugs are simply instruments, like microscopes, telescopes and telephones. The biologist does not sit with his eye permanently glued to the microscope, he goes away and works on what he has seen.[1]

(Alan Watts)

5

A peak experience can produce more questions than it resolves, as shown in the account below, and in these cases further spiritual exploration is another way of trying to make sense of it all.

DMT and the Temple of Life

I have done many psychedelics – LSD, mushrooms, peyote – but DMT makes these seem like children's toys. After reading everything I could find on DMT, the descriptions seem to fall far short of what happened to me. I inhaled *one* toke of DMT and was immediately catapulted into another dimension.

Now, I am not a religious person at all, but I found myself (or, rather, what I had become) in what I can only describe as 'The Temple of Life'. I was in a sort of white dome, with jewelled walls, covered with liquid diamonds. I felt overcome by an enormous sense of maternal love. I think it was coming from my girlfriend.

Confusion set in and I started to question the validity of it all. I could not recall how I had gotten there, or what I really was. In fact, when I opened my eyes, reality was utterly transformed, beyond all my powers of description. 'Biosphere' is the word that comes to mind. My girlfriend looked like a machine-goddess, her face glowing with iridescent patterns of symmetrical colour. I kept looking out the window, as the scene out there was not as I knew it to be. In fact the landscape was so completely alien that I couldn't accept it and kept saying, 'This can't be real'. It was *not* psychedelic, this was something *very, very* different.

The speed with which I came down was very surprising; I found myself walking up and down, shaking my head in utter disbelief. I now feel that I entered some hyper-real dimension, which also felt incredibly 'techno-spiritual'. I am left with a feeling of, 'What the hell are we? Why are we here? What is this experience all about? Why is humanity in the state it is? Who or what is responsible for this? What is the meaning of the temple?'

I am infused with joy at having experienced this. I am still in awe.

(Gary, aged 32, from America)

The majority of people who responded to the survey said that their entheogenic experiences had led them to explore spirituality in other ways. In some cases the experience had acted as a trigger:

I've always been relatively spiritual but these experiences have made me more active in my spirituality. For example, actually buying incense and using it, actually attempting meditation, not just leaving all these things in the 'One Day' box and never getting round to doing these things.

There was a clear bias towards solitary spiritual paths. Three in particular stood out: yoga, meditation and martial arts (t'ai chi and aikido). Yoga was described as a 'slow process compared with acid [but] once the dhyana state is achieved, you can have as many free trips as you want because the dhyana state is very similar to deep acid experience'.

Traditional religions were mentioned by very few respondents. One said that 'I have become more interested in (liberal) Judaism'. Another replied: 'I will always wonder if my first "e" trip (the closest I have ever felt to God) was due to the fact that I was to be baptised the very next day as a Catholic'. Another took up Buddhism.

Following initial 'ego death/clear light' experience, I explored the writings

from various mystical/contemplative traditions, eventually settling on
Buddhism, with particular interest in the Zen schools, and finally taking up
formal practice with the London Buddhist Society.

Most were still exploring possibilities, seeking a path which would recognise,
mesh with, and develop further the experience they had had. One respondent
said: 'I was previously very anti-religious, anti-spiritual, anti-mystical. I have
looked into wide and various areas, including Magick (Aleister Crowley), nature
worship, and even the Bible...my future areas of inquiry are Buddhism and
Sufism. I guess I'm a little eclectic.' Another said 'we (my wife and I) have
included a number of native American and pagan practices in our spiritual life,
but are not part of any organised group or church. I guess you could call us
spiritual pragmatists.'

Other respondents did not feel it was a matter of cause and effect so
much as entheogens and an interest in spirituality working in tandem. For
example:

> I was always spiritually inclined, and in the environment of my youth, drugs
> were the only way I knew to get more information about what exists
> beyond my 'skin-encapsulated ego'. As soon as I was able to connect with a
> meditation teacher, I stopped using drugs altogether for a time, and
> applied myself to drug-free means of inner exploration. Now, I am learning
> to balance the discipline of spiritual practice with the discipline of using
> sacramental catalysts.

5

There is still much to be learnt about the 'best way' to use a psychoactive,
and it may be that there are as many ways as there are individuals using psychoactives. By his or her very nature the 'psychedelic explorer' will seek to
venture into unknown territory. This chapter offers a snapshot of the myriad
ways that psychoactives are used by individuals for spiritual exploration, and
how some of those experiences were integrated. The accounts here show that
it is not necessary to have an established structure, such as a church, in which
to explore spirituality using psychoactives. But it is important to have some kind
of support network, be it friends, family, or Internet-based allies, to help one
make sense of an experience afterwards and, possibly, to help guard against
the occurrence of an inflated ego after an especially enlightening experience.

6

Rave Spirituality

I show you all alive

a world where every particle of dust

breathes forth its joy.

William Blake

We are all the Rainbow tribe

All colours, all races, united as one,

We dance for peace

and the healing of our mother earth.

Peace for Tibet,

Peace for all nations and

Peace within ourselves.

As we join as one on the dance floor

across the world

Let us connect heart to heart.

Our love is the power to transform

Our world.

Let us send it out,

Now...

Earthdance Prayer for Peace

Rave culture, often portrayed as purely hedonistic, is frequently regarded as a spiritual event by those involved. Raves are likened to trancelike tribal rituals where ravers celebrate their unity and shared uplifted state, freely giving and receiving from one another. Terence McKenna, author of *True Hallucinations and Food of the Gods*, views the rave as an explosive re-emergence of the repressed human drive to free consciousness from its unnatural ego-centred state. He sees the natural state as having been regulated out of existence except in a diluted form in churches, sports stadia and clubs. The modern manifestation of this state is the rave, which involves entering an altered state of collective consciousness through the ingestion of drugs, through physical activity and through sensory bombardment by technological artefacts such as hypnotic, emotional, loud music, light shows and smoke machines.

> Raving can be viewed as a transcendental mind-altering experience providing psychic relief to alienated people in a secular, repressive and materialistic society. Ecstasy and other drugs are the keys that unlock the doors to these desired states of consciousness...a deeply desired escape from the constraints of the self and normal behaviour. To stretch the religious metaphor, DJs are the high priests of the rave ceremony, responding to the mood of the crowd, with their mixing desks symbolising the altar (the only direction in which the ravers consistently face). Dancing at raves may be construed as the method by which ravers 'worship' the God of altered consciousness.[1]
>
> **(Russell Newcombe)**

In this chapter the spiritual dimensions of rave are considered from a number of different angles. First, we look at settings of a rave that can foster spiritual overtones. Secondly, the feelings of unity brought out in a rave, on both the individual and the collective level are illustrated with personal accounts. The participatory aspect of rave is shown through two accounts which vividly describe the process of setting up a party, one on a beach in Santa Cruz, USA, the other in South Africa. Finally, the possible implications of this form of contemporary spirituality are considered, both on an individual level and in terms of collective consciousness.

'Rave' as a term is not uncontroversial. Many people prefer 'dance culture' or 'clubbing' – words which more accurately describe the diversity of the area.

They feel that 'rave' is outdated, describing a particular type of dance event set in the early years of the evolution of dance culture. Many also feel that the word has been appropriated by the media and as such comes with baggage in the form of negative connotations. Clubbing or partying are seen as more neutral words: it is possible to tell your straight workmates on a Monday morning that you were out 'clubbing' at the weekend without raising any eyebrows – describe it as 'raving' and media-hysteric images of drug-addled kids defying the law by dancing to repetitive beats in a warehouse might spring to mind.

However, here the terms 'rave' and 'raving' are used simply because they seem most accurately to describe the kinds of events and states of mind discussed. 'Dance culture' or 'dance scene' encompasses a huge range of genres and attitudes, from massive commercial superclubs with their own merchandising and associated industries, to squat parties. The main focus here is on the more underground (or commercial-underground) scene which usually features a relaxed door policy, no dress code, and where, generally, Ecstasy rather than alcohol is the drug of choice.

In this chapter the psychoactives used are discussed less than in previous chapters. The connection between raving and drug use is taken as given: in a Release dance survey 87 per cent of those questioned at dance events planned to take an illegal drug on the night they filled in the questionnaire.[2] Ecstasy and cannabis were the most popular drugs with those questioned, with amphetamines and LSD some way behind in popularity. Cocaine, ketamine and mushrooms were also mentioned.

While it is possible to make the assumption that the majority of people at a rave will be on one or more psychoactive substances, raving is not simply about finding a sociable atmosphere in which to take drugs. According to the Release survey, drug use was only the fifth most popular reason for attending events, after music, socialising, the atmosphere and dancing.

6

Spiritual settings

Setting is a crucial factor in influencing an entheogenic experience. Some clubs attempt to bring out the spiritual side of rave by consciously creating spaces which are conducive to spiritual expression. In London, Escape from Samsara, Pendragon, and Return to the Source are renowned for providing an environment in which the spiritual element in rave can be explored more fully.[3]

Pendragon, for example, coincide their nights with the full moon and each night commences with a ritual. They use pagan imagery in their flyers, urging clubbers to 'invoke the tribal Celtic spirit' and celebrate festivals such as Samhain and Lammas.

Return to the Source organisers see the dance floor as a sacred space and prepare it accordingly. A crystal, symbolising cosmic energy, is hung above it, spring water from Glastonbury is ritually sprinkled, and American Indian sage is burnt to cleanse the energy. Return to the Source describe their vision:

> The all-night dance ritual is a memory that runs deep within us all; a memory that takes us back to a time when people had respect for our great mother earth and each other. Dancing was our rite of passage, our shamanic journey into altered states of reality where we embodied the Great Spirit and the magic of life...
>
> The ancient memory has reawakened, the all-night dance ritual has returned. At Return to the Source, it is our vision to bring back the dance ritual. A ritual is a sacred act with focused intention. We aim to create a modern day positive space, created with love where we can join as one tribe to journey deep into trance, just as our ancestors did...[4]

The sense of community which arises out of being at a festival may well add an extra dimension to an already excellent setting. In the festival described below, the care and love the organisers had put into their party (which they have held once a year for the past eight years) was heightened by the fact that everybody had spent that day together relaxing.

> I attended a party in an old country house set within acres of grounds. We had all spent at least all of that day camped in the grounds, enjoying treatments such as massage and osteopathy, taking part in yoga and t'ai chi workshops, or just chilling out by the swimming pool. The build-up to the evening's party was carefully orchestrated. As the sun set an enormous bonfire was lit and it was surrounded by fire dancers who later led the party-goers across the lawn to where fireworks were going off across the lake. As the last firework burst into the sky, lasers, projected from the house, cast the party-goers into a trippy wonderland of light, smoke and images projected and imagined. Drummers led the revellers along a path leading to the house, lit on each side by fire torches. As we entered the hallway of the house, white-clad children and adults were playing bells and

humming on the main staircase which was decorated with flowers. In front of us was an altar covered in fresh petals and crystals. Further into the house and each room was carefully decorated with branches, leaves, flowers, dreamcatchers. In the largest room, packed full of people dancing to hard trance, a large screen flashed the words 'one love'. There was a tangible feeling of connectedness between the people dancing together in that room...

(Buttercup, a 25-year-old English woman)

While the care put into preparing a dance space is important, the power of sound should not be forgotten as music is, after all, the defining feature of rave. A skilled DJ will weave a narrative with sound, bringing everyone up to a heightened state of euphoria, cutting layers away, both responding to and creating the mood of the dance floor.

The more magical techno activists understand the power of the gnosis of trance, and may use lots of tricks and techniques to 'direct' the energy of the dance in a certain direction. Sound is the most obvious one but artists have buried crystals under dance areas, used static visual art or computer-generated visuals, or most recently, I've found myself dancing on a black floor covered in a 22-pointed star – the artist is perhaps a Qabbalist – and this is the first time I've found myself 'dancing' in orgiastic communion with others. Meditative rituals often open and close gatherings.

It's incredible to be in an environment with a couple of hundred other playful crazies, possessed by the sounds, as you writhe and shake wildly in unison with a dozen or so other people who have suddenly found their minds in the same sonic whirlpool. I'm sure we're all 'seeing' or 'understanding' the experience in many and varied ways but there is a moment when powerful energies – life forces and spirits and under-standings – are created and exchanged and shared with those around you.

6

(bigk, an Australian woman)

Organisers may choose to hold a party in a venue which naturally has spiritual overtones, such as a church or monastery. While some people might be shocked to discover a Christian church being used for a rave, others may find it especially fitting. Here, Nicholas describes what for him was the 'ultimate spiritual rave':

It was in a 600-year-old monastery in Normandy, but everyone and everything came from Britain, even blocks of ice for the ice sculpture. Our host, Jane, had spent most of her working life organising events for other people, which gave her plenty of opportunity to dream up her ultimate party...and this was her dream come true.

About 500 of us arrived on Friday after a night on the ferry, and were allocated cells last used by nuns some years before. There was ambient music, food that was simple but delicious and beautifully served, such as fresh bread, ripe Brie, and lots of salad and fruit, all artistically arranged.

Besides the chapel, the party was spread over several other rooms including a dungeon (shoes off, incense and ambient music); an 'Arabian Nights' tent lined with hangings where you could sit on cushions and help yourself to a variety of teas, and a room whose walls were covered with brilliant fluorescent paintings depicting aspects of good feelings: hearts, dancers and (my favourite) a 'love bug', an insect made up of hearts that appeared to be zooming towards you and about to hug you.

The chapel altar had gone, but Jane made her own to display goddess statues and precious personal items that she had asked guests to bring. It was lit by candles and several carefully placed strobes that each gave a different glimpse of the statues by lighting them from different angles. The altar was the focal point, with speakers either side and DJs hidden away behind it. The result was that we all faced it and danced in praise of the goddess icons, as it were. The music was consistent non-stop techno, and the dancing quickly got going and carried on and on.

The main day was Saturday. There was a torch-lit procession with people grouped according to their star sign, each led by someone dressed in costume; a brief play and a band outdoors, then the procession led us into the chapel whose stone arches and pillars were lit by hundreds of candles. At this point my E started to take effect and the feeling was of being part of a pilgrimage that had reached its goal where we celebrated by dancing to the goddess altar.

Every hour or so I would go out to help myself to water – there was even a sacred spring with the reputation of having healing powers, where some people filled their bottles. And at the same time I would go down to the lakeside to see the progress of the ice sculpture. This started as two large blocks of ice and was carved with heated rods, lit by gas flames, and with microphones picking up sizzling and cracking sounds. The changes the

ice went through were so fascinating that some people spent the entire
night watching.

I felt that the altar, and being in a church, provided just what was
missing from other dance venues: a worthy focus for our spiritual attention.
But the atmosphere also relied on everything being done with love and
care, and the fact that we were all together for so long.

A venue which has been specifically designed to evoke the spirit certainly helps
give atmosphere to a dance event, but the mind-set of participants is also a
crucial factor. Here Nicholas describes a church service:

The venue was a fair-sized Gothic-style church, an active Christian church,
and the service was described in the church programme as 'Trance Dancing
– an ancient practice which invites the spirit to embody us and to heal us
through external spiritual ecstasy...The spirit knows the moves and once
awakened, the spirit takes over...Trance dancing has nothing to do with the
expectations of others and all to do with revealing our timeless existence.'

We arrived at 11 p.m. The church was complete with all the usual
Christian ornament. At first glance all looked normal, but the front few
rows of pews had been removed to allow room to dance, some cushions
and blankets were placed on the floor of a carpeted side chapel as a chill-
out area. A sound-system and mixing desk was set up at one side of the
front of the nave, and the pulpit was used to house projectors aimed at the
back wall...all rather low-key, including the volume of sound. A nice touch
was that the DJs' names were displayed on the board designed for listing
the hymns to be sung.

6

About sixty people turned up, mostly in their forties although there
were some in their twenties, and the majority were men. As the clock struck
midnight, we congregated in front of the altar for the opening meditation.
They had decided not to have a leader or 'priest', so this was followed by
people taking turns to suggest little rituals like holding each other's hands
in silence and 'toning'.

Then the music took over; people started dancing and the atmosphere
suggested that entheogens were enhancing the experience for several
people: certainly no one drank alcohol as that was specifically forbidden in
the rules of admittance. Once dancing, I immediately felt more at home in
spite of a stiffness in my back, but after a while I found that even my back
became fluid and it was a real pleasure to bend it. My arms are normally

kept safely below shoulder level, but they rose higher and higher until they stretched up to the roof followed by my gaze as I celebrated the glory of being in such a magnificent place – and my loose neck. The grandeur of the building seemed to bring out my most sweeping, uplifted movements and I felt great respect for the church itself.

We were still dancing when seven o'clock came. Lights went on and the reinstatement of the church was efficiently organised, with the pews being moved back into place and screwed down again. Fresh coffee was provided and some people had brought breakfast, which was shared. Hugs were given and people dispersed.

That kind of event does not happen easily. The organisers carefully approached the church council and outlined what they wanted to do. 'Will there be drugs?' 'We certainly won't dispense or encourage them though we know of no way to know what people may have taken before they come in. In any event, there will be no alcohol.' The local authority was consulted about a dancing licence, but it turned out that churches are exempt; police were told about the event and asked to relay any complaints to the organisers' mobile.

All the careful preparation paid off. The church council agreed without being told any lies and one or two came, including a retired bishop. They saw it as a way of attracting new people into their church, and in fact one or two have since returned to attend Sunday services.

Afterwards I asked myself whether this had been the truly 'spiritual' experience I had been anticipating and hoping for. Possibly, but no more than events I have attended in disused warehouses and under railway arches! Yet it had another, unexpected effect on me: it had dissolved my prejudice against Christian churches. All my life I had regarded them as sterile monuments that made me feel uncomfortable, but that night I had felt very much at home. A week later I walked into one and put it to the test: yes, I felt much less defensive.

Using the power of the rave setting to attract new people to church was possibly taken to its limit by the 'Nine O'Clock Service', a Church of England congregation in Sheffield, England. Now defunct, due to abuses of power by their leader, this was a community involved in ground-breaking experimental worship. This was no church hall disco – members were extremely professional in their approach to 'rave worship', and combined personal knowledge of the club scene with the technical ability to produce video and slide backdrops, graphics and sets. They shocked many of those who watched them at the 1992 Greenbelt Christian arts festival with their postmodern service/performance 'Passion in Global Chaos'. It combined multi-media technology with postmodern theology, loud techno and bikini-clad dancers. They also held regular services in a club, using rave-style flyers in a bid to attract clubbers to the church. Music with uplifting lyrics was chosen but the words were related to the experience of God, rather than an Ecstasy-high, as drugs were not permitted. This description of a service, from a book about the rise and collapse of the congregation, indicates the emotional power of the setting:

> ...into a different world, the world of primeval techno: darkness and druidic white-robed figures around an altar resembling a crescent moon coming out of partial eclipse with the sun, surrounded by a circle of pillars. When one's eyes have adjusted to the ultra-violet light, hundreds of black clad figures peer out of the darkness swaying to the swirling, strangely ethereal breaths of ambient techno. The world outside has dissolved into synthesiser and computer-generated mysticism...The crescendo builds and the white-robed Reverend Chris Brain, techno shaman, moves to the centre...[5]

Unity and community

At a rave, no matter who you are, you feel a sense of 'connectedness' with all those around you. Your energy becomes part of a greater circle of energy and love. You feel free to be who you have always wanted to be, because nobody is judging you. They're experiencing the exact same rush of happiness and when you leave the rave, you carry that free spirit and high energy out with you. You incorporate it into all facets of life, making things a little bit better.

6

Raves have allowed me to 'touch base' with reality and humanity. People are beautiful. People ought to tell other people that they are beautiful more often. The love and bonding experienced at raves needs to be carried out into the world. We are the visionaries, and it is our job to slowly change society. There was a women's movement, a sexual revolution, and many other giant steps taken by previous generations. It is now time for the next revolution, the one back to realising the beauty of humanity.

(Pete, aged 26, from America)

The sense of mind and body being at one is a key factor in rave spirituality. Roger Griffin, who lectures in history at Oxford Brookes University, describes this as the oldest and newest parts of our brains reconnecting. The limbic layer of the brain deals with fight or flight, and responds to rhythm. The neo-cortex layer works with abstract thought and awareness. When these parts link up, mind and body are working together creating unity within the self. A feeling of acceptance grows, of oneself and of all around. Griffin sees this experience as having benefits beyond the immediate sense of well-being: 'With this union the regenerative experience of years of therapy are packed into a few hours of release and internalised deep within the body memory as a reservoir of hidden psychic strength.'[6] The result is a sense of joy, of bliss even. This aspect was remarked upon by a Buddhist monk whom Nicholas took to a rave:

> I invited Bertrand to a dance party where he took some ecstasy. It was the first time Bertrand had taken the drug except while meditating, and he was surprised at how different the experience was. Beforehand, he said he could hardly stand the noise, but after the drug took effect he could see the value of the volume in drowning out distractions. As the drug took effect his face changed expression from curious to happy and he exclaimed: 'I can see what it's all about, this is like walking meditation. These people are meditating only they don't realise it. They are in the same state. They are completely in the "here and now", moving spontaneously without thinking about it.' Far from it being alien to his experience, he saw that everyone was totally aware yet absorbed in their dance without self-consciousness or internal dialogue, and that this was the very essence of meditation. He had once been a guest at an American Indian ceremony which provided the feeling of tribal bonding by the use of a drug and monotonous beat, and thought that the rave was comparable, although it missed the Indians' cultural framework and focus.

The individual sense of wholeness can expand into a feeling of collective unity. It is this experience which makes a rave feel like so much more than the sum of its parts. It manifests itself as a feeling of overwhelming sense of unity, of connectedness with all things, while the sense of self is retained. It is almost as if one has tapped into a form of collective consciousness. This can happen at an outdoor gathering:

> Like the old pagan festivals, we're all in this together, this is our planet, She

is indescribably beautiful, gigantic, we are atoms of that Living Goddess. Personally I can't see a better way to help people learn a love, respect and reverence for Nature than the classical open-air all-night Rave. Can you imagine what it felt like with 20,000 people going for it and actually feeling together, and the power of a people together...and then dancing the sun up?! It is awesome, it is religious, and it is life-changing.[7]

(Fraser Clark)

Or it can be equally powerfully felt within a club setting:

The hug

I was at a party in Vancouver, with all my friends, celebrating my time there, and saying goodbye to a scene that had transformed my life, taught me the meaning of love again, and generally just blown my mind.

At some point in the morning, I was swimming through the music across the dance floor, having been pretty engaged in some meditational stuff, when I ran across a couple of friends on the floor, and proceeded to give them both a hug. We were all trancing pretty heavily, and as I stood with my arms around my two buddies, looking at the ground, I felt that familiar rush of good vibes coming on. All of a sudden, I looked up and found that we were surrounded by 20–30 other people, all hugging in on us, creating a huge circle, the most gigantic hug I have ever been in, and everyone just pouring their love and good vibes, not only into the hug, but out into the rest of the party, and the rest of the world as well. As I looked around at these beautiful people, a space cleared in the middle of the hug, and I started turning around, with one hand in the air. Someone outside the hug grabbed my hand and squeezed it, then came into the hug. All of a sudden, the music started to peak, and I began to spin, and let off a huge yell, and, as my yell and the music peaked at the same time, the entire group broke up as one, and everyone just started bustin' out insanely, leaping up and down, whooping and whistling, and then the whole party was yelling, and it was all on all over again.

Despite all the amazing things that have happened to me in the short time I have been involved in this scene, this was the wildest, most beautiful, crazy one, with love pumping out, with a vibe so thick the air seemed like water, a party where everyone felt so comfortable and so at one, and the hug just peaked it all.

(Andy, aged 24, from Canada)

6

These feelings of unity, both within oneself and with all around, can lead to a rave setting becoming a sacred time and space. This feeling may be accentuated by the way in which time characteristically takes on a different dimension in both psychoactive and mystical experiences. A minute can seem like an eternity while at the same time ravers frequently puzzle at the end of a night about where exactly the previous seven hours went. There is a sense that collective time transcends individual time. It is visionary, mythical time that spans the darkness of the night and welcomes the dawn of the new day and beyond; this is common to many rituals throughout history and throughout different cultures.

The sense that a rave can be seen as being 'outside time', combined with its tendency to be a place in which there is almost total understanding and acceptance of altered states, means that it can also seem to be outside society, or outside the normal bounds of society. It has the potential to become, in Hakim Bey's words, a *temporary autonomous zone* (TAZ) – a spontaneous emergence, and maximisation, of pleasure, freedom, energy and excitement uncontrolled by oppressive hierarchies.

DIY culture

A rave is not easy to organise. It may take place somewhere not specifically designed for large parties. For legal reasons the location may only be announced at the last minute, making advertising and logistics difficult. But rave is a participatory culture – it works because of the involvement of all those who have felt the vibe and love it. At its best, it is not a passive consumable.

These next two accounts bear testimony to the way in which, for those involved, rave truly is special.

> For me, the idea of a small, do-it-yourself ritual gathering was a natural extension of what I had found several years ago in the rave scene. Although the large, colourful raves that I started to attend some six years earlier did provide some amount of spiritual transcendence, I was always searching for something more pure and real. I found myself enjoying smaller parties, and I quickly learned that the more energy you put into a gathering, the more energy you would get back.
>
> This was definitely in my mind as I sat in the 'staging area' for this

evening's event, a friend's flat in Santa Cruz. Myself, and about twenty
friends who I had met through the rave scene in the Bay Area, were all
psyched up for this evening's festivities. As more people arrived, we started
to make some rudimentary plans: who would control parking, when to
update the voicemail number, what the DJ order would be. All along there
was a sense of excitement and anticipation.

Around midnight we make final preparations and leave Santa Cruz,
heading north on the lonely Highway 1. Tonight I was with two new friends
from Nottingham, England. I had met them over the Internet and they were
visiting the Bay Area to check out the scene here. I was determined to
show them a good time. The site is a completely isolated stretch of beach
with a gated path leading down to the beach from the highway. Here the
scene is chaotic and exciting. To make these gatherings happen, everyone
takes responsibility for a certain part of the production. Everyone is
depending on everyone else, because one mishap can render the whole
adventure useless. In trying to drag an entire sound system 300 yards
down a broken path, while at the same time hiding 300 people and their
cars from being spotted by authorities, the number of things that can go
wrong is substantial. But everyone keeps a positive attitude, and everyone
is driven by some force within them to make the impossible come true. I
quickly park my car by the gate and unload the generator, extension cords,
and a variety of props and camping equipment, then park with the other
cars, out of sight across the highway. A small team of people are using
flashlights to ID cars that look like they are looking for the gathering, and
then park them safely off the road. Without these people, a passing
highway patrol would certainly see at least a few mis-parked cars and come
to shut the gathering down.

Soon, the sound system arrives and teams of people start the long
process of moving sixteen sound cabinets, amps, turntables, the generator,
blacklights, water, brewing pots, banners, stands, tents, sleeping bags,
firewood, fresh fruit, etc. down to the beach. I am taking full responsibility
for powering this party, so once I have the generator in place, started, and
extension cords running to a power strip and illuminating a small lamp, I
feel relieved. In the mean time, two audio technicians are combing through
their boxes of interconnects and plugs to figure out the best way to merge
the two sound systems we are using. Another group of people are setting
up the blacklights and figuring out how to best position them to illuminate

6

the two fluorescent art banners we have put up on either side of the speaker stacks. I get my tiki torches and arrange them in a sacred pattern around the dancing area, adding a tribal feel to our production. A team of girls are quickly placing many sacred objects on our altar in front of the DJ, including an orange fluorescent Buddha with a necklace of chasing LEDs. Several random drummers are providing the beat while we work.

At around 1.30 a.m., the first beats are emanating from the speakers. Once the final tweaks are done to the sound system, the first DJ starts his set and the ritual is under way. Only now could all those involved finally take a deep breath, relax, and enjoy what they had created. I walk around being social, meeting up with friends, checking on some little details, meeting new people. It is always interesting to see what kind of people make it to an event like this, one that you only promote by small flyers at other small gatherings. After making some new friends, and concluding that this party is 'go', I find one of the other key people involved with producing this gathering for the sacrament. He is eager to tear me off a single square of Q-Bert, a variety of acid that got its name from the 3-D cube design on the blotter that resembled the early '80s video game.

Goa trance music is our current obsession. It has a quality that is quick, light and spacy. The beat and sounds make one feel as if they are bouncing off the stratosphere. Rough, growling, grizzly synthesiser sounds cut like a rusty knife deep into your brain and into your soul. These sounds penetrate you, get into you, touch you deep in your head. An hour after ingesting Q-Bert I am grooving out relentlessly on the beach. The gathering is at critical mass, maxing out at around 300 people. The temperature has dropped substantially, forcing participants to generate their own heat by dancing. Time distorts tremendously in the vibe of this gathering. Dancing feels so right, so good, that one can continue for hours on end and think nothing of it. Two o'clock, three o'clock, four o'clock, the hours pass quickly and I enjoy the sheer pleasure of dancing in this environment that I have created for myself and my guests. The pulsating Goa beats drive my body directly. My brain is taken out of the loop of controlling my body. Instead, there is a direct connection between my aural nerves and my twitching leg and arm muscles. My body is so tied up with dancing, that my brain is no longer concerned about its physical limitations. With the body taking care of itself pulsating to the beats, my brain is free to soar out into higher and higher dimensions of trancedental bliss. Dancing isn't something I have to force my body to do...it is simply what I want to do most. There is no thought of rest. No thought of pause. I am in the most satisfied state I have ever experienced, and I want it to continue. Thanks to years of trance-dancing, my body is fully capable of dancing non stop for a six-hour stretch, so I let the beats push my body further and further...at the same time, my brain becomes increasingly detached from my physical body, my spirit soaring through higher dimensions of pleasure. This is everything I crave in life, dancing hard to ripping beats.

By 5 a.m., the first hints of the next day are peeking over the eastern horizon. By now, only those people fully into the vibe are left. Anyone not into the party has either gone home or crashed out under a warm sleeping bag. Emerging from my trip, I can start to connect with those around me. Simple eye contact, glances, moving in sync with other people, is all it takes to confirm that they are in the same ecstatic state you are. There is some sort of energy field surrounding the party. It is warm and womb-like. It's like the generator is not only powering the sound system, but also somehow powering this energy field. I am gripped by a sense of love and warmth. I know that there is nobody on this deserted stretch of beach who will stop our gathering before sunrise. As the distant lights of dawn slowly illuminate those around me, I see nothing but wide smiles and utter, total, complete joy. It is in this state that I fully understand vibe...the feeling I get whenever I am in proximity to numerous other people in ecstatic states. Looking at the joy others around me are experiencing causes me to dance harder, which in turn forces them to dance harder, and the feedback loop continues, driving us further into that state of transcendental bliss. Pre-dawn, the universe is in complete order, everything has worked out this evening and there is nothing left for us to do except enjoy it and push it further. Endorphins flood my body, naturally pushing me higher as the acid starts its long, slow retreat.

6

There comes a time when you feel so at peace with yourself and the beings around you, that you cannot possibly imagine it could get better. It is when you are proved wrong that you know you really are having a genuine spiritual experience. With the DJ spinning the perfect track, the sun finally makes its ascent over the horizon. The first rays of solar energy hit with the impact of a laser, piercing deep within me. I look around for the first time at the illuminated environment surrounding me...waves of the Pacific ocean gently crashing on the white sand beach. The lighthouse in the distance. The rolling grassy hills inland...beautifully costumed and decorated people all around me. It is as if Mother Nature, or Gaia, or God, or whatever you wish to call the spirit that encircles this planet – with all of its infinite duties of spinning the earth around the sun, keeping balance between a trillion living organisms – has stopped, and paused, for just 60 seconds, and acknowledged me as a life form. For the first 60 seconds of the new day, Gaia has decided to show me, one mere human, all of her beauty and glory in one concentrated burst. For 60 seconds I am floating above the earth below me, experiencing the most sheer beauty I have ever imagined experiencing in my life. Everything around me is pure light, pure positive energy, pure love and pure beauty all at once. For 60 eternal seconds I am being touched by the hand of God. For 60 seconds Gaia is saying to me, in her own language of light, 'I acknowledge you as a human...I am here and I am real.' For 60 seconds I glimpse into heaven, eternity, or however else you can describe the highest level of human perception of what it means to be a living being on this planet.

But it is not just Gaia I am getting energy from. As someone who helped make this happen, I am getting a little piece of everyone else's bliss. For all that shit I went through early that day – getting the generator and hauling it over a mountain in rush hour traffic, spilling gas, lugging it around – I am getting tenfold return on my efforts. I can only imagine the energy return the friend who gave me the acid is getting...or the DJ spinning the music...

As the morning continues, the scene on the beach is still a true celebration of simply being alive on this planet. A few girls strip off their clothes and run naked, doing cartwheels and backflips, on the wet sand. There was not a lot to say to each other, just smiles and hugs. Even though the intensity slowly receded, the feeling of some sort of electrical force around the gathering continued. We all felt connected.

One might think that after being awake for some twenty-four hours straight, dragging a sound system down to the beach, and then dancing for some seven hours on end would make the job of dragging all the equipment up to the highway difficult. But with the magical vibe still flowing though us, and with everyone chipping in, it was actually quite easy. Slowly everyone packed their piece of the party into their cars and one by one we departed the beach. I took my time on the way home, stopping often along Highway 1 just to peer at the waves crashing on the rocky shoreline, and ponder how amazing it is to be alive on this planet.

(Joe, American, aged 24, working as a computer engineer)

Rave in South Africa

I was fortunate enough to be part of an underground beach party on the shores of Kwazulu-Natal, South Africa. Our party took place at an area called Virginia Beach, just north of the port of Durban. The party had been planned almost a month before by a like-minded group of individuals calling themselves Kindred Spirit. We were all part of the underground dance culture in Durban, inspired by the Goa trance parties taking place in our own country and all over the world. Coming from various corners of the rave culture (clubs, gatherings and so forth), we were all brought together by a common goal – to create the ultimate outdoor party for our fellow party freaks.

Our black and white flyers went out around a week before. We called our gathering the Longest Moon, because our party was to fall on the night of the longest full moon. The day of the party began with us collecting a large number of poles, scaffolding and UV banners from a house in Durban. We arrived at the site around 10 a.m. and held a small meeting, discussing where to set up our party. Others arrived with generators, lighting and sound systems. The basis of all our organisation was teamwork – we all worked together with a common goal in mind. A teepee was set up and a scaffold wall was built at a 90 degree angle to the bank which led down on to the beach, effectively cutting off the party from anyone who did not wish to be there. UV banners were tied to the scaffolding and UV string was strung across the roof of the area. A large firepit was dug into the middle of the area to keep everyone warm (although it doesn't really get *that* cold in Durban). Fire, I believe, has great spiritual significance within such a culture so it was also serving another purpose.

6

By around 5 p.m. the venue had been completed – the police had, a number of times, popped past on routine patrols and seemed to have no problem with what was taking place. By nightfall, everything was working and we had organised two large UV blowers so it was all glowing wonderfully. Party-goers had begun arriving. Our DJs spun into action and the party began in earnest – all in all, a total of about 400 people arrived at the party that night. The full moon shone down upon us and the sea crashed around us. Many of the party goers sat together and smoked our local ganja, or took a little sliver of a Dr Hofman, incredibly psychedelic LSD. Together we connected and danced the night away. A massive dreamcatcher hung above the fire and the world connected and began spinning in tune to the incredible energy that existed on the beach as we danced and drummed under the skies.

Many of the people who had come together that day to organise the gathering had met for the first time – now they had experienced the spirituality of the earth together. As dawn broke, together we cleaned the beach and made sure there were no traces of our presence left on the sacred earth. All that remained was the burnt firewood and the memories of what had taken place. I was honoured to be a part of such a celebration of life – one where the negativity of our modern societies' attitude towards mind-expanding substances had not made an impact. Although narcotics police had made their presence felt at the party by confiscating one or two people's stashes, they had not made any arrests or attempted to shut down the party. Perhaps they, too, had felt the serenity and energy of what was happening.

The incredible thing for me is that I made such great friends at the gathering – I met like-minded souls who are, to this day, still good friends of mine. I truly believe that the Earth Goddess, or whichever gods it is that we claim created this earth, smiled upon us that night and saw that what we were doing was good. Dancing under the stars is a thing which we have done since the beginning of time and is happening all over the world. Substances such as LSD, marijuana and Ecstasy are drugs which, used in the correct context and with the right people, serve merely to show us that peace, love and unity are the only ways in which we should be living our lives – and they help us to celebrate the greatness which is creation.

(Alex, aged 26, a South African man)

Implications of rave spirituality

'If the truth can be told so as to be understood it will be believed.

The emphasis of house music and rave culture on physiologically compatible rhythms, and this sort of thing, is really the re-discovery of the art of natural magic with sound. That sound, properly understood, especially percussive sound, can actually change neurological states, and large groups of people getting together in the presence of this kind of music are creating a telepathic community, a bonding, that hopefully will be strong enough to carry the vision out into the mainstream of society. I think the youth culture that is emerging in the Nineties is an end of the millennium culture that is actually summing up Western civilisation, and pointing us in an entirely different direction; that we are going to arrive in the third millennium in the middle of an archaic revival, which will mean a revival of those physiologically empowering rhythm signatures, a new art, a new social vision, a new relationship to nature, to feminism, to ego – all of these things are taking hold, and not a moment too soon.

Terence McKenna with the Shamen: 'Re: Evolution' (1992)

From the accounts above it is clear that rave has the potential to enable a spiritual experience for many people, but does this have any implications beyond the specific rave situation? Does the spiritual energy dissipate on come-down? Is it a weekend phenomenon? How do those feelings relate to 'normal' life?

Among 137 ravers surveyed by Nicholas concerning the effects of Ecstasy on their lives in general, a significant number reported 'increased spiritual awareness', some adding that they felt closer to nature, calmer and more appreciative of life itself. In the Release survey, among the positive benefits of Ecstasy use that respondents said they had experienced were increased happiness and confidence, feeling more in touch with their body, heightened compassion and empathy and feelings of oneness with the world.[8]

As with any peak experience, thought and work are required to integrate the 'rave high' into everyday life. Roger Griffin has described the time between raves as a 'suspension bridge': at first you only see the gap until the next peak experience, until the realisation dawns that you can thread peace, love and smiles in between the peaks, interweave them in and out of everyday life...[9]

6

The longer-lasting implication of all the positive aspects of rave could be summed up in the ravers' mantra: PLUR (standing for Peace, Love, Unity, Respect). A contributor to the uk.music.rave Internet newsgroup, gave this definition of PLUR:

PEACE: The reason we like the music that we do, and dance like we do, is because it helps us achieve a state of inner peace, particularly peace with ourselves. For me the music that catalyses this state has a sticky label on it that says 'Goa trance', sometimes 'psychedelic trance', and includes 'tribal trance'. Being able to dance the way we do is being able to be four years old again, to be free of ego like we were before self consciousness took control. When we dance free of ego, we are at peace with ourselves, and at peace with all those around us.

LOVE: It means you can turn to a complete stranger who's sipping a bottle of water, and they'll see your sweat dripping and ears glowing and your eyes dark and deep, and they'll smile and offer you the bottle. It means people not only call out to you 'Are you OK mate?' when they hear you heaving your dinner in the toilet cubicle, but they care about the answer.

UNITY: I think this one shows the widest gap between the aspiration and the realisation. There still seem to be anorak wars between disciples/ acolytes of various stylistic sub-genres, by people who've forgotten that preferring green to blue or liking cardamom more than coriander is not a sign of intellectual underendowment and spiritual inadequacy. For me the concept of unity is not us against them, but trying to give 'them' a glimpse of the wonderful space we experience at a good party.

RESPECT: Sometimes I fantasise about a club with coat pegs all round the periphery, where everyone just hangs their stuff and it's still there when they come to wear it home. Hey, and you can even leave your money in the pockets – now that's *respect*.

The notion of PLUR is idealistic and aspirational, and many clubbers reject it for this reason. But the following account gives one man's story of how PLUR affected him and what it means to him now.

I will always remember the night at the Que club where I first sat down with someone and actually started to talk about what was going on in my life and I guess this is where PLUR really became meaningful to me. For a long time that night, I totally poured my heart out. The fact that I'd done quite a lot of drugs meant that I wasn't worried that I was talking to someone who was basically a stranger, and the fact that they were in a similar situation meant that they didn't think that someone they hardly knew was telling them really very personal things. Instead they listened to me with total openness and made me feel confident enough to focus on and identify where my problems were coming from. For that short time I totally dropped the shield that I'd built up over the past months and really started to confront feelings which I'd kept bottled up for a long time. It was a hugely emotional experience for me, as it was for the person I was talking to (lots of tears and hugs were shared) and I don't think that in any other situation I would have been able to do this. The feeling of friendship and support that I now get from friends, both old and new, that I've met through clubbing has really made a difference to my life, it's made me realise what PLUR is really about.

PLUR is a way of putting into words an emotion that is far more than just Peace, Love, Unity and Respect. It's the feeling that I get when I know that I'm sharing an experience with people who, for that instant, are opening up their minds and dropping all the negative attitudes and emotions that seem to be a constant part of our society today. They are joining together without prejudice or hate. It may only last a few seconds or it may not happen at all...but when it does, everyone feels it. Everyone is equal and everyone shares the same feeling. It's like looking into a world where total, complete and unconditional peace and love is really possible, you catch people's eyes and you see that sparkle that says 'I know how you feel, and I feel the same!' and suddenly your faith in people is restored, you realise that despite all the shit that goes on in the world true PLUR is possible, if only we could take the time to look up from our mad hectic lives, and stop chasing our materialistic ideals that just fuel the hate and anger that prevent us from accepting people for who they are.

I'm sure that many of you will be thinking that this is just a result of the drugs. But I believe the drugs are a catalyst; they break down the barriers and open the doors, but it's the people that make the magic happen. It's a shame that this is only normally possible because of drugs, but that doesn't make the feeling any less valid. It's experiences like this that have allowed me to examine emotions and feelings that normally are kept locked away. Each time this happens I leave feeling that little bit more refreshed and that little bit more invigorated. Each time I take a little bit of that feeling with me, and use it in my everyday life.

PLUR is a real, positive and constructive emotion that I've come to associate with club culture. It's not always possible to achieve and sometimes I forget what it means, but I know that it's there...no matter what anyone says, I've felt it and I know that I'll feel it again, and one day I hope that I'll be brave and strong enough to let go and keep it with me all the time.

(Dan, aged 19, a British student)

Dr Mary Anna Wright, a sociologist at City University, London, uses the concept of 'metanoia' – a transformation in thought – to explain the impact of rave on the lives of those involved. She believes that rave, particularly within the context of the use of MDMA, has inspired many personal revolutions:

> I have met hundreds of people within the dance scene who have had profound experiences caused by a combination of drugs, music and communal euphoria. Such ecstatic experiences may not be intentional but always have a deep impact on those who share them. Interviews with people involved in all genres of dance music have revealed what I believe to be a pharmacological shaping of culture. This means interactions within dance culture are largely based around the effects of MDMA. Some people have taken these effects further. I have seen many projects motivated by involvement in dance culture embedded in the empathic tenets of peace, love, unity and respect. I think it is important to use metanoia, to take experiences imbued on the dance floor and allow them to inspire each day.

But can these 'personal revolutions' have a wider impact on society? Nathan, an English raver, feels that the longer-term effects of rave spirituality lie in the way in which rave culture and lifestyle encourage a merging and deepening of spirit between those involved and, by implication, in society as a whole:

> Since I started raving in Manchester, I have noticed a difference in the way *some* sections of the raving community operate. Our lives are intertwined in a way normal society couldn't imagine, indeed sometimes I find it hard to remember where the boundaries are in normal society. Seriously deep problems, be they emotional, psychological, or real-world type, can be discussed with people not that close, the level of privacy, ownership of property etc. required is far less, and the level of physical contact is much greater. I'm trying to describe an awareness, a very, very slow realisation, that living this lifestyle may have a deeper, spiritual consequence. It could be argued that by being this way with each other, we are actually allowing our spirits/souls/essences/consciousness/whatever to become more intertwined and actually merge in some way (or just to become more aware of their unity, depending on your point of view). Living the culture that comes with raving, and regularly having fairly intense experiences together, as well as causing the quite apparent increase in love and happiness, may also have some even deeper spiritual impact.

(Nathan, aged 23, working as a researcher in computer science)

It has even been claimed that the collective spiritual energy generated at a rave can and should be used to produce a change in collective consciousness. The Earthdance Project, devised by Chris Dekker of Return to the Source, is an example of this being put into practice. Earthdance is an annual 'global dance party for planetary peace' held for the first time in 1997 and encompassing over twenty different countries. Dekker's ideal is that all around the world, people will be 'dancing as one tribe united with a common vision for peace and planetary healing'. Proceeds from the night go to Tibetan charities and at midnight GMT a Prayer for Peace,[10] written for the occasion, is played simultaneously around the world, with Internet and video link-ups allowing many thousands of people to share in the experience.

Dekker describes the moment of the Prayer for Peace in 1997:

> It was an incredible moment of togetherness, knowing that everyone around the world was linking up at that precise moment affirming the same prayer for peace. In London the Sushumna ritual dance group made a circle in the centre of the dance floor visualising light entering the planet as the track began. The energy was very powerful and more people began to make bigger circles, some holding their arms in the air, cheering when it finished. It was a moment that inspired feelings of hope and unity, a glimpse into the possibility that as a collective we can make a difference.[11]

Further projects, based on the Earthdance ideal, are envisaged.

Some may question the extent to which raving can be a spiritual experience. It is a very different setting in which to take a psychoactive substance and explore mysticism than, for example, the Santo Daime or Native American Church. It is a collective rather than solitary path, and the psychoactive substance taken is generally Ecstasy, which, on the whole, does not open the way to overwhelming visions. What it does do is open the heart. Feelings of unity (with self and with others), of sacredness and awe, a positive mood with deep feelings of peace are all important elements in a mystical experience and these are evident in ravers' accounts. In this light, raves are very much part of contemporary spirituality.

6

7

Before, During and After

A mind that is stretched by a new experience can never go back to its old dimensions.

Oliver Wendell Holmes

What you take in by visionary experience you must give out by love and intelligence in daily life.

Aldous Huxley

Sometimes spiritual experiences come out of the blue. They are unconnected to what happens before or after them. This can have a value, if we are aware enough to be conscious of what is going on at the time. Intellectual understanding does not necessarily validate what has happened and can sometimes even detract from its worth. As Joseph Campbell said in an interview with Bill Moyers: 'People say that what we are all seeking is the meaning for life. I don't think that's what we're really seeking. I think what we're seeking is an experience of being alive.'

People who take psychoactives do look for this experience. However, it is natural to want to make sense and good use of an experience so going into a psychoactive experience with a spiritual focus, having it guided in a caring way and consciously integrating it into one's life afterwards, can give the experience a lot more value.

A form of ceremony or ritual can help to connect body and spirit, the material and the etheric world. The whole ceremony can be just a moment of silence before taking the sacrament and a time of thanksgiving afterwards. Or it can be very elaborate and involve days of fasting, cleansing and praying, ceremonial songs and dances and therapeutic evaluation sessions. The idea is not for the ceremony to take over, but to use it to establish a more spiritual focus.

Here ritual is defined as 'a ceremony done with the express purpose of connecting with spirit in order to mark times of transformation'. This suggests that a spiritual connection is actively sought and change welcomed. It is important to realise this when doing spiritual work with psychoactives. Profound changes can take place and not everyone is ready for this. A change may bring a valuable addition to one's life, but also involves a letting go of old patterns. It is possible to experience an unexpected release of bottled up emotions. Well established values in one's life may become questionable and lead to confusion. Perceptions of one's identity and the world one lives in may alter dramatically, requiring adjustments on all levels. When an experience is labelled 'bad' it is often because of the resistance to releasing the old, and the fear of the unknown. To enter a spiritual connection requires trust. It is therefore important to prepare for a psychoactive ceremony in a way that provides optimum potential for letting go and trusting, in a safe environment and with sufficient support. This is what we will look at in this chapter.

Set and setting

Spiritual experiences are special events. There is no known way that they can be induced reliably, although various religious techniques, such as meditation, can help to create a situation where they are more likely to occur. Similarly, certain drugs can act as catalysts for accessing a suitable state of mind. But, unlike pharmaceutical drugs whose effects are (generally) predictable, the effect of these drugs depends largely on the state of the user and their environment at the time.

The conditions that determine the effect of a psychedelic are often referred to as 'set and setting'. 'Set' refers to the mind-set of the participant: their beliefs, hopes, fears and expectations. 'Setting' describes the conditions under which the drug is used. The ability to let go requires conditions where one feels safe, so the actual location has to be one where it is possible to feel at ease and no interruptions will occur. But that is just the beginning. To be accompanied by somebody trustworthy, who will look after the person making the psychoactive journey, is most important for many people, although some prefer to be alone. This person is called a 'sitter': literally someone who sits with the user. The role of the sitter is to serve: to provide security and comfort without intruding.

Set

The ideal state of mind is a sincere yearning for a spiritual experience. But to acquire that state is rather like telling someone to relax: it can't be done to order, and many people are simply not spiritual seekers. Those who do have a practice, a way of stilling and centring themselves, may choose to do that as their preparation. For others, a period spent beforehand in an undistracted state, such as a walk in nature or perhaps an hour in a float tank, has been most beneficial.

Setting

The ideal setting is more tangible and can be created.

The first thing is to look after one's body. Although some shamanic techniques include sleep deprivation, generally it is seen as beneficial to be well rested and physically fit. Fasting is often recommended, especially if it helps to avoid stomach discomfort and nausea.

7

Doing some bodywork before a ceremony is popular. Partly because sitting for a long time can make the body stiff, but also because being grounded in the body reduces the risk of getting too disconnected and experiencing difficulties in coming back to daily reality afterwards. Yoga, t'ai chi or dancing can be practised before, after and sometimes during a journey. Particular clothes can help to focus the intention, much like a priest dressing for a service or an actor for a play.

Just as in other spiritual gatherings, the venue itself needs to be secure. That means a place where there will be no disturbances. The obvious place for many people is at home, because home is where most people find it easiest to let go. Others prefer to be outdoors in a natural setting and away from man-made distractions.

The focus for the ceremony can be a physical object. This serves a similar function to icons, statues and symbols in churches. The object can vary enormously from drawings and crystals to cuddly toys. During the ceremony, if one is distracted or confused, the object can be used as a reminder of one's focus and intention.

Protection from unwanted energies is a concern for many people. Through the use of psychoactives, people's energy centres (chakras) can become more open and there is a greater chance of connections with various psychic energies, good *and* bad. An old and widely used technique for protection is for the user to visualise an egg of white light around himself. The light will penetrate the darkness and absorb it, thus preventing negative energies from coming too close. Fears are notorious for attracting more fearful energies, so the more protected and loved the user feels, the more protected he indeed is. Crystals, medicine bags, Aura Soma* pomanders or mantras and visualisation techniques are also used for the purpose of protection.

Getting stuck in an experience, as if a tape is played over and over, or being confronted by a repeated, fearful image are quite common occurrences in a psychoactive experience and can produce a lot of anxiety. Paying attention to breathing before, during and after the session has helped people to keep the experience flowing. For the experience to end as positively as possible it

---

* Aura Soma is a company that produces coloured liquids used for cleansing and protection of the energy field that surrounds the body.

is important to return to a loving space. Pictures of loved ones, objects of beauty with a positive sentimental value and the presence of dear friends can be of assistance. As in any spiritual context, cultivating a sense of gratitude for the experience and those who helped provide it will promote a positive attitude.

Here some experienced entheogen users describe their ideal set and setting. The first considers setting more important than set:

Set

My intent whenever using entheogens is to gain as much power from the drug as I can. I approach the event with the expectation that I will have a powerful, meaningful spiritual experience. Beyond this, I make no effort to direct or manage my thoughts in preparation for the journey. If I have stresses or concerns (e.g. if I've been working hard, or a friend is sick) I make no effort to relax my mind: I have found that the only important component of my mind-set going into the trip is my direct expectation of the trip itself, and not anything else going on in my head. Sure, if I've got problems I may dwell on them while I'm travelling, but I don't see that this affects the power or the value of the experience. In short, despite conventional wisdom on the subject, I don't believe that mind-set has so great an influence on the power of the experience (although it obviously affects the direction the experience takes). The only existing state of mind I need to gain the most value from the medicine is the will to do so.

Setting

I have played with a number of entheogens, and have always found that the most important contributing factor to the experience is physical setting. I am highly conscious of other important contributing factors to an entheogenic experience – who travels with you, what sounds you surround yourself with and what refreshments you prepare for yourself – but nothing seems as important to me as where you are. In my experience, there is *no way* that an entheogenic experience constructed indoors, or even within sight of concrete can be half as powerful (and enjoyable) as one built somewhere beautiful (in a forest, on a beach, on top of a mountain) with no cars, no roads, no houses, buildings, overflying planes. Tripping indoors can never compare to tripping in nature. I have found this to be true with every single entheogen I have experimented with, particularly mushrooms. Every outdoor mushroom experience I have had

7

has been ecstatic, while every indoor mushroom experience has been difficult. While with other entheogens, I have gradually learnt from experience that tripping in nature away from the concrete jungle I live in is somehow much more powerful and enjoyable than being in a house, a warehouse, a backyard or even a suburban park, with mushrooms this understanding is much more clearly communicated.

(Tim, American)

Other people find the state of mind, the set, the most important factor in entering a psychoactive experience:

A lot of creation of setting certainly shapes and is shaped by set. For entheogenic work, I have noticed that stuff which I have been thinking/ worrying about and doing lately seems to come up and/or colour my experiences. I tend to try to spend at least the day before an entheogenic experience reading something that I would like to think about or wouldn't mind diving into.

I pick out ritual clothing to wear, which consists of clothing that I really like for one reason or another, is comfortable and loose around my stomach (I tend to find tension focused in my abdomen a lot and this seems to be made worse by tight-waisted pants). I personally like simple, all natural fibre clothing. I have specific clothes that I wear for entheogenic work. I usually fast the day of the experience (mostly to limit my stomach discomfort).

I find that if my space is cluttered and/or dirty, I can find myself thinking or worrying about the mess. I find that if I clean/straighten before any entheogenic work, I am much happier. I like to light candles or incense as a marker of the shift to a relaxed state of mind. I tend to pick out music to play based on what kind of mood I think I'm heading towards. Sometimes I like to just listen to the noises of the world.

I usually begin my work by sitting in meditation/contemplation about what it is I'm about to do, reflect on why I'm doing it, try to think of the path the entheogen took through the world to get to me. I then think about what I hope to accomplish. I write down the date and time and anything that I've been thinking about. I have a few ritual objects I like to have around.

I always have my blanket with me. I find that there is nothing quite as comforting as being able to wrap myself in my favourite blanket when I want to. I usually have picked out clothes I would wear to go outside (a jacket or hat or whatever) so I don't have to go fumbling about.

I think about the Code of Conduct concept we've been working on: 'When I engage in spiritual practices designed to bring about profound changes in consciousness, I will consider my intentions and will choose carefully the occasion and location for the practice. I will be well informed about the mental and physical effects, anticipate reasonably foreseeable risks to myself and others, and employ safeguards to minimise these risks.'

I almost always find that I need to lie down for the onset and peak of most entheogenic experiences, so I don't usually like to do much entheogen work outside of spaces where I can lie down (at home or somewhere homey).

I also write down some of the insights, thoughts, visions that I have. I spend the time after the experience reflecting on it, reflecting on my ideas about what it was for and how that turned out. I think of ways of remembering insights. I associate them with words, phrases, try to think of mnemonics for bits of images, etc. I use those insights in my daily life, whether I need to tell someone something, behave differently, etc.

I also take vitamins of various types throughout and after the experience or drink herbal tea because I tend to experience fairly unpleasant side/after-effects from most entheogens – headaches, muscle soreness, stomach discomfort, and general drainedness. For most entheogens, these effects do not persist longer than two sleeping periods after the experience.

(Earth Erowid, American)

Choosing a sitter

Some people feel confident enough to take psychoactives on their own, but the majority prefer to do it with a friend or a group of people. Traditionally, plant medicines are taken with a shaman, someone who knows the substance/teacher and can keep the space safe. In modern times this could be a friend, a therapist or a leader of a workshop. The guide can give structure to the session and sometimes takes the substance as well in a smaller dose to tune in to the psychoactive state. He can also stay neutral and be a fair witness or fulfil the caring role. This is generally called 'sitting for someone'. To be a sitter during someone's psychoactive experience is a responsible role.

7

> The role of the psychedelic guide is perhaps the most exciting and inspiring role in society. He is literally a liberator, one who provides illumination, one who frees men from their life-long internal bondage. To be present at the moment of awakening, to share the ecstatic revelation when the voyager discovers the wonder and awe of the divine life-process, is for many the most gratifying part to play in the evolutionary drama. The role of the psychedelic guide has a built-in protection against professionalism and didactic one-upmanship. The psychedelic liberation is so powerful that it far outstrips earthly game ambitions. Awe and gratitude – rather than pride – are the rewards of this new profession.[1]

Most people choose a friend as a sitter. It needs to be someone you can trust enough to reveal your feelings and needs to without having to impress or be polite. A willingness to serve appears to be the most important quality for any sitter, who has to devote himself unreservedly to those in his care for as long as it takes, with his own comfort coming a long second. Sitting for someone is not to be seen as a duty, but more as a generous offer of giving someone a treat. It is a job that can be very boring, since it may appear as if nothing is happening for long periods of time. However, the sitter has to stay alert, be prepared for emergencies and know how to respond. Cleaning up vomit or worse, having to tolerate the same music repeated endlessly or waiting for hours whilst the user is staring in space may all be part of the deal. After the experience, follow-up work may be needed and most people appreciate a sitter who will be available to talk to about the experience some time later. It is usually preferred if this person has experience with the substances involved, but what is considered most important for the sitter is a willingness to look after the user whatever may happen. Here are a couple of examples from Nicholas's experience with sitters.

> My very first acid trip was in the company of two college friends, a happy couple called Julian and Kay: caring, homely people who I could turn to when I was down. Julian soldered his circuit boards and Kay knitted a sweater, every now and then asking if I was all right. Although I felt that I was on a superior plane to them, the 'observer in me' was aware that my 'superior' state depended on being able to let go, and that they provided the reassurance I needed to do that.

Many years later I tried ayahuasca with a sitter who was very experienced but had no interest in me apart from the money I was paying him. At one point I asked him for reassurance that it was safe to explore the dark side, only to find that he had gone to sleep. My adventurous explorations came to an abrupt halt and I felt paranoid, rejected and physically ill.

Another option is to choose as a sitter a qualified therapist who offers sessions with psychoactives. Eleanor, an underground therapist working with psychoactive substances, explained why she thinks it is important to have a therapist as a guide:

It's very easy to deceive yourself when taking these substances alone. There is a risk that you can avoid looking at difficult things, because you're not being guided in certain ways to face and confront things. The way I do the work is very strong, we push people up and against their resistances and their fears so they can face, confront and go through them.

In any case the sitter needs to be prepared to listen to fears and hopes beforehand, sit through the whole journey and help with grounding and integrating afterwards.

Deciding who to sit for

To be chosen as a sitter by a group of friends is an honour but also an enormous responsibility. Before saying yes, that person needs to make it clear where their responsibility ends as, in the worst-case scenario, the drug could trigger a psychotic episode. Whether this seems unlikely or not at the outset, it is still a possibility and the sitter must be committed to seeing the user through it. This could involve days rather than hours of care, finding professional assistance, or even being questioned by the police. Thoughtful preparation minimises the risk of anything going wrong.

People who are healthy, well grounded, successful in their work, have a stable relationship and happy home life are least likely to get into trouble, especially those with no current or previous psychiatric problems. This is the baseline; the further a person deviates from this ideal the more risk is involved in taking a psychoactive. It does happen that people manipulate to get what they want and participants may not always be entirely truthful about their intentions. For this reason sitters sometimes interview participants at length before agreeing to assist with a session.

Sitters have to guard against being affected by something going wrong. Legally, a sitter is in the clear if she simply offers services as a friend, without payment and without supplying, administering or encouraging the use of any illicit substance. But the problem may not be the law so much as one's conscience. It is not uncommon to feel inadequate or guilty for not having given the required support. Limits need to be defined beforehand and clarity must be established as to how much responsibility the sitter is prepared to take.

Preparation

A responsible sitter will have read up about the chosen psychoactive and collected as much information as possible even if she has personal experience with the substance. She ought to be prepared for any known side-effects and able to answer questions like 'Will it get any stronger?', 'How much longer will it last?' and 'If I take more, will it last longer or will the effect be stronger?'

Knowledge of basic first aid is another requirement. It is obviously important to know when someone really needs emergency treatment, recognise conditions like panic attacks and the difference between emotional and physical effects. See the medical section at the end of the book for more information about first aid.

Because people generally feel more secure in their own home, a visiting sitter will make herself familiar with the house rules and could ask questions like: 'What would disturb the neighbours? Do the windows or curtains need to be closed? Should the doorbell or be phone switched off? Where are things like blankets, cleaning cloths and drinks kept? How do the lighting, the heating the CD player, etc. work?

Psychoactive workshops

Some people offer group sessions. It is advisable to check out their credentials and meet them beforehand, since not everyone is trustworthy. The obvious pitfall is that some people do love to play the shaman and pride gets in their way. This is a dilemma: the more confidence the leader expresses, the more likely that he will induce the right conditions for people to have beneficial spiritual experiences. And the more they believe that he is a great shaman, the more easily he will gain their confidence. This makes it terribly tempting for leaders to bluff or bullshit. Some will tell stories showing that they have great powers; others credit their brew with particularly fine ingredients, and so on. With the shamans in the Amazon our checking-out procedure often involved asking them to sing an 'icaro' – a power-song. We could usually tell from the way they sang whether or not they had integrity and a spiritual connection. If we felt the song was a routine action or they seemed impatient or too eager to sell us their services, we would be careful. If we were moved by the song or felt almost as if another presence was working through the shaman, we would trust him. Modern workshop leaders should come under the same scrutiny. Some people are charismatic leaders and it is easy to give your power away to them. If they truly serve a spiritual purpose, they will have a modesty about them and will not allow you to put them on a pedestal.

The following sums up what participants we spoke to have found important about the way workshops were conducted:

Workshops have their own culture. Participants expect attention, caring and a chance to share experiences afterwards. The leader has to have the ability to vet participants beforehand (besides asking about medical contraindications), be attentive and sensitive to their needs, and tell people what to bring for their own comfort and whether they can drive home or stay the night. All the usual hallmarks of good workshop practice apply.

People also like to know what they can expect from the leader in terms of support. Can they ask for a neck massage or for their hand to be held? Can they discuss the situation if they get 'stuck', and is there any 'after sales service'? Can they phone up later to discuss what happened?

7

It is nice to learn a bit about the other participants, but without it becoming superficial. A good way is to invite each person to talk about their hopes and fears for the session.

Whatever the form of the ritual, it has to be clear to the participants what is going to happen and what behaviour is expected: this provides security, which makes people feel reassured. One must agree on ground rules beforehand. These often include the following: keep confidentiality in the group; do not do anything that might cause damage or upset neighbours, do not leave the session until the end; sexual feelings may be expressed but not acted upon. There is also general clarification of boundaries around interacting with other participants. If participants are allowed to interact it is useful if they are made aware that even a whispered conversation can be very disturbing to others who may be in a state of heightened sensitivity. Additional rules may be added if the sitter or participants want these. For example, Ann Shulgin suggests that if a participant encounters a 'door marked death' during their trip, they must agree not to pass through it.[2]

It is a mistake for workshop leaders to copy what they have experienced in the jungle. Amazonian shamans can get away with 'doing their thing' without caring about what participants are doing, but this is not acceptable in a workshop. Visitors have to accept how people behave in their own country, but these practices are often not acceptable back home.

People like personal attention. If each participant is visited during the session, it is easier for them to express their needs.

Good leaders will prepare people for the possibility of unpleasant experiences and how to work through them. Like all sitters, they need to be well informed and usually give people detailed information about the possible effects of the drug. What does it taste like? Is it likely to make you feel nauseous, and for how long? Is it best to throw up or keep it down? How long does it take to come on? and so on.

Often people appreciate the opportunity to share their experiences, and participants might want feedback to help them to integrate their trip. This may be straight after the session, or next day.

Some examples of the worst experiences in workshops:

- The 'shaman' went to sleep.
- A leader helping me did so in a seductive way.
- I was placed where others had to step over me to get to the loo.
- People arrived and were never introduced or told what to do.
- The leader cuddled his girlfriend and ignored the group.
- The person next to me made a lot of noise and was not asked to stop.

- Vomit bowls were too far away and shared, and I was constantly afraid that my neighbour would be using it when I needed it.
- The leader asked the group what they would like next, which made me feel very insecure, since I was not able to make decisions.
- The ritual was never declared ended; people just drifted off.
- The leader seemed scared when asked for reassurance, and this made matters worse.
- The leader asked for payment towards the end of the session but before the effects had worn off.
- The leader lectured me, interpreting the experience for me.

Some of the best experiences:

- We were given carrot and ginger soup beforehand to settle our stomachs and to make our vomit less offensive.
- An elaborate ritual helped us to orientate and become grounded.
- All the participants travelled by boat for two hours on the way to the venue, giving us a chance to reflect and get to know the others.
- The helpers included doctors and psychiatrists.
- There were almost as many helpers as participants.
- The helpers were so attentive that our needs were anticipated: I felt cold and a blanket was put over me; later I felt sick and a bowl was brought.
- The ritual was in daylight in a beautiful, secluded house with a beautiful view.
- The music was carefully chosen, mixed and played through several large speakers.
- The leaders were a married couple, a bodyworker and therapist.
- Adult-size nappies (diapers) were provided to allow participants to let go more completely.
- We met the next day in the park to share our experiences.
- We were made welcome guests, given lunch and invited to stay on until we were ready to face the world again.

7

Bad trips

Bad trips are naturally the biggest worry for people taking psychoactives. But what is a bad trip? There are two sides to the issue, the physical and the mental.

Physically, a trip may turn bad if the user proves to be allergic to the substance involved. Someone in poor health may also be more susceptible to the toxins that are contained in quite a few psychoactives. Whilst this may be equally true of many common foods, it is generally easier to obtain information about those than about illegal psychoactive substances. Being well informed about the physical effects of a substance is essential for those who take this path seriously. Some of the symptoms such as tremors, shaking, sweating, blurred vision, severe nausea, vomiting, jaw clenching, hyperventilating or paralysis occur as a normal by-product of certain psychoactives and are usually short-lived. However, if these symptoms persist without direct relation to the substance taken or for longer than expected, then it is important that medical help is sought urgently otherwise physical damage can result and the user is truly having a bad trip.

Here the role of an experienced guide becomes self-evident. The sitter needs to be well informed about the physical effects of the substance as well as the user's health. She will also have to be able to distinguish between a real physical danger (see medical and first aid chapter for symptoms) and an imagined danger caused by terrifying visions and thoughts.

The mental side of what people term a bad trip is far more complex. Generally, if one feels insecure through circumstances in one's life or environment, it is not a good time to embark on psychoactive journeys. Feeling mentally stable is a better state from which to depart but even then it may not be possible to avoid a bad trip. However, what feels bad at the time may be perceived as valuable afterwards.

In a discussion group several people exchanged their views about bad trips. Robert Forte, one of the participants and editor of the book *Entheogens and the Future of Religion*, offered some ideas:

> A bad trip is simply one that the experiencer, or their guide, is not
> prepared for and/or fails to negotiate with ordinary reality. It has nothing
> to do with content.

There are potential problems inherent in making long-term commitments while under the influence of a psychoactive:

Someone can have MDMA for example and fall in love, make love, get pregnant, married, whatever, only to find they should have waited...I'd call that a bad trip.

To avoid trips turning bad it seems important to test one's revelations in ordinary reality:

> The most frequent bad trip: experiencing some 'mystical real' and then believing you are 'enlightened'. There are lots of inflated psychonauts. In some mystical traditions, such as Vipassana (insight) meditation, experiencing momentary enlightenment is regarded as 'corruptions of insight' (bad trips) because of the unfortunate tendency to mistake them for the end of the path, when really they are just more self-generated, conditional illusions.

It is generally recognised that facing rather than fighting a bad trip is a better way to deal with it and may actually turn it into a positive experience. A good sitter will be able to offer reassurance and help to prevent panic attacks (which can make people believe they are dying when they are not). Even though the effect of a psychoactive may be disturbing for quite a while, the chemical workings of the substances are always limited in time and the sitter needs to remind the user, who may be caught in a tangled web of fears, that the effects of a bad trip will pass.

Some experiences on a psychoactive are so overwhelming that it is impossible to function for days afterwards. In these situations help from professionals needs to be sought. A spiritual teacher or a therapist who has experience with psychoactives may be more suitable as a helper than someone who will give out sedatives without further support.

Anyone who is seriously exploring the spiritual aspects of psychoactives would do well to read Alexander and Ann Shulgin's books *PiKHAL* and *TiKHAL*, especially the chapter 'Places in the Mind' in the latter, which gives clear descriptions of the various states one can find oneself in and offers invaluable advice. Ann points out that:

7

> some forms of alterations of consciousness can happen to anyone anywhere, without warning and having no apparent cause. Psychedelic drugs can help open a person to an experience of euphoria, just as they

can open him to deep sorrow, empathy and humour, cosmic meaningfulness and total confusion. Again, it isn't the drug that creates the experience; it's the drug that opens the door to what is already resident inside the person.[3]

Facing fears is an integral part of opening to more love. Every spiritual experience has an element of the unknown, which can be frightening. Not all fears are founded and some can be bridges to a space of greater acceptance and trust. If one is guided through the darkness into a loving space, the outcome can become positive and the likelihood of a spiritual connection greater.

'Come to the edge', he said.

They said: 'we are afraid'.

'Come to the edge', he said.

They came

He pushed them...

and they flew

(Guillaume Apollinaire)

Integration

Set and setting are important, but paying attention to integrating the experience afterwards is even more so. The experience needs to be given a place and meaning. A spiritual experience is often hard to put into words and this may make integration more difficult. Understanding one's own process and devising ways of getting through it with appropriate help, if necessary, reduces the risk of permanent emotional damage.

It is common to pass through three stages in the integration process. The duration of each stage varies greatly from person to person.

In the first stage although the chemicals are no longer active the feeling is still intense and often it is hard to describe what is going on. A lot of processing happens unconsciously, but it needs time to surface. This is potentially a vulnerable time for the user, since it is hard to express one's needs. At this stage sitters need to be extra alert, patient and loving. It is not a time for asking too many questions. It is a gentle and often non-verbal stage, but simple, non-invasive touch like holding a hand can be comforting.

After this first stage, which can last from a couple of hours to a few days or even weeks, all sorts of thoughts can pop up at odd times and it may be helpful to have a notebook nearby for writing and drawing in order to remember the experience. This is a very creative stage if one can avoid becoming judge-mental about what happened during the session. It is a good time to express feelings through artwork, painting, dancing, singing, etc. Abstract shapes and colours often help express images and ideas that are still uncoordinated in the mind and hard to verbalise. People also portray visions seen during their session. The Huichol Indians in Mexico, who use peyote as their sacrament, always create something after a journey. Their beautiful yarn paintings and bead-masks help them to bring the otherworldly experience into this world.

In the third stage the experience comes more fully into consciousness. At this point it becomes easier to verbalise and people who are used to keeping a journal tend to write accounts of what happened. It is the time where one tries to make sense of the altered state of consciousness in the context of one's daily life. For some this is liberating, for others it is difficult since it may require a redefinition of one's life. For this reason there is a tendency at this stage to distort what actually happened and try to fit the experience into a pre-conceived framework of established values. A sitter who was present at the time could help to put things in perspective.

Help in integration

Sometimes it may be impossible to get to the third stage because feelings are so disturbed that communication is difficult. This is when people need pro-fessional help, preferably from a therapist who has experience with the psychoactive concerned. Actively seeking help in this state is a valuable stage of the integrating process and not to be seen as a weakness of any kind. The journey may have had such a deep impact that it just takes a little longer to get back to daily life, but it may also have been the key to a beautiful trans-formation process. The chrysalis doesn't know it will become a butterfly...

In tribal societies there was always help from experienced elders. Integrating the experience on one's own can be hard work at the best of times.

7

Journal-keeping and art are helpful media. Bodywork can help one to feel grounded in the material reality again. If the psychoactive journey leaves one with the need to reconsider one's perceptions and values in life, a psychotherapist may be of assistance.

Eleanor, a therapist, feels that:

> Meeting people in between the psychotropic sessions is very important, because that's the place you can keep the insights and the awareness alive and help people to see where they might be slipping back into unconscious patterns, that are not beneficial to them to keep. What we're doing in these consultations is loosening the soil, preparing the soil so that the medicine doesn't have to work so hard to get in there. We are also at the same time integrating the material from the previous session. I feel this is vital. I am not really willing to work with people unless they are willing to commit to it as a process.

Many people advocate a spiritual discipline like meditation or yoga to help with the integration of a psychoactive event.

Ronald is a 40-year-old psychiatrist, who works in a fairly standard psychiatric setting in America. His hobby and intellectual passion has been the use of psychedelics in psychiatry and religious practice. Influenced by Ram Dass, Roger Walsh and Stanislav Grof, he has explored the meditative and psychedelic paths and believes that

> if you use psychedelics repeatedly, even in a sacred context, then it would be much enhanced by some kind of mental discipline. It's good to have a complementary practice of some sort such as meditation, some way to train your mind. I think that's a good exercise for anybody and people that just have no kind of practice or exposure to a spiritual discipline...well, they don't seem to get as much out of it. I realise that there are a lot of exceptions and having been in the Buddhist meditative community, I have also seen a lot of screwed-up people and a lot of people avoiding life and their problems. But being among all these people who are into psychedelics, I saw that some people there didn't necessarily transform their lives either. They were more interesting people generally, they were more risk taking, they weren't safe and content with a little narrow view of reality, but they had problems like everybody else. So I saw a lot of people

who thought they were getting a lot out of it but who seemed to be progressing really slowly, with a lot of narcissism and a lot of 'aren't we special, don't we know more than the rest of the world' ego inflation. Meditation isn't magic. I see life as a journey and meditation is a path that you just have to walk down and keep practising. I guess people do get enlightened but I think even then you still have to keep walking. And sometimes experiences with psychedelics are less spiritual and more psychological. As I got more into my body, I realised I needed bodywork and started seeing a bioenergetic therapist and I began to see that, for a lot of people, taking psychedelics is an attempt to leave their body. I see development as a spiral thing where sometimes you have spiritual experiences and then go back and have psychological experiences and childhood experiences. The spiritual seems to pave the way: if you have that faith then it's easier to go back down and deal with the really painful realities of living existence.

For most people the integration process will be easier if they have the chance to be part of a group that meets regularly or have people they can talk or write to after their explorations. Traditionally, psychoactives are taken within a community and whether this community is composed of therapists, friends, fellow ravers, church or an Internet discussion group, it will help prevent feelings of isolation and loneliness, and as such enriches the psychoactive experience.

Robert Jesse is the founder of the Council of Spiritual Practices (CSP). He graduated from Johns Hopkins University in 1981 with a degree in electrical engineering and worked in a management role with Oracle Computers, a software company, until he took leave to set up the CSP. One of the areas of interest of the CSP is 'to study the potential roles of entheogens in spiritual development'. In an interview with Nicholas, Robert spoke about the importance of a spiritual community:

7

Entering into an exploration of consciousness in the company of other people who can support, challenge and encourage you may actually be a healthier model to follow than taking a completely solo path. I've felt that very much to be true in my own explorations. From the standpoint of CSP's goals, I think there's often greater good to be had from people conducting this kind of exploration within a group with some continuity, rather than a group of strangers who converge for a night or a weekend then go their separate ways (the 'entheotourism' model). Of course there is a place for solitude in a spiritual practice. But I sense that, in a backlash against the perceived shortcomings of organised religion, the pendulum, for some people, has swung too far in the direction of individualism.

The cocktail party – Nicholas's account and Anja's integration

Paying attention to set and setting increases the chance of having a valuable time, but there is no guarantee of an easy or pleasurable time. The following account is from an extremely well prepared workshop Nicholas and Anja attended. Nicholas had an interesting but not always comfortable time. Anja had a rather unpleasant time for most of it. However, by consciously working through the integration process this turned out to be a session that provided valuable insights. Nicholas describes what happened:

We were told when and where to turn up, to fast the previous day, to bring sleeping bags and photos of people close to us and that the session would involve mushrooms and LSD with ketamine as an optional extra.

We soon learned that this was no amateur event but was organised by extremely well qualified people in their forties, including a research psychologist and two practising psychiatrists. They were in fact following on the work of the late Salvador Rocquet who used to run a centre for such events in Mexico until he was stopped by the local police. Several of them had attended many of his sessions before starting to run their own.

The participants were similarly well established professional people including a research scientist, a film director, the wife of a well known therapist and yet another psychiatrist.

We arrived at 6 p.m. and had time to relax and learn more about the event before it began at eight. There were nearly as many helpers as participants, all busily preparing for our session, and I was impressed to see that the sound system not only had four speakers but was equipped with a mixing deck.

After a brief silent meditation on our intention while holding hands, the night's session began by us filling in two questionnaires. These were the Hartman Values test, and consisted of eighteen statements which we had to place in order of how true they were to ourselves.

Next we were given three sheets of paper and asked to draw 'me', 'my shadow' and finally God.

Lastly, we had to write the answers to the questions: 'Who am I?' and 'What do I want to get out of this session?'

Our responses were collected and we were asked to get to know one another by discussing our hopes and fears for the session. I said I wanted to make use of all this professional support to open up more than ever before, as I believed that letting go was the key to having a valuable spiritual experience. The others all had rather similar hopes except for one: he was on a quest to find hidden treasure. He had spent a whole night in an Inca sacred temple where he had had a vision of a hidden vault very close to him, but having failed to locate it with echo-sounding equipment he hoped to use the session to re-enter the vision and this time to remember the details of where it was located.

Meanwhile we could see into the next room where our answers to the values test were being fed into a computer for analysis while other staff went through our drawings and writings. This was a little disconcerting and made a clear separation between 'us' and 'them'. At the time I thought that this was purposeful, but on reflection I think it was a mistake.

Eventually we were told to end our discussion and that we should hold silence until the session ended next day. We spent some time outdoors with some movement and song under the stars.

When we returned the room was prepared for us. It had been laid out with our sleeping bags placed where we should be; no choice. Incense as used by shamans in Mexico was lit and passed round. Finally we were asked to settle in our places and were presented with a bowl of dried psilocybin mushrooms. A slide show unexpectedly began; images, mainly religious, were flashed on the wall as we ate our mushrooms. They were dry but chewy and tasted very nice, perhaps because I had not eaten for over 24 hours by then. It was now midnight.

7

Soon we were told to put on our blindfolds and to keep them on in silence for the whole night, no exceptions. If we wanted anything we should raise a hand and one of the staff would come (and lead us to the bathroom if necessary).

I was never quite sure when the mushrooms started to take effect as they were mild and came on very gradually. I tried to get comfortable but my head kept being brushed against, so I wriggled away only to find that my feet knocked against someone else. People kept stumbling into me, and even though I realised they were being led to the loo, this made it hard to relax. The music was loud, and I found the choice surprising; instead of harmonious chords smoothly transporting me into a sacred space, I found it quite disturbing, creating suspense-like film music. That led me to see the whole event as some kind of experiment in which we were the guinea pigs: the psychological test, all these doctors discussing us behind our backs, not being allowed to take off our blindfolds, the upsetting music...What was going on? Fortunately the paranoia was short-lived and I was able to come to terms with being on the main road to the loo and let go a bit more.

By now the music was more uplifting and I began to enjoy it. I expected the effect to come on stronger and allow my internal dialogue to dissolve, but instead I found it intensified. I became annoyed by my perpetual chatter and felt it was blocking any deeper experience. For ages, I seemed to be in a state where on one hand I thought: wow, this is the way to hear music! and on the other: so what? This is not what I came here for. I was later told that this mushroom stage lasted for three and a half hours.

The change was marked by someone popping a small sweet pill into my mouth and whispering, 'Hold this under your tongue.' I knew it was acid and was ready for a change, especially one that might dissolve the internal dialogue. I waited for a change and I think it happened, but the truth is that I can't remember!

One and a half hours later again another whisper: 'We need to get your shirt off for an injection in your arm.' I wore a buttoned shirt between a long-sleeved vest and sweater which got hopelessly tangled after the injection. I was aware of their attempts to sort out my clothing in the few seconds before the drug took effect, but fortunately my earlier paranoia was over and I laughed at their predicament.

Almost immediately I was aware of a rattle as though someone was flipping through the pages of a magazine behind my ears. In fact I had a visual image of this as though each page contained a philosophical statement or question concerning my identity. These kept pace with the pages being flicked: first a question, then an answer that led to a further question on the next page, and so on.

First I asked 'Who am I?' answered by, 'The one who is asking', then, 'How do I know that exists?' answered by, 'Asking is proof of existence', then, 'Do I only exist to ask?' answered by... These questions flashed through in a seemingly logical way but leading to less and less grounded conclusions. I then tried to take stock of what was happening and questioned whether I was certain there was a 'Me'. Yes, I felt sure. But 'Me' was not part of my body, a realisation that made me aware that I should be concerned, although I actually did not care. I tried to visualise my body lying there so that I could identify with it, but without success. I moved my limbs just to check they were part of me, but I was still left unconvinced. They existed, but might be anyone!

If 'Me' did not mean my body, then what did it mean? Perhaps it was just part of some amorphous being-ness. And what of my body; could that exist without 'Me' returning to identify with it? I certainly existed. Yes, in my reality I did exist without my body, but would I exist in another person's? I felt as though I could just as well return to another body or not at all... What then? I felt as though I was walking along a cliff top, aware of the danger but also finding it seductive.

I reached a state where I was convinced that my existence was in the balance, and that it was my choice, which depended on my belief, that would determine whether I continued to exist as an entity or sink back into that amorphous collective consciousness, or whatever it was. It was as though I was both Schrödinger and his cat! Most of this was verbal although I did have an image of my existence as a point swinging on a thread that was bound to break, and that my destiny depended on where it landed.

Intellectually I knew this was of the utmost importance, but since I was observing from outside of 'Me' I could see that it really didn't matter! There was no emotional content to make me hang on to my identity. Whether that point, that essence of 'Me', was united with my body or dripped back into the pool was not significant because it did not imply any loss. I decided, but only just, to come back.

7

As the ketamine wore off, I returned to enjoying the music. This time I felt more indulgent without interference from internal dialogue and the sound was simply superb. The Tibetan monks were singing in magnificent, sumptuous halls. The synthesised pan pipes were exquisite in each component of that subtle combination of sounds that made up each note, and the notes were pitched and so subtly spaced as to form a pattern with its own beauty in addition to the music made up of notes. What an incredible sound system! I wanted to curl up with Anja, but did not feel at liberty to do so.

Finally, my blindfold was gently lifted and I was offered some juice. By then I thought I was 'back to baseline', but as I tried to sit up I realised how spaced out I was, and in fact this lasted all day. The time was now 9 a.m., and for the next three hours we took turns to relate our experiences.

I looked over at Anja, nervously at first in case she was in another space. But she connected and we stared into each other's eyes without blinking. It became a game as to how close we could get without breaking the unwritten rules in the several hours that followed, during which people related their experiences.

A woman was crying for the loss of expressing her love to her husband and children whose photos she held: she had shown her shadow side to them for years, and grieved over lost opportunities to express her love for them. This had tormented her until she was given LSD; that had changed her view to seeing the opportunities for softening in the future. She had also felt sexual in the session and realised that she could enjoy her sexuality by herself, she did not have to depend on another person.

Then the man who wanted to locate the treasure spoke. He was in a completely different space: he said that he had been given the answer, the answer to so many of the world's problems and it was of vital importance, yet it had slipped away as he was coming back. It was a technique concerning the interaction of isotopes of heavy metals. He sweated as he struggled with intense frustration as he tried to hang on to the fading 'knowledge' and bring it back. I felt sympathy for him: I saw him as an alchemist who had just been handed the 'philosophers' stone' on a plate and had dropped it, but the others were not impressed.

Another man enthusiastically told us how he had vomited, and the bits in his vomit represented bits of rubbish that he was getting rid of. He had also seen the importance of keeping close to his relations. The scientist experienced a lot of imagery about his past, and felt that he was able to file it away usefully. Everyone reported a profound experience of some kind.

Anja's reflections, a few months after this workshop:

The workshop obeyed all the rules about set and setting. Everyone was well prepared through intellectual, emotional and physical work. The space was well prepared, the carers extremely competent, the build-up carefully timed, the integrating process comprehensive. And yet...I can't say I enjoyed the experience.

The slight initial paranoia in thinking that we might be used as guinea pigs went completely out of proportion when I took the mushrooms. This was triggered by the fact that someone bumped into me, hard and painful, which made me feel totally unsafe for most of the trip.

> I feel a big bang on my right shoulder blade, ouch! They must be playing games with me. The music is loud and threatening. A thumping sound, like a rubber ball and I become alert. In suspense I wait for the next blow. It does not come. Finally I lie down again. I feel ever so small, not able to act or defend myself. Then I feel a soft pad under my hand, should I feel, explore? I am very tentative. Are they playing with me? Trying to get me to react? Should I react? The pad moves in a kind of strange way. It goes up and down rhythmically. It reminds me of throbbing. I don't feel safe, so I retract. I feel things pressing against my hand and arm. Where is my boundary – where is my space? I feel jumpy, alone and vulnerable.

Upon reflection, I realise I was confronted with a couple of deep-seated issues here. One was trusting that people won't harm me. The second was claiming my right to have a space in this world. I was not aware of the extent to which these fears were still buried inside my unconscious, but they certainly presented themselves in their full glory during this session.

I clearly went through the three stages of integrating this experience.

In the first stage the feeling was so overwhelming that I could not get a grip on it at all or find the words to talk about it. I had no idea how to get out of my feeling of deep insecurity. I was fortunate that I had Nicholas, who just accepted my feelings and gave me love and comfort till I was ready to explain and talk. If this had not been the case, I think I might not have felt secure enough to let my fears be and would possibly have suppressed them or even felt haunted by them. Luckily this did not happen, so I could use this uncomfortable period to face what was really going on inside me and learn from it.

Later I realised how important it is to give myself time and not have to get back to doing things quickly, so I can be gentle with myself in that state. It also brought home to me the importance of people who deeply love and care for me, to surround me after a big inner journey.

I wanted to understand what had happened, mainly to reassure Nicholas who had been so patiently sitting by me, but found that when I tried to explain in words what was going on it never sounded quite right. After some time, I started doodling and playing with coloured pens. Abstract shapes and colours reflected my mood best. The feeling of being trapped in one spot where people could invade my space, which had been so strong during the trip, was still lingering. I like dancing and found it helped me to move out of this feeling. Later we went for a stroll in the countryside and I was given a massage. After several pots of tea, I finally opened up enough to be able to talk a bit.

It wasn't till we came back home, a week later, that I really began to understand what happened. In writing, I experienced the whole nightmare again and was shivering for hours afterwards. However, at this stage I had moved on and was at least able to put it into words. A few days later I read my account again and still felt my breath getting shallow, but began to understand more what had been going on.

When we evaluated the session immediately afterwards, I was the only one who did not think much of it. I knew that this was supposedly the most perfectly prepared workshop I could have wished for and it had been quite an adventure to go through this psychedelic cocktail, but I had come out with my inner defences stronger than ever. 'Nobody is gonna mess with me any longer' was my feeling. My boundaries were rigid and I did not see that as a very spiritual attitude. It was only through the long integration process that I managed to transform what I had initially not even recognised as fear into an ability to expand my boundaries and become more trusting in the process of life.

A structure in which to take psychoactives

Many people feel the need to contain a spiritual experience within a structure that relates it to the earthly experience of life. Mainstream faiths help fulfil that role for the majority, and the need is no different for those who seek spirituality through the means of psychoactives. In tribal cultures this was understood, but in the modern world support structures for this work are sadly lacking. This is a fundamental problem which can lead to drugs being taken heedlessly and without respect, which in turn leads to much despair and suffering.

New ways need to be found by those who want to search for the ultimate high using the path of psychoactives. Set, setting and integration are as important now as they have always been in the various religious traditions. As people create their own ceremonies for this work, new structures will emerge. Hopefully they will be based on wisdom that honours experienced elders, sacred places, integrity and truthful intent. Much further thought needs to be given to these concepts if psychoactives are to fulfil a greater spiritual function in our society.

7

8

Practical Information

Just say know.

LSD had indeed been known to cause psychoses... in people who haven't taken it.

Timothy Leary

Medical information

This section contains medical information specifically related to the use of psychoactives. It does not pretend to give comprehensive advice but explains the problems that can occur through taking such substances.

Legal information

The legal consequences of drug-use are set out here, with details of what to expect if you are arrested, in Britain, on suspicion of possession, supply or production of an illegal substance. The debate over drugs and the law is also introduced.

Glossary

Some of the terms used in this book are explained here, within the context of using psychoactives for spiritual purposes. This is a limited selection – the subject is vast – but a number of encyclopedias are listed later, in the bibliography, and these provide comprehensive definitions and etymologies.

Resources

This section provides contact addresses for those who seek further information on any of the areas covered in this book. We have included details of websites, religious groups, periodicals and drug-law reform groups. Please do use your own judgement when seeking further information – be aware that your details may appear on an email or mailing list which may not be confidential and could be accessed by law enforcement agencies if you are entering a legal grey area. The web addresses listed were correct at time of going to press, and the sites contained helpful information. However, the Internet is growing rapidly and sites may have since changed.

Annotated bibliography

This is an extensive bibliography, with a short excerpt of each book where possible. We would like to thank the Council for Spiritual Practices for allowing us the use of their chrestomathy, or collection of literary passages, from which most of the books were chosen.

Medical

*Prevention
is better than cure.*

This section contains medical information specifically related to the use of psychoactives. It does not pretend to give comprehensive advice but explains the problems that can occur through taking such substances.

Paying attention to health

The intention of this book is to provide information about the use of psychoactive substances for spiritual purposes only. We have made it clear throughout that drugs have the potential to cause serious harm. However, given the possibility that some people nevertheless choose to take drugs, we urge anyone considering taking a psychoactive substance to read this section very carefully.

Those who intend taking psychoactive substances for spiritual development need to look after their general health to minimise risks. A healthy lifestyle involves stress levels being kept to a manageable level, having a supportive network of friends or family, eating good food containing plenty of vitamins and minerals, having uninterrupted sleep and maintaining a good balance between relaxation and exercise.

A weakened immune system probably increases the physical risks of drug-taking as does acute or chronic disease in general.

In the case of psychoactives it is definitely advisable *not* to take *too much* or *too often*.

8

Risks

From a medical point of view there are undoubtedly risks in taking psycho-actives. Risk taking is inherent in life and it is up to the individual to assess the level of risk for themselves.

Narcotics (opium and opium derivatives like heroin) can be extremely dangerous and highly addictive. Depression of breathing is a common problem with these substances. The dangers of stimulants (cocaine, tobacco, coffee, amphetamines) and depressants (alcohol, barbiturates, GHB, cannabis) are often but not necessarily dose related and adverse reactions to them may occur at any dose. Someone who has taken too many stimulants for their con-stitution will be overexcited, may sweat profusely and may have tremors. Depressants can also affect the breathing, which becomes much shallower than normal, the pulse may get weak and rapid and the person's skin may feel cold and clammy.

The risks of most hallucinogenic substances (such as LSD, DMT and mescalin) are of a psychological rather than a physical nature although there is a considerable risk of accidental, physical harm during psychological dis-turbance resulting from the use of such substances. What is commonly labelled as an hallucination during a psychoactive experience is strictly speaking not of that nature, since the person nearly always knows that what he perceives is not reality but the effect of the substance he has taken. If someone is truly deluded, this awareness is not present.

Various methods of administration

There are various methods by which people take psychoactives. Injecting is by far the most risky one. Since the drug goes straight into the bloodstream, a lot of the body's defence systems are bypassed. This may intensify the effect, but also makes it far more dangerous. Needles should always be sterile and never shared, since there is the danger of contracting hepatitis, HIV or other lethal infections. Those with cardiovascular problems (for example a faulty heart valve due to previous infection) are at a particularly high risk of serious disease when using drugs intravenously.

Smoking or snorting may seem safer but in fact the drug moves even more rapidly to the brain than through injecting because of highly rapid absorption from the lungs. This may partially account for the strong addiction patterns amongst those who smoke. Anyone with a lung disorder (for example chronic bronchitis or asthma) is taking particular risks by smoking psychoactives or any substance.

Taking these substances orally gives the body the most chance to respond in its own way and is therefore somewhat safer. However, those who suffer from chronic liver disease or partial kidney failure are also at considerable risk of an adverse drug reaction because of an impaired capacity to break down or excrete drugs.

Psychological problems

In the chapter 'Before, During and After' we pointed out the importance of set, setting and integration in relation to minimising psychological dangers.

Someone who uses psychoactives to escape from a mentally troubled state is more likely to find himself further in trouble, rather than getting relief, since many of the substances intensify the mood the taker finds himself in already.

It is extremely dangerous for people with a history of schizophrenia or severe psychiatric illness to take any of the substances mentioned in this book, unless as part of a highly controlled, medical treatment programme. It is questionable if what is often seen as a state of psychosis during the course of a trip can indeed be labelled as such. Psychoactives may bring existing patterns to the surface, but rarely cause a complete mental breakdown if taken with the right guidance.

If the substance is taken with spiritual intention a certain frame of mind has already been adopted through which the experience can be contained.

Even in these situations **panic attacks** may occur. Feelings of anxiety are more likely to emerge if someone is taking a substance for the first time and is not familiar with its effects or the setting. It is important for those surrounding the user to stay calm and reassure her. This may avert a panic attack. If someone does start to panic and breathing becomes difficult it is even more important to stay calm and regulate the person's respiration by breathing in a slow rhythmical fashion with them, maybe gently holding their feet to give them some reassurance and reminding them in a relaxed voice that the experience is of a passing nature. They should not be given sedatives, tranquillisers

8

or other psychoactive drugs except by a trained health care professional (e.g. a paramedic or emergency physician). If the person stays conscious and is breathing sufficiently, it is probably best to keep them where they are rather than moving them to a hospital emergency unit.

Flashbacks and paranoia afterwards are usually symptoms of inadequate integration of the experience. Flashbacks, such as a sense of *déjà vu*, are quite common to everyone in daily life, whether they have ever taken psychoactives or not. If paranoia lasts for a long time after the effects of the drug have passed, professional psychotherapeutic help needs to be sought.

Physical problems

Poisoning

Taking too much of any substance can lead to problems and the classic symptoms of poisoning may be seen. The most common ones are vomiting and breathing problems. For some psychoactives, however, vomiting is predictable because they act as purgatives and this is considered healthy. If there is blood in the vomit, abdominal or chest pain or dizziness then professional help should be sought immediately. Taking far too much of any substance can lead to coma and death.

Asphyxia

This occurs when not enough oxygen reaches the body tissues (including the brain) and can be life threatening within minutes. If asphyxia is due to objects in the mouth, very gentle efforts to remove them may be undertaken with the co-opration of the victim, although care must be taken not to exacerbate the situation by pushing the foreign body deeper into the throat. In the windpipe, foreign bodies may be dislodged by a slap between the shoulder blades or a Heimlich manoeuvre. Asphyxia can also result from swelling of the throat, which is harder to deal with. Tight clothing should always be loosened and the person should be brought into fresh air, although this should never distract one from attending to the primary problem, that of ensuring a clear airway. In severe cases the person may show blueness of the lips and stop breathing altogether and an ambulance should be called immediately.

Allergic reactions and shock

There is always a risk that a person is allergic to a substance and that some people may have an adverse reaction to drugs for 'non-allergic' reasons (for example they may have diagnosed or unsuspected liver or kidney problems). The most common symptom is itching and swelling, not so different from what people with nut allergies or hay fever experience. In extreme cases, particularly when injecting a drug, someone may develop anaphylactic shock. This is a severe reaction that can develop within a few minutes of taking a substance. Most commonly it is a reaction to bee stings or penicillin. Panic attacks can affect the breathing and increase the heart rate: calming the person may have a regulating effect on their breathing. Anaphylactic reactions, on the other hand, tend to begin with a sense of fearfulness or angst, followed by wheezing, coughing or difficulty in breathing, an itchy rash (particularly about the face and lips) and, thereafter, dizziness, vomiting or diarrhoea. Collapse can occur within seconds. The patient must be put in the recovery position (on one side, the underneath hand placed under the head and the top leg bent forward at the knee) and medical help must be sought straightaway. Some people who have previously had anaphylactic reactions may carry their own supply of adrenaline with them. If they are unable to inject it themselves, the ambulance service controller may be able to advise bystanders on its use.

Hyperthermia – getting too hot

This occurs particularly if people take drugs while dancing for long hours or in very hot climates they are not used to. People who find it hard to sweat or who are taking certain medication (for example antidepressant anticholinergic medication) may be especially prone to this condition (hyperthermia). Many people find it difficult to sweat in a very humid environment like a club or a tropical climate. The sufferer needs to rest in a half-sitting position in a cool place and be fanned or supplied with cold water compresses.

More serious problems occur when the body temperature gets above 42 degrees C. Our blood starts to form tiny clots that stick to the artery walls. The process uses up the clotting agent in the blood, so that there is nothing to prevent bleeding. There is the potential for continual blood loss from the small blood vessels within the body, but clotting factors and platelets in the blood constantly form aggregates or thrombi to repair the damage. Overactivity of this process can result in stroke and other complications; underactivity can result in blood haemorrhage into the tissues, for instance causing bruising, blood loss or haemorrhagic stroke. Triggered by a range of infections, diseases and traumas is a condition called *disseminated intravascular coagulation* (DIC) in which there is blood clotting within small blood vessels. Paradoxically, because this process uses up the various clotting factors in the blood faster than they can be made, severe bleeding may then result. People can bleed to death in this way...

Those who sweat profusely may lose too much salt (sodium) and can end up with muscle cramps. This can be alleviated by sipping water containing no more than a level teaspoon of salt per litre of water. A far more serious condition is swelling of the brain. Sodium holds water in the body's veins and arteries. Without it we tend to lose water into the body's tissues, and swell. The brain, encased in the skull, cannot swell a lot. It becomes compressed and puts pressure on the brain stem which controls heart and breathing functions. This can be fatal. Isotonic drinks, unlike pure water, will help replace some minerals like sodium and preserve the balance of fluids in circulation. Eating crisps or salted peanuts will also help replenish sodium levels.

The danger of overheating while on Ecstasy, in particular, has been well publicised. Fewer Ecstasy-users are aware that it is possible to drink *too much* water. For the reasons mentioned above, too much pure water can dangerously dilute sodium levels. If one is taking Ecstasy and is not in a humid environment, dancing or involved in other exercise then it may not be necessary to drink large amounts of water. Liquids (e.g. water) should be seen as an antidote to dehydration, not an antidote to the effects of Ecstasy or overheating. Deaths due to Ecstasy seem to be related to excessive drinking of water, excessive consumption (massive repeated dosage) or ill-understood idiosyncratic reactions in users. Such deaths may be impossible to prevent for medical reasons (and are comparable to the deaths which occur after marathon running in fit young adults).

Things to watch out for:

- disorientation in time and place: the user can't say where he is or what day it is;
- drowsiness and lack of response to commands like 'Open your eyes'

or 'Squeeze my hand';
- anything which looks like fitting;
- breathlessness or difficulty in breathing;
- they feel abnormally hot to the touch, even though they have been in a cool environment for some time.[1]

Hypothermia – getting too cold

Technically, the body temperature should fall below 35 degrees C for hypothermia to occur. This is not likely, but some people lose their sense of temperature on psychoactives and a sitter needs to monitor the environment. The user may start shivering. This is the body's natural response to feeling cold and actually regenerates heat so it is a good thing. When shivering is replaced by lack of muscle co-ordination and this is not a direct effect of the substance (for example with ibogaine) the sitter needs to make sure that the user stays warm by providing blankets and heating.

Pregnancy

In general it is not good to take psychoactive substances during pregnancy or while breastfeeding, although in some of the Brazilian churches pregnant women do drink ayahuasca.

Specific substances

MDMA can lead to heat stroke and dehydration when used in long dance rituals in a hot space without adequate intake of fluids. It may also cause convulsion or seizure in those who have not previously been known to be epileptic (the mechanism of this is unclear but may be related to dose). Longer-term effects of the drug (particularly in relation to depression and memory) are still being researched, but it is clear that people with weak liver and kidneys have to be extra careful. It has also been established that body temperature is a key factor in toxicity risk and potential harm can be reduced by keeping cool.

GHB (gamma-hydroxybutyric acid) has depressant (anaesthetic) actions that depend very acutely on dose. Respiration is depressed and this can lead to lethal coma if combined with other depressants such as morphine and other opiates, or alcohol.

SSRIs (selective serotonin reuptake inhibitors), mainly used as antidepressants, should not be mixed with other MAOIs (whether antidepressants or otherwise) since these drugs can have interactions. Medical drugs used as SSRIs include fluoxetine (Prozac™) and paroxetine, but some psychoactive agents have actions overlapping one or other group so potentially can be dangerous in combination (harmine, harmaline, 2CB, mescalin, MDMA, MDA). For example, Prozac and Ecstasy in combination could cause a hypertensive crisis (or a severe sudden rise in blood pressure which may lead to a stroke, blindness or kidney failure). Several weeks' gap should be left between the chronic use of one such drug and another.

Ayahuasca, because it contains harmala alkaloids, including harmaline, which act in part as monoamine oxidase inhibitors (MAOIs), at least theoretically is contraindicated for individuals taking the same wide variety of other drugs that are contraindicated for patients being treated therapeutically (for depression) with MAOIs. Such drugs include antidepressants of the non-MAOI type (especially SSRIs including Prozac™), sympathomimetic amines (e.g. ephedrine and pseudoephedrine for colds, levodopa, a form of dopamine, by prescription for Parkinson's disease), prescription opiate analgesics including pethidine (meperidine in USA) and possibly some NSAID analgesics, some anti-migraine treatments, some anti-ulcer treatments, also the amino acids tyramine and tryptamine – whether as drugs, in foodstuffs or as psychoactive agents. It is the presence of tyramine in certain foodstuffs that leads to the prohibition for patients taking most MAOIs – because of the risk of hypertensive crises – of foods including ripe cheese, meat and yeast and soya bean extracts (e.g. Bovril and Marmite), 'high' game and fish, and possibly red wine and other foodstuffs. But, of course, appropriate trials have not been conducted, so it is not known which of these drugs and foodstuffs possess the most risk.

Mushrooms can be very poisonous and hard to identify. One should not eat them without making sure that they are edible and safe.

First aid

First aid is applied in emergency situations, whilst waiting for medical help. First aid is not a way of treating the patient, so it does not involve giving them medication. If they ask for it, you may of course hand someone their own medication which they take regularly, for example in the case of an asthma sufferer. First aid is mostly about what *not* to do, rather than about trying to save a situation which should be dealt with by the medically trained.

For sitters and those who are around people who use drugs, taking a first aid course is a good idea.

When to act?

- when someone causes damage to themselves, other people or their environment ;
- when someone becomes unconscious;
- when someone has unusual breathing problems;
- when someone acts extremely out of character.

What to do

- Keep calm.
- Send for an ambulance.
- Put them in the recovery position (on one side, underneath hand under head, top leg bent at knee).
- Talk to them and reassure them.
- Take details, if possible, of their name, how long ago they took the substance and how much they took.
- When the medical/ambulance people arrive pass on as much information as you can and give them an example of the substance taken, if available (one that you found: it should not be in your possession).

What not to do

- Don't walk the person around or keep them moving.
- Don't give them drinks.
- Don't make them sick.
- Don't leave them alone.

8

Mixing drugs can be dangerous, as it can be very difficult to identify what the problem is if anything goes wrong. Mixing drugs includes prescribed or over-the-counter medication.

In all cases of loss of consciousness an ambulance needs to be called immediately. For an ambulance in the UK dial 999.

Other useful numbers:

National Drugs Helpline: 0800 77 66 00

Samaritans: 0345 90 90 90

Legal

The prestige of the government has undoubtedly been lowered considerably by the Prohibition Law. Nothing is more destructive of respect for the government and the law of the land than passing laws which cannot be enforced.

Albert Einstein

Let us declare nature to be legitimate. All plants should be declared legal and all animals for that matter. The notion of illegal plants and animals is obnoxious and ridiculous.

Terence McKenna

Most of the psychoactive substances mentioned in this book are illegal in English-speaking countries. This section sets out what the consequences of such activity could be, with details of what to expect if you are arrested, in Britain, on suspicion of possession, supply or production of an illegal substance. The debate over drugs and the law is also introduced.

In different countries the law may slightly differ on each individual drug. In Britain drugs are *scheduled* under the Misuse of Drugs Regulations 1985 and *classified* under the Misuse of Drugs Act 1971.

There are two schedules. The drugs in Schedule I (such as LSD and MDMA) are seen to have harmful effects which outweigh any potential value, and these drugs may not be prescribed. Drugs which fall into Schedule II (such as medical opium and diamorphine) can be prescribed but only under very tightly controlled conditions.

Drugs are divided into three Classes (A, B and C) and the relevance of the Classes is in relation to the maximum penalties that may be imposed for possession or supply of these drugs. In Britain, LSD, MDMA and other phenethylamine derived substances, 2CB, DMT, mescaline, opium, heroin, and coca leaves are all Class A drugs. The Class of a drug is intended to say something about the relative harm of that drug, and harm may be sociological (i.e. drugs that are liable to give rise to a social problem) as well as pharmacological.

Whether the drugs within a Class are all equally harmful is a matter of debate. However, from the point of view of the law, *all* the substances within a Class are treated as equal and those in Class A have the strongest penalties attached to them.

Different courts may vary their verdicts, but the maximum penalty for possession of a Class A drug is seven years' imprisonment. People who have no previous convictions are more likely to receive a fine than a prison sentence. The police do not always bring cases to court and a person may instead be cautioned. A caution may sound like a mere telling off, but is actually quite a serious affair because it forms part of a criminal record. This may negatively affect the chances of, for example, getting a job or a loan in the future.

Production and possession with the intent to supply is regarded as an even more serious matter and the maximum penalty for Class A drugs is life imprisonment and confiscation of assets (except for assets proved not to have been acquired as a result of drug trafficking). It would be unusual to receive a life sentence for a drugs offence, but some sentences for importing Class A drugs on a massive scale have certainly been very high (twenty-five years plus).

Any passing of drugs can be interpreted as supply. Looking after someone else's drugs, giving them back to them, sharing a substance or handing it in for testing purposes are all seen as possession with the intent to supply. Money does not need to be involved for one to be convicted, but if one is found to have sold drugs then a prison sentence is almost certain.

Allowing one's premises to be knowingly used for the production or supply of a Class A drug could result in a fourteen-year prison sentence.

Class B drugs (amphetamines, if not injected, and cannabis) are regarded similarly in the legal system, but they do not attract such heavy fines. However, the penalties are still substantial: the maximum penalty for possession is five years' imprisonment and for production and supply is fourteen years' imprisonment. The fine for both is unlimited.

In Britain, if the police reasonably suspect you are in possession of controlled drugs, they may stop and search you, although this should not be on the basis of stereotyping (such as style of hair, clothes etc). Intimate searches are allowed only if you are formally detained.

To ensure that proceedings are properly followed it is important that both sides (police and suspect) keep detailed notes of everything that happened, preferably with witness reports. Anything that is said may be used in evidence in court. However, if you choose not to say anything, this too will be mentioned should the case go to court. For this reason people often insist on their right to have a solicitor present during questioning.

A warrant is not always necessary to be able to search premises; for instance, if the maximum term for the offence is five years or more (under Section 18 of the Police and Criminal Evidence Act 1984). However, the police do have to give information about their powers to search premises and the occupant is normally allowed to be present. Again, record-taking is of vital importance.

It is not an offence to tell someone about a past experience with drugs. However, to generally admit to taking Class A or B drugs may technically lead to a 'Past Possession Charge', although this would be unusual. For this reason,

8

people who use psychoactives responsibly never disclose names of participants, leaders or places with respect to psychoactive use.

Contacts for more detailed information on the law, police guidelines and the Criminal Justice Act are given at the end of this section. The Internet website 'The Lycaeum' has information on controlled substances in the USA.

Drugs and the law – the debate

The general argument for prohibition is that the public at large needs to be protected, especially the weak and uninformed. Opinions on this issue vary greatly and to go into this in any depth involves discussing concepts such as the right of the individual and the role of the government, which fall outside the scope of this book. We limit ourselves to providing more information about the spiritual uses of these substances. We do, however, hope that this book will contribute to a debate about whether there is an argument for legalising psychoactives in order to facilitate a spiritual experience.

The debate has hardly begun. Only in America has this issue been discussed, around the legalisation of peyote as a sacrament in the Native American Church. There are many questions that need to be asked. Can spirituality be exempt from the law? Should psychoactives be legal only within a spiritual context? How would we define this context? Are some substances better suited than others? What effects may legalisation have on other members of society? And many more...

When Nicholas talked to Robert Jesse, founder of the Council for Spiritual Practices, some of these issues came up. Robert Jesse's view was as follows:

> Nearly everyone agrees that society has a legitimate interest in the health and safety and welfare of its citizens. Whether right or wrong there is a great deal of fear that entheogenic substances, plant and chemical, are dangerous, even though they may not be organically harmful. It is apparent that some susceptible individuals, quite rarely even apparently healthy individuals, can suffer adverse effects from entheogens that may last days, weeks, or a lifetime. The risks do appear to be minimised when the substance is used with appropriate screening, preparation and supervision, and when the practice is embedded in a context that provides ongoing support. This is precisely how the religious traditions work that have well developed ways of guiding people on paths towards mystical awareness.

The training and practices offered are calibrated to the participant's ability to benefit from them, and they take place within an ongoing, supportive social context...One of the things that will help increase the amount of wisdom in our culture about entheogens is for people to take prudent steps out of the closet. Being progressively more open about the graces that people have received through their use of these sacraments seems so important. It also seems important to acknowledge the risks, limitations and traps of using plants and chemicals in spiritual practice – to avoid single-mindedness and true-believerism. It's such a fascinating field, worthy of sober and balanced study.

But sober and balanced study is still thin on the ground. This is partly due to the fact that it can be difficult to talk openly about a psychoactive experience because of the legal status of psychoactives. The result is a vicious circle: information is hard to come by because of the current legislation, but without more information being available, a balanced debate is unlikely to ensue.

Further information

The British charity Release does a wonderful job in providing information on drugs and the law, including emergency help. Its advice line is open from 10 a.m. to 6 p.m. Monday to Friday on 020–7729 9904, and its emergency line is accessible at all other times on 020–7603 8654. Its website, which contains Release's famous 'bust-card' (detailing your rights should you be arrested on a drugs charge), is at http://www.release.org

Britain now has a government-appointed 'drug czar'. If you have comments on the legal status of psychoactives in Britain you may wish to contact his office. The address is:

Mr Keith Hellawell (Drug Czar)
Room 61/2 Government Offices
Great George Street
London
SW1 3AL

If you would like to take a more active role in changing the current political climate of opinion on drugs in Britain, Transform is a group campaigning for a 'more effective drugs policy'. Their address is:

8

Transform
1 Roselake House
Hudds Vale Road
St George
Bristol
BS5 7HY
Tel: 0117–939 8052
http://www.transform-drugs.org.uk

Glossary

Unknowingly we voyage in a labyrinth,
a macrodimensional maze of living
electrical force, cloaked by a thick
layer of ordinary life.
Our most serious obstacle is the
uncontrollable urge to convert
everything to the familiar, to reduce it
all to the level of the primate brain;
to reject the living, breathing reality of
the totality of all possible attention.

E.J. Gold

8

Addiction: dependence on a drug with continued, probably excessive, usage of it. This results in the individual becoming accustomed to the drug, with detrimental effects (e.g. psychological and/or physical withdrawal symptoms) on ceasing to take it. Additionally, the individual may become tolerant to it, requiring higher dosages over time.

Adulteration: the addition of cheap or impure substances.

Afterglow: state of total peace and contentedness that can follow on the heels of a psychedelic experience.[1]

Amphetamine: synthetic central nervous stimulant. It comes in pills or as powder. The effects (increased mental activity and physical energy) last about four hours and the comedown can be harsh. It is a Class B drug (unless it is prepared in a form for injection). Also known as amp, sulph, speed and whizz.

Amyl nitrite: a volatile liquid that can be inhaled. It dilates the arteries, causing a sudden drop in blood pressure. The high is short, lasting only a few minutes. Also known as pearls, poppers (due to the popping sound when you break the glass ampoules it sometimes comes in) and snappers.

ASC: altered state of consciousness.

Ayahuasca: meaning 'vine of the soul', also called yajé and caapi, is the name given both to the main ingredient and the potion made by mixing two sorts of ingredient. The first ingredient is prepared from the species of the jungle vine, *Banisteriopsis*, genus (mainly *Banisteriopsis caapi*, formerly known as *Banisteria caapi*), and contains the psychoactive beta-carboline (tryptamine derivative) alkaloids harmaline and harmine. The second ingredient is one or more of a number of plant species that contain psychoactive tryptamine alkaloids, mainly DMT (dimethyltryptamine). Normally, the second type of ingredient is inactive when taken by mouth, being broken down in the gastrointestinal tract by enzymes with monoamine-oxidase activity, but the harmala alkaloids in the first ingredient have monoamine-oxidase inhibitor (MAOI) activity, protecting the second ingredients, so the two have a synergistic activity. But, because of this MAOI activity, there may be complications for those individuals taking certain other drugs (see p. 228).

Bad Trip: unpleasant journey on a psychoactive. See 'Before, During and After' chapter for more information.

Bufotenine: a psychoactive substance contained in the venom of several toad (*Bufo*) species. Poisonous when taken orally, toad-licking is outlawed in many American and Australian states. The venom is usually extracted by squeezing various glands, and is then dried and smoked.

Cannabis: *Cannabis sativa* is the most commonly used variety. The tops of the plants produce a sticky aromatic resin, which can be pressed and then smoked or eaten. The female plants are preferred and can be dried and smoked directly. THC (tetrahydrocannabinol) is the main active ingredient. It is neither simply a stimulant nor a depressant and produces very different effects in different people.
THC can be good for nausea (it has been used to help with chemotherapy treatments) and has helped with asthma (although smoke may irritate), muscular cramps and glaucoma. Some people who live with multiple sclerosis have benefited from the use of cannabis. Also known as hemp, marijuana, pot, grass, weed, dope or resin, it is a Class B drug.

Clean: to be in that state of body which results from having declined the use of any psychoactive drug for a period of time.[2]

Cocaine: a psychoactive alkaloid, made from the leaves of the coca plant (*Erythroxylum coca*). It is snorted, and is a Class A drug.

Coming down: the effects of a drug wearing off.

Contact high: a drug-free observer becomes aware that (s)he is experiencing some effects of the material being used by others. This can also happen to animals and there is no known scientific explanation for it.[3]

Crack cocaine: derived from cocaine, this is smoked and gives a shorter, stronger burst of stimulation than cocaine. Even more addictive than cocaine, this is a class A drug.

Crash: depression after a high from taking a psychoactive.

Datura: roots, seeds, leaves and flowers from various *Datura* species (especially *Datura stramonium* – thornapple), all used for psychoactive purposes. They are often added to brews or can be chewed or smoked. The plant is very toxic in overdose and effects can be quite dramatic and frightening. Up to a couple of days after taking datura physical symptoms may be noticeable such as dry skin, eye and intestinal disturbances and affected heart rate. The belladonna alkaloids hyoscyamine (atropine) and hyoscine (scopolamine) are the main active components. A number of other solanaceous plants (e.g. deadly nightshade, black henbane, mandrake) have similar components and actions.

Dealer: someone who sells (drugs).

DMT: dimethyltryptamine is a psychoactive tryptamine alkaloid and was first synthesised in 1931. It also occurs naturally in many plant species including *Banisteriopsis*, *Psychotria* and *Virola* species. It is inactive orally (being broken down in the intestinal tract before it reaches the bloodstream) unless combined with an MAOI (monoamine oxidase inhibitor) which inhibits the working of the enzyme. DMT can be snorted or smoked. The effects are strong, immediate and short-lived (about twenty minutes). It is a Class A drug.

Dosage: the required dosage of a psychoactive substance may vary greatly according to body-weight, metabolism, experience and the setting. Myron Stolaroff describes dosages for various substances in *The Secret Chief*, but he took these in strict psychotherapeutic settings, and they were of known purity.[4] At a party or alone at home it would certainly not be advisable to take such high dosages. In addition, people tended to take higher doses in the 1960s than they generally do now. Increasing the dose may not necessarily get one 'higher'. Lowering resistance by calming oneself through relaxing, breathing, focusing and meditating can increase the potency of the psychoactive effect.

DPT (dipropyltyramine): is a short-acting tryptamine alkaloid which is smoked as a sacrament by the Temple of the True Inner Light in New York.

Drug: a substance taken to alter one's physical or mental state.

DXM (dextromethorphan hydrobromide): is contained in many over-the-counter cough-suppressing medicines. In low doses the effect is similar to alcohol, producing carefree clumsiness with a touch of psychedelic speediness. On higher doses dissociation and more psychedelic effects can be felt. Lasts between four and eight hours.

Entheogen: a psychoactive substance used for spiritual purposes. The word was coined by Jonathan Ott *et al.* in 1979. In Greek the word *entheos* means literally 'god (*theos*) within'. The Greek root *-gen* denotes the action of 'becoming'.

Hallucination: a convincing reality which only the person experiencing it can see/hear or interact with. People who hallucinate do not realise that what they see is not reality. Shulgin

argues that this phenomenon is very rare on psychoactive substances.[5]

Harmaline: a psychoactive beta-carboline alkaloid that, together with harmine, occurs in the *Banesteriopsis caapi* vine, *Peganum harmala* (Syrian rue) seeds and other plants. It is an MAO inhibitor and it is usually not taken on its own, because one needs to take a lot for it to have a psychedelic effect and it often makes people vomit. It is used together with DMT (making this active orally) or sometimes with LSD or psilocybin to give the trip an 'earthier' quality. Harmaline is not classified in Britain.

Heroin: a Class A drug which is a derivative of opium, containing a number of opiate alkaloids including morphine and codeine. It may be smoked or snorted, but is most commonly injected. It is highly addictive. Other dangers include the risk of overdose from unusually pure batches of the drug and poisoning from contaminants, in addition to all the risks associated with needle use.

High: euphoric or ecstatic state of consciousness.

Ibogaine: the root of *Tabernanthe iboga* and several other plants in the *Apocynaeae* genus. It grows in Africa where it was originally used by the Pygmies. Trips can last twenty hours (longer in the Bwiti initiation rites) and tend to be profound. Traditionally, it is used to get in contact with ancestors. It has been used to treat addictions. Ibogaine is not classified in Britain; it is a Schedule I drug in America.

Intoxication: the state of being under the influence of a substance.

Junkie: heroin addict.

Jurema: a DMT and harmaline combination, like ayahuasca, but prepared with *Mimosa tenuiflora* seeds and Syrian rue or vine.

Ketamine: a synthetic, legal drug and (to date) not a controlled substance, although it is under regular review in Britain. It is used as an anaesthetic mainly for animals and also for humans (especially children). Most people choose to inject it, but it can also be snorted or smoked or swallowed. It has dissociative effects which last for about half an hour. Also known as Ketalar, K and Special K.

LSD: lysergic acid diethylamide is a synthetic drug, although lysergic acid itself is a chemical that is found in ergot, a fungus that grows on grains. Dr Albert Hofmann first made LSD in 1938. Working for the Swiss drug company Sandoz, he was searching for new medical drugs. In 1943 he accidentally discovered its

8

psychoactivity. LSD was used therapeutically until the 1960s, when it became a popular street drug and a driving force behind the hippie movement and the 'summer of love'. The effects are purely psychedelic, with strong sensory perceptions and time distortions. Many people say they see the intrinsic energy patterns of nature and connect with the deep truth of the soul. A trip lasts six to twelve hours. 'Bad trips' do occur, usually when either the set or setting is unsuitable for the trip. Whilst LSD is not advised for pregnant women (due to its potential to induce uterine contractions), no evidence has been presented that it damages physical health. It is a Class A drug.

MDMA: the substance methylenedioxymethamphetamine (methylenedioxymethyl-amphamine) is generally known as Ecstasy but also as Adam and XTC, and is taken in pill or powder form. Pills often have a logo imprinted on them and are known by that logo, such as 'Doves' or 'Mitsubishis'. MDMA was first patented in 1914 by Merck but only became popularly known after its rediscovery by the 'Godfather of E', Alexander Shulgin, in the 1970s. It has actions fairly similar to amphetamine and releases serotonin, noradrenaline and dopamine, which break down fear barriers and leave the user with feelings of love and empathy. It lasts for about five hours. It was originally used in therapeutic settings but is now best known for its role in the rave scene. It is a Class A drug.

Mescalin: can be obtained in synthetic form, but is mostly consumed as the active ingredient of the peyote (*Lophophora williamsii*) or San Pedro (*Trichocerens pancha*) cactus. Aldous Huxley's mescalin trip was the inspiration for his books *The Doors of Perception* (1954) and *Heaven and Hell* (1956). It is a Class A drug.

Microgram: one-millionth of a gram.

Milligram: one-thousandth of a gram.

Mushrooms: various species are psychoactive. The common 'fly agaric' toadstool (*Amanita muscaria*) has long been known to be poisonous and hallucinogenic, and was formerly used by Siberian shamans. It contains several active alkaloids. Some quite unrelated *Psilcybe* species are highly psychoactive, of which the first discovered, *Psilcybe mexicana*, was traditionally used by the Mexican Indians as a sacrament. Various Psilcybe species have been referred to as 'magic mushrooms', notably 'liberty cap' (*Psilcybe semilanceato*), and these all contain as active ingredients the tryptamine (indole) alkaloids psilocybin (psilocybine) and psilocyn (psilocyne) which are Class A drugs. It is illegal in Britain and the USA to knowingly

possess hallucinogenic mushrooms. They can be eaten fresh or dried and are often made into tea. The effects last for four to six hours. Other mushrooms containing these alkaloids include *Psilocybe cubensis* and *Conocybe cyanopus*. In all cases it is essential to be thoroughly conversant with mushroom identification since some other highly poisonous species may be similar in appearance.

Mystic: someone who seeks divine union outside ordinary reality.

Nitrous oxide: also called laughing gas, this is inhaled as an anaesthetic but also used for its psychoactive properties. The effects last as long as the gas is breathed. It causes loss of muscle control and needs to be mixed with oxygen to be safe to breathe for more than a couple of minutes.

OD: overdose.

Opium: comes from the opium poppy (*Papaver somniferum*). It contains morphine (from which heroin may be chemically derived). Opium is a Class A drug.

Peyote: is the common name of the mescalin-containing cactus *Lophophora williamsii*. It grows in Texas and Mexico and is used by the Huichol Indians as a religious sacrament and as the inspiration for their art. It has a very bitter taste and may be eaten directly as buttons or as powder. It is sometimes made into a paste with water, or drunk as a tea.

Psilocybin: (psilocybine), the main psychoactive tryptamine (indole) alkaloid found, together with psilocyn (psilocyne) in *Psilcybe* species and certain other 'magic mushrooms'. They are tryptamine (indole) alkaloids first isolated in 1958, and are Class A drugs in Britain, and controlled substances in the USA.

Psyche: the non-physical human mind. Sometimes identified with soul.

Psychedelic: comes from a Greek word that literally means 'mind manifesting'. A psychedelic experience can be produced by one's body, such as through a fever, or by ingestion of a psychedelic substance. Psychedelics produce both open- and closed-eye visions and can give a new dimension to other senses, such as touch and hearing. Examples of psychedelic drugs are LSD, psilocybin and DMT.

Psychoactive: literally means activating the psyche. A psychoactive substance will affect one's mood and perception. Substances like alcohol, tobacco, coffee and chocolate are technically speaking all psychoactive. Examples of illegal psychoactive drugs are MDMA, marijuana and amphetamines, as well as heroin and cocaine.

Rave: a large party of people coming together to celebrate, usually with loud music, dance and the use of psychoactives.

Shaman: healer/priest.

Salvia divinorum: is a member of the sage (*Salvia*) family and the active ingredient has been identified as an unusual diterpena alkaloid, salvinorin A. It is generally smoked and effects start within thirty seconds. The peak will be reached within a minute and typically continues for two to three minutes. Severe distortions of time and space are often felt. The Mazatec Indians of Oaxaca, Mexico are the only people known to use *Salvia* in rituals at the present time. It is not classified in Britain.

San Pedro: the mescalin-containing *Trichocereus pachanoi*, or San Pedro, cactus is found in the mountains of Peru, Bolivia and Ecuador. Sometimes it is mixed with other plants like coca of brugmansia leaves. Generally the cactus is cut and reduced with water to a slimy brew. As far as we know it has been used by the shamans since the beginning of the Andean civilisation, which is at least 3,000 years ago.

Sniff: to inhale the fumes of a drug.

Snort: to inhale powder.

Solanaceae: a family of plants that include some species containing psychoactive constituents, mainly the solanaceous or belladonna alkaloids hyoscyamine (atropine) and hyoscine (scopolamine). Examples include *Datura* species (especially *Datura stramonium* – thornapple), the nightshades (especially *Atropa belladonna* – deadly nightshade), *Hyoscyamus niga* – black henbane and *Mandragora officinarum* – mandrake. But many other members of this large family, such as potatoes and tomatoes, do not contain these alkaloids.

Tolerance: the decrease or loss of response to a drug, due to recent or prolonged exposure to it.

Trip: the experiences resulting from taking a psychedelic.

2CB: comes in pill form and is similar to MDMA but is more psychedelic and less empathic. It also inhibits the sexual response less than MDMA and allows more intellectual thought patterns. It is a Class A drug.

Withdrawal symptoms: occur as a result of ceasing to take a drug, and are the result of becoming dependent on a substance. They may take the form of psychological withdrawal symptoms (e.g. extreme anxiety or dysphoria) or physical withdrawal symptoms (e.g. muscle tremor, goose pimples, diarrhoea, vomiting) or both. With some drugs the former are more evident (e.g. cocaine, amphetamine) but with others both are evident (e.g. nicotine, morphine). Marijuana has no very evident withdrawal symptoms.

8

Resources

Space is big. Really big.
You just won't believe how vastly hugely
mind-bogglingly big it is.

Douglas Adams, *The Hitch-hiker's Guide to the Galaxy*

The web addresses listed were correct at time of going to press, and the sites contained helpful information. However, the Internet is growing rapidly and sites may have since changed.

Organisations

Council on Spiritual Practices
POB 460065 (Dept. PRL)
San Francisco CA 94146–0065, USA
(415) 285 9000
(415) 285 9030 fax
csp@csp.org
http://www.csp.org
The Council on Spiritual Practices is dedicated to making direct experience of the sacred more accessible to more people. CSP has no doctrine or liturgy of its own.

Erowid
http://www.erowid.org
An excellent website dedicated to providing accurate information on the uses of entheogens as a tool for spiritual and personal growth.

Hanuman Foundation
524 San Anselmo Avenue no. 203
San Anselmo, CA 94960, USA
(415) 457 8570
(415) 454 4143 fax
rdtapes@aol.com
http://www.RamDassTapes.org
Promotes spiritual well-being through education and service. Ram Dass's tapes are available from here.

Heffter Research Institute, Inc.
330 Garfield, STE 301
Santa Fe, NM 87501, USA
(505) 820 6557
(505) 992 8260 fax
george@heffter.org
http://www.heffter.org
Non-profit research into the use of psychedelics to explore the connection between mind and brain.

The Albert Hofmann Foundation
1278 Glenneyre Street, no.173
Lagune Beach, CA 92651, USA
(310) 281 8110
inlaguna@sprynet.com
http://www.hofmann.org
Dedicated to furthering the understanding and
responsible application of psychedelic substances in the investigation of both individual
and collective consciousness.

Hyperreal
http://www.hyperreal.org
Excellent database of drug information. Good
starting point on the Internet.

Ibogaine
http://www.Ibogaine.org
European mirror web page:
http://www.Ibogaine.Desk.nl
A wealth of information on ibogaine, including
how it can be used to treat addiction.

Island Group
849 Almar Ave, STE C–125
Santa Cruz, CA 95060, USA
(408) 427 1942
(408) 426 8519 fax
island@scruznet.com
http://www.island.org
News, views and articles from psychedelic
pioneers.

Timothy Leary
http://www.leary.com
Take a trip with a virtual Leary around his web
home.

John C. Lilly Homepage
http://www.garage.co.jp/lilly
Information on Lilly's work with ketamine and
dolphins.

The Lindesmith Center
400 West 59th Street
New York, NY 10019, USA
(212) 548 0695
(212) 548 4677 fax
tlcweb@sorosny.org
http://www.lindesmith.org
Drug policy research institute. The website has
a searchable database of library documents
focusing on drug policy.

The Lycaeum
director@lycaeum.org
http://www.lycaeum.org
European mirror web page: http://www-
europe.lycaeum.org.

'An on-line village of entheogenic enthusiasts'
with an excellent collection of links.

MAPS – Multidisciplinary Association for Psychedelic Studies
2121 Commonwealth Ave, STE 220
Charlotte, NC 28205, USA
(704) 334 1798
(704) 334 1799 fax
info@maps.org
http://www.maps.org
Membership-based non-profit research and
educational organisation doing great work
assisting scientists and researchers around the
world to design, fund, conduct and report on
research into the healing potential of psychedelic drugs and marijuana.

Release
388 Old Street, London EC1 V 9LT, UK
(020) 77295255
(020) 7729 2599 fax
info@release.org.uk
http://www.release.org.uk
Release provides a range of services dedicated
to meeting the health, welfare and legal needs
of drug users and those who live and work with
them, including a twenty-four-hour legal
helpline.

Religious Experience Research Centre
Westminster College
Oxford OX2 9AT
01865 253592
Centre founded by Sir Alister Hardy to collect
and archive accounts of religious experience.
They continue to welcome new accounts.

Nicholas Saunders
http://www.ecstasy.org
Accessible, objective, authoritative and up-to-
date information on MDMA (Ecstasy) including
Nicholas's books on-line.

The Scientific and Medical Network
Gibliston Mill
Colinsburgh
Leven
Fife KY9 1JS
Scotland
01333 340492
01333 340491 fax
SciMedNetwork@compuserve.com
http://www.cis.plym.ac.uk/SciMedNet/home.
htm
Promotes open exploration in science and
human experience. Interesting publications and
conferences.

8

Daniel Siebert's *Salvia divinorum* site
http://salvia.lycaeum.org
Lots of information on this legal psychoactive plant.

Transform: the Campaign for Effective Drug Policy
1 Roselake House
Hudds Vale Road
St George
Bristol BS5 7HY
0117 939 8052
http://www.transform-drugs.org.uk
Does what its name says! Membership-based organisation with a good quarterly newsletter.

Religious and spiritual groups

Friends of the Forest
Centre for Human Development.
Amsterlveenseweg 27 1054 Amsterdam, Netherlands,
(206) 905394
(206) 830129 fax
info@friends-of-the-forest.nl
http://www.friends-of-the-forest.nl
Therapeutic work with ayahuasca and jurema and indigenous wisdom. Also involved in forest conservation work. Holds regular rituals in Amsterdam.

The Peyote Foundation
POB 778
Kearny, AZ 85237, USA
http://www.win.net/~peyote
Promotes education on peyote use, sells pottery, supports the non-racist spiritual use of peyote.

Santo Daime Amsterdam
(206) 161413
cdsmaria@cistron.nl
The Santo Daime Church in Amsterdam, which holds regular meetings.

Santo Daime Homepage
http://www.geocities.com/RainForest/5949/
Website for the Santo Daime Church world-wide.

Takiwasi Homepage
http://www.cosapidata.com.pe/empresa/taki/taki.htm
The Takiwasi Centre in Peru treats drug addicts using plant medicine such as ayahuasca.

Temple of the True Inner Light
http://www.dorsai.org/~soma/
New-York based psychoactive-using Church.

UDV Homepage
http://www.udv.org.br/udvpag01-ing.htm
Website for the Uniao Do Vegetal worldwide.

Rave on the Internet

Escape from Samsara
http://www.fridge.co.uk/escape.htm
Website of the London-based trance club.

List of Rave Mail Lists
http://www.hyperreal.org/raves/rml/
As the name suggests...

Pendragon
http://www.hal2000.demon.co.uk/pendragon.html
'Invoke the tribal Celtic spirit' – website of the London-based trance club.

Rave Links on the Internet
http://rave.ml.org/umr-faq/resource.html
Good starting point on the Internet for rave sites.

Return to the Source
http://www.rtts.com
Website of the London-based trance club that organises the annual 'Earthdance for planetary peace'.

Spirit of Raving
http://www.hyperreal.org/raves/spirit/
Stories, links and lists about rave spirituality.

Booksellers

Mind Books
321 S. Main Street no. 543 (dept. PRL)
Sebastopol CA 95472, USA
(800) 829 8127
(707) 829 8100 fax
books@promind.com
http//www.promind.com
Wide selection of mind-manifesting books.
Speedy service. Run by knowledgeable and
friendly people.

Natural Products Co.
POB 1251 (Dept PRL)
Occidental CA 95465, USA
Jonathan Ott's books.

Transform Press
POB 13675 (Dept. PRL)
Berkeley CA 94712, USA
(510) 934 2675
Books by Alexander and Ann Shulgin.

Periodicals

Eleusis
c/o Museo Civico di Rovereto
Largo S. Caterina, 43
38069 Rovereto (TN)
Italy
eleusis@lycaeum.org
http://www.lycaeum.org/eleusis
Twice-yearly publication which is scholarly yet
very readable. A forum for the collection and
propagation of information on the relationship
between humans and psychoactive plants and
compounds.

The Entheogen Law Reporter
POB 73481
Davis CA 95617-3481, USA
telr@cwnet.com
http://users.swnet.com/specming/page6.html
Dedicated to providing legal advice on the use
and possession of psychoactives.

The Entheogen Review
564 Mission Street, Box 808
San Francisco CA 94105-2918, USA
'The journal of unauthorised research on
visionary plants and drugs'.

Gnosis
POB 14217
San Francisco CA 94114-0217; USA
(415) 074 0600
(415) 974 0366 fax
http://www.lumen.org
Explores spiritual and esoteric paths.

High Times
Trans-High Corporation
235 Park Ave S. 5th floor New York NY 10003
Probably the best known magazine dedicated
to cannabis.

MAPS Bulletin
Always interesting and informative reading from
the newsletter of the MAPS organisation (see
'Organisations' for details).

The Resonance Project
323 Broadway Ave East no. 318
Seattle WA 98102, USA
resproject@aol.com
http://www.reproject.com
High-quality magazine covering psychoactives,
consciousness, counterculture and reviews.

Shaman's Drum
POB 97
Ashland OR 97520, USA
(541) 552 0839
sdrm@mind.net
Quarterly magazine about shamanism.

Annotated Bibliography

Thus, the task is

not so much to see

what no one yet has seen,

but to think what nobody

yet has thought about that

which everyone sees.

Schopenhauer

This bibliography is mainly compiled from the chrestomathy of the Council on Spiritual Practices website (marked C) and the Mind Books catalogue (marked MB) with a few additions from other sources.

This is by no means the ultimate selection of books. Both the chrestomathy and Mind Books have many more titles you may be interested in. Of course, a good browse in your local library or bookshop may provide pleasant surprises too.

The chrestomathy is compiled by Thomas B. Roberts and Paula Jo Hruby. They have done an excellent job in selecting excerpts from many books and we have only been able to print a short version of each of them. For the full list contact the CSP.

Mind Books is run by Bob Wallace. Their mission is to 'help the mind evolve' and you can order a wonderful selection of books about mind-manifesting substances directly from them. (We received ours only three days after sending an email to the States.) For more details see p. 245.

The Adventure of Self-Discovery: Dimensions of Consciousness and New Perspectives in Psychotherapy and Inner Exploration, by Stanislav Grof (Albany, NY: State University of New York Press, 1988)
'Several profound personal experiences with psychedelic substances and clinical observations of their effects in psychiatric patients attracted my attention early in my professional career to the remarkable healing and transformative potential of nonordinary states of consciousness. Systematic exploration of the theoretical significance and practical value of these states has been the central focus of my research for over three decades.' (C)

Aldous Huxley: Moksha: Writings on Psychedelics and the Visionary Experience (1931–1963), ed. Michael Horowitz and Cynthia Palmer (New York: Stonehill, 1977)
'The publication of *Moksha* presents for the first time an authoritative collection of the prophetic and visionary papers of Aldous Huxley – his writings on mind-altering drugs, psychology, education, politics, the collective unconscious and the future of mankind.' 'One is reminded, as one reads these descriptions of the mescaline experience, of what is said of the next world in the various religious literatures of the world.' (C)

Altered States of Consciousness, ed. Charles T. Tart (Garden City, NY: Doubleday, 1972)
The readings in this collection cover a wide range of ASCs (altered states of consciousness) including those generated through psychedelic drugs. Chapter 23 by Walter Pahnke, 'Implications of LSD and Experimental Mysticism', reports on the Good Friday Experiment. (C)

Amazon Healer: The Life and Times of an Urban Shaman, by Marlene Dobkin de Rios (Bridport, Dorset: Prism, 1992)
'Trance is very well known among many adult men in the Amazon, who seek out such personal experiences by means of drug plants, either out of curiosity or to heal themselves of a witchcraft-induced disorder. Thus, despite the influence of several hundred years of Christianity, animistic beliefs continue to flourish side by side with Catholic doctrine.' (C)

American Mysticism from William James to Zen, by Hal Bridges (New York: Harper & Row, 1970)
'When certain proponents of psychedelic ecstasy, including experimental subjects who report their experiences, state that these drugs induce what they term "mystical experience," they seem to mean merely heightened sensual perception, psychological insight, or religious feeling, or a blend of the three. By my definition these are not, either singly or together, mystical experience, although it is nearly always accompanied, to be sure, by religious feeling.' (C)

El Arte de los Huicholes (The Art of the Huichols), by Ramon Mata Torres (Guadalajara, 1980)
'A nierika is a round or square offering made of wood or paper board. It has one or both sides covered with wax and, pressed into the wax, designs in yarn representing whatever the Huichol is asking of the gods...From these magic little tablets, or nierikas, there developed some thirty years ago the large yarn paintings, which one see in expositions and in those shops where Huichol art is sold. The intensely vivid colours in the pictures are based on the images and the colours seen after eating peyote. The colours in the embroidery on Huichol clothes are based on peyote dreams too.' (C)

Ayahuasca, by Ralph Metzner (Thunder's Mouth, 1998)
'Hallucinogens, Consciousness, and the Spirit of Nature. Scientific essays and first-person accounts of ayahuasca use. Chapters by Eduardo Luna, Dennis McKenna, Jace Callaway, and others.' (MB)

Ayahuasca Visions: The Religious Iconography of a Peruvian Shaman, by Leis Eduardo Luna and Pablo Amaringo (Berkeley, CA: North Atlantic

8

Books, 1991)
'Years ago, Peruvian Pablo Amaringo took the shaman's path. Today, he paints from a photographic memory the intricate, detailed visions he experienced under the influence of ayahuasca. Anthropologist Leis Eduardo Luna provides an introduction to the Peruvian Amazon and its ethnobotanical tradition, the use of ayahuasca in a shamanic context, and background on his long relationship with Pablo Amaringo.' (C)

Be Here Now, by Ram Dass (San Cristobal, NM: Lama Foundation, 1971)
'In these few years we had gotten over the feeling that one experience was going to make you enlightened forever. We saw that it wasn't going to be that simple. . . . we realized then that what we needed to do was to create certain kinds of environments which would allow a person, after being into another state of consciousness, to retain a certain kind of environmental support for new ways of looking at himself.' (C)

The Call of Spiritual Emergency: From Personal Crisis to Personal Transformation, by Emma Bragdon (San Francisco: Harper & Row, 1990)
'Intent on coming to terms with the Pandora's box of my inner world, I also sought explosive techniques of expanding my consciousness. After nine months of being at the monastery, when I was living in San Francisco within the Zen Center community, I asked Allan, my dear friend, to initiate me into the world of LSD. As the trip began, I became wondrously ecstatic. Coming back down into ordinary consciousness was traumatic...Which drugs can be used therapeutically, and which drugs are harmful? All drugs, conventional and unconventional, have the capacity to give us new information about ourselves, from coffee which speeds us up, to LSD which takes us dramatically past the boundaries of our ordinary mind, to alcohol which reduces our inhibitions.' (C)

Changing My Mind, Among Others, by Timothy Leary (Englewood Cliffs, NJ: Prentice–Hall, 1982)
'Dr. Leary has selected excerpts from his own lifetime writings, putting each one in its real life context...Leary offers 25 years' worth of essays, chapters, and transcripts reflecting his eclectic views on the nature of man.' (C)

Chemical and Legal Guide to Federal Drug Laws, by Alexander Shulgin (Ronin Publishing, 1992)
The official list of illegal (and legal) drugs. Each has a CSA schedule, drug code, class, synonyms, and chemical structure. Plus many details of federal drug law, illegal precursors, federal register citations, and more. Good reference, by the master chemist.(MB)

Chemical Ecstasy: Psychedelic Drugs and Religion, by Walter Houston Clark (New York: Sheed and Ward, 1969)
'It is not so much the statistical chance of things going wrong in the use of the psychedelics that produces the witch hunt, the hue and cry against those who misuse them. It is the fear of the unknown, of the "forms that swim and the shapes that creep under the waters of sleep" that so terrorizes the ordinary man, both educated and uneducated.' (C)

The Chemistry of Mind-Altering Drugs: History, Pharmacology, and Cultural Context, by Daniel M. Perrine (Washington: American Chemical Society, 1996)
'this book of necessity explores much more than chemistry. In addressing so broadly human a topic as the mind itself and the drugs which affect it, it becomes impossible to understand the effects of such drugs outside the total context, and especially the cultural context, of their use...When some experts were asked to apply the standard psychiatric definition of addiction to such substance usage or behaviors as eating chocolate, jogging, shopping, sex, work, watching television, or mountain climbing, many of these proved to be just as addictive as marijuana and much more so than LSD...The very suggestibility and claimed in-depth confrontation with Self and Other intrinsic to the action of the drug probably makes the exclusion of all painful encounters an impossibility; the same can be said of psychoanalysis and religious mysticism.' (C)

Come Blow Your Mind With Me, by Andrew M. Greeley (Garden City, NY: Doubleday, 1971)
'So, psychedelia takes man away from the ordinary into the really Real, [and this] as any reader of Mircea Eliade knows, is precisely what religions have always attempted to do – to transcend the finite, ordinary, and confused of their everyday existence and bring man in touch with the basic realities of the universe. Whatever else it may be, psychedelia is a religious movement.' (C)

The Cosmic Serpent, by Jeremy Narby (New York: Tarcher Putnam, 1998)
'DNA and the Origins of Knowledge Molecular biologist works with ayahuasca shamans and concludes they were given the knowledge of the DNA double-helix. Combines personal adventure, study of Amazon ethnobotany, and

investigation into sources of knowledge, intelligence, and consciousness. Extensive notes, bibliography, and index.' (MB)

Current Perspectives in the Psychology of Religion, ed. H. Newton Malony (Grand Rapids, MI: William B. Eerdmans, 1977)
'This is an illustration in a commonplace, contemporary person of the influence that religion may have in the transformation of personality. I have seen and studied such phenomena in ordinary men and women, and in many persons undergoing a religious experience under psychedelic drugs. The psychological study of religion is as fascinating as man himself, and as compelling as his fascination with God.' (C)

Dance of the Four Winds, by Alberto Villoldo and Erik Jendreson (Destiny Books, 1995)
'Secrets of the Inca Medicine Wheel. Explores use of ayahuasca and San Pedro by Quechua shamans in Peru and how they teach Villoldo. He works to master four traditional inner realms (or bodies), such as freedom from the past (south) and fear of death (west). Captures the many-world perspective and viewpoint of these plant shamans.' (MB)

The Discovery of Love: A Psychedelic Experience with LSD-25, by Malden Grange Bishop (New York: Dodd, Mead (distributor), 1963)
'Last week I had the most profound experience of my life. I took LSD-25, one of the newest psychedelic drugs. From this single experience, which lasted about ten to twelve hours, the whole scope, depth, and direction of my life have changed miraculously. Indeed, a miracle has happened to me...Psychedelic is a very descriptive word for the drug and the action it has. It is from the Greek and means literally soul revealing, or images of the soul. This is exactly what LSD does, when used as it was with me. It reveals the soul.' (C)

The Doors of Perception, by Aldous Huxley (New York: Harper & Row, 1970). First published 1954.
'The best essay on psychedelic experience.' (C)

Do Psychedelics Have Religious Implications?, ed. D.H. Salman and R.H. Prince (Montreal: R. M. Bucke Society, 1967)
'The particular problem we are to study in this conference is the impact of psychedelics upon religious experience.' (C)

The Drug Experience: First-person Accounts of Addicts, Writers, Scientists and Others, ed. David Ebin (New York: Orion Press: 1961)
'CHARLES BAUDELAIRE. "...A final, supreme thought bursts forth from the dreamer's brain: 'I have become God!' "
THOMAS DE QUINCEY. "The Malay has been a fearful enemy for months. I have been every night, through his means, transported into Asiatic scenes."
JEAN COCTEAU. "I am describing a cure: a wound in slow motion."
ALDOUS HUXLEY. "We walked out into the street. A large pale blue automobile was standing at the kerb. At the sight of it, I was suddenly overcome by enormous merriment...Man had created the thing in his own image..."
ALLEN GINSBERG. "I have to find, among other things, a new word for the universe, I'm tired of the old one..."
GORDON WASSON. "May not the sacred mushroom, or some other natural Hallucinogen, have been the original element in all the Holy Suppers of the world?" ' (C)

Drugs and Mysticism: An Analysis of the Relationship between Psychedelic Drugs and the Mystical Consciousness, by Walter N. Pahnke (Cambridge, MA: Harvard University Press, 1963)
'This experiment is popularly known as "The Good Friday Experiment"...With increasing frequency, books and articles have been appearing which make the claim that certain chemical substances (most notably mescaline, lysergic acid diethylamide, and psilocybin) are capable of inducing under appropriate conditions 'mystical' or 'religious' experience. Such claims have met with skepticism from many religious people, and rightly so. This investigation was undertaken, therefore, to study in an empirical way the similarities and differences between experiences described by mystics and those induced by these drugs' (C)

Drugs and Pastoral Care, by Kenneth Leech (London: Darton, Longman & Todd, 1998)
'The idea of an association between drugs and spirituality seems almost indecent to many people. However, much drug use, and much of the motivation for drug use, is connected with the search for meaning and identity – in other words, for spirituality. Kenneth Leech argues that those who work with drug users need to counteract the prejudices and misrepresentations which shape and distort public attitudes and political policies.'

E for Ecstasy (1993) (out of print)
Ecstasy and the Dance Culture (1995) (out of print)
Ecstasy Reconsidered (self-published at 14

8

Neal's Yard London, by Nicholas Saunders, 1997)
All three books deal with MDMA, its effects and uses. Some of the most authoritative and comprehensive works on Ecstasy. Full of practical information and first-hand accounts. *Ecstasy Reconsidered* includes many contributions from leading specialists in the field.

The Ecstatic Adventure, ed. Ralph Metzner (New York: Macmillan, 1968)
'In *The Ecstatic Adventure*, thirty-eight people from a broad spectrum of backgrounds and beliefs tell what it was like for them by describing their own experiences with hallucinogenic drugs – mescaline, LSD, peyote, psilocybin. Some of the trips are hell, others ecstasy...' (C)

The Ecstatic Imagination: Psychedelic Experiences and the Psychoanalysis of Self-Actualization, by Dan Merkur (Albany, NY: State University of New York Press, 1998)

'My first contention is that psychedelic drugs induce an alternate state – not restricted to consciousness – that consists of intense fantasying. Depending on the dosage, the fantasies may or may not reach pseudohallucinatory intensity. Beyond the induction of a state of intense fantasying or, to introduce a synonymous term, a state of reverie, the drugs themselves do nothing. They do not alter perception, or release forgotten memories, or induce psychoses, or anything else. All of the mental phenomena that are produced by psychedelics are fantasies.' (C)

The Encyclopedia of Psychoactive Substances, by Richard Rudgley (London: Little, Brown, 1998)
Accessible and entertaining, the encyclopaedia includes over 100 entries covering, amongst other things, the chemical and botanical background of each substance and the effects – both physiological and psychological – on the user.

Entheogens and the Future of Religion, ed. Robert Forte, (San Francisco: Council on Spiritual Practices, 1997)
'These writings aim to direct attention to the distinctly sacred nature of these substances with the hope that religious-minded investigators, policy architects, and the concerned public will take note. It is our hope that this book will contribute to an honest reappraisal of the historic and modern significance of entheogens so that they may be used accordingly in today's world by those seeking to cultivate their spiritual awareness.' (C)

Enzyklopädie der Psychoaktiven Pflanzen, by Christian Ratsch (AT Verlag, 1998)
Comprehensive encyclopaedia on psychoactive plants. Latin and common names, chemical, botanical, historical information, preparation and identification, ritual and medicinal uses, fully illustrated. In German, this may be translated into English in the future. An excellent book.

The Essential Psychedelic Guide, by D.M. Turner (San Francisco: Panther Press, 1994)
'My philosophy has been to use the psychedelic, spiritual, ego-loss experience to break down my limitations and definitions of myself, to keep my identity from stagnating, then to rebuild and develop in the manner I choose, a wiser, healthier, happier ego.' (C)

Event Horizons of the Psyche: Synchronicity, Psychedelics, and the Metaphysics of Consciousness, by David Bruce Albert Jr., (Riverside, CA: University of California, Press 1993)
'This study presents a metaphysical theory of consciousness. The theory developed in this study is unique because it is founded upon both the biology of the human nervous system, and the experiences of transcendent reality that form the core of mystical and religious thought. It takes as its foundations the existence of alternative realities, or "worlds", found in spiritual theories, and the pharmacology of neurotransmitters in the brain. Specifically, this theory is offered as an explanation for those cases in which an individual is exposed to some psychoactive substance, and subsequently reports having had a mystical experience...That psychoactive plants have played a role in the evolution of human consciousness is an inescapable conclusion, if we are to take evolution theory seriously.' (C)

Exploring Inner Space: Personal Experiences under LSD-25, by Jane Dunlap (London: Victor Gollancz, 1961)
'Written by a well-known scientific authority whose books were so popular the publisher refused to let her use her correct name. Jane Sunlop describes in detail five outstanding experiences under the influence of LSD. There probably does not exist more beautifully written and profound descriptions of remarkable LSD experiences.' (Myron Stolaroff, *The Secret Chief*, 1997)

Exploring Mysticism: A Methodological Essay, by Frits Staal (Berkeley: University of California Press, 1975)
'While reports of miracles are quite common in

the major religions, the attitudes toward them vary a great deal...It is not surprising that the religious use of drugs has not met with the approval of religious establishments. Institutionalized religions are not so much concerned with the religious or mystical experience of individuals, as with society, ethics, morality and the continuation of the status quo...In general, the parallels and differences between drug-induced experiences and the states of mind reached through meditation or other mystical exercises deserves close experiential study. Even if the differences turn out to be fundamental, the known similarities require an explanation.' (C)

Facing West from California Shores: A Jesuit's Journey into New Age Consciousness, by DavidToolan (New York: Crossroad, 1987)
'Even in the universities of the Catholic ghetto in which I grew up, where metaphysical speculation was highly approved, the general assumption was that the noumenal order of things could not be perceived. Is metaphysics a matter of "immediate perceptions"? Without argument? Psychedelics provided the gate-opener for just this announcement. In every one of my five trips, I left ego control behind rather rapidly. The energy had the quality of ethereal dazzling light, sheer, glorious golden splendor. At the same time it did not occur to me to think of the Hebrew tradition's Shekhinah, God's effulgent "glory" – but I would now understand it in such terms.' (C)

The Feast of Fools: A Theological Essay on Festivity and Fantasy, by Harvey Cox (Cambridge, MA: Harvard University Press, 1969)

'We drink alcohol not just because we like its taste but because it produces a certain state of consciousness. Nor is our society particularly opposed to inducing other desired states of consciousness (or unconsciousness) with substances in addition to alcohol. We quaff caffeine to cajole our brains into awakening in the morning. We drag on a pipe to relax. We order a martini to help clinch a business deal or madeira to speed a seduction. We pop Sleep-eze or sip warm cocoa to encourage slumber. But when it comes to the well-publicized drugs now increasingly used by young people, we suddenly turn angry and petulant. We serve champagne at wedding receptions but put people behind bars for smoking marijuana.' (C)

50 Years of LSD: Current Status and Perspectives of Hallucinogens, ed. A. Pletscher and D.

Ladewig (New York: Parthenon, 1994)
'Profound uncertainty surrounds peak experiences. It has often played havoc with attempts at measurement. Yet when these numinous moments occur there is great healing. To meet the challenge of understanding this potentiality, we need a broader frame of analysis, a new paradigm, one that forces us to describe all the variables in the clinical situation to understand what the relevant ones are.' (C)

Flesh of the Gods, ed. Peter Furst 1990 (revised)
'The Ritual Use of Hallucinogens. More detail on specific cultures: tobacco in Venezuela, ayahuasca in the Amazon, San Pedro in Peru, Peyote and Psilocybe in Mexico, fly-agaric of the Aryans, Cannabis many places, Iboga in Gabon, plus an overview of hallucinogens and shamanic origins of religion. Furst, Schultes, Wasson, Reichel-Dolmatoff, La Barre, other contributors. Bibliography and index.' (MB)

Flight from Reality, by Norman Taylor (Duell, Sloan & Pearce, 1949)
Worth hunting out. Very comprehensive book about psychoactives, rare for its time. Bibliography fascinating for its historic value.

Flowers of Wiricuta: A Gringo's Journey to Shamanic Power, by Tom Soloway Pinkson (Mill Valley, CA: Wakan Press, 1995)
'This journey with Huichol shamans of Mexico and other "medicine teachers" from North and South America leads through a mystical doorway into realities far beyond the ordinary, guided by "wisdom elders" who know how to transform darkness, fear, suffering, and death – the shit of our lives – into fertilizer to nurture the blossoming process. I am writing this book now to help me remember. It is too important to forget. It is my life.' (C)

Food of the Gods: The Search for the Original Tree of Knowledge, by Terence McKenna (New York: Bantam; London: Rider, 1992)
'McKenna reviews the history of drugs in the East and West...He ends with a master plan for resolving contemporary drug problems, examining why the pursuit of happiness is illegal if it involves plants found in nature and addressing the continuing furore over legalising.'

Forest of Visions, by Alex Polari De Alverga (Rochester, VT: Inner Traditions, 1999)
'Ayahuasca, Amazon Spirituality, and the Santo Daime. New book about the Santo Daime Brazilian ayahuasca church.' (MB)

Forgotten Truth, by Huston Smith (New York:

8

Harper Collins, 1992)
'The Common Vision of the World's Religions. Good introduction to metaphysics: levels of reality, levels of selfhood, limits of science, by a noted author. The real gem is the appendix, The Psychedelic Evidence, where Smith uses work by Stan Grof and Otto Rank to show how psychedelic experiences illuminate spiritual realities. Excellent synthesis of psychedelics with religious values.' (MB)

From Chocolate to Morphine, by Andrew Weil and Winfred Rosen (New York: Houghton Mifflin, 1993)
'Everything You Need To Know About Mind-Altering Drugs. Comprehensive, accurate, practical information about using mind drugs. Includes history, uses, problems, and alternatives for drugs in general, and specific chapters on stimulants, depressants, psychedelics, marijuana, and other drugs (PCP, ketamine, nightshades, etc.) Describes drugs in each class, gives benefits, risks, suggestions, and precautions. Glossary and index. Highly recommended.' (MB)

From Religious Experience to a Religious Attitude, ed. A. Godin (Chicago: Loyola University Press, 1965)
'With considerable consistency subjects of experiments report that the drugs do not seem so much to produce such experiences as to uncover or release them. People, on recovering from the effects of the drugs are not so apt, as with alcohol, to say, "I was not myself!" as to declare, "I was never so completely myself!" If this is the case, then it is of considerable significance that so often the drugs mediate either genuine mystical experience in many people, or something so very similar that the two cannot be distinguished.' (C)

Ganja in Jamaica: The Effects of Marijuana Use, by Vera Rubin and Lambros Comitas (Garden City, NY: Anchor, 1976)
'Dragons in dark caves, Justice Oliver Wendell Holmes once reminded us, are far more fearsome than when they are seen in daylight. How refreshing it is, therefore, to have available an objective study which not only exposes but also demolishes many emotional and "fright-symbolic" dragons which have clouded our perspective in recent years with reference to cannabis.' (C)

Gateway to Inner Space: A Festschrift in Honor of Albert Hofmann, ed. Christian Ratsch (Bridport, Dorset: Prism Press, 1989)
'For thousands of years, psychedelic drugs have been used during sacred rituals in almost every ancient culture throughout the world.

Ethnopharmacological research has shown that the aim was to attain direct spiritual experience, during which the individual made contact with higher worlds in order to gain knowledge and wisdom for his further life. In Western industrialized societies, where spiritual experiences are no longer an immediate aspect of our culture, it is hard for us to understand the unity of this continuum of experience.' (C)

The Good Death: The New American Search to Reshape the End of Life, by Marilyn Webb (New York: Bantam, 1997)
'For many, the first glimpses of the transcendent power of dreams or controlled images arose with psychedelic drugs. And so, many therapists and physicians are now beginning to consider using these drugs as a means for helping patients prepare for death.' (C)

Grist for the Mill, by Ram Dass and Stephen Levine (collaborator). (Santa Cruz, CA: Unity Press, 1977)
'After you know of the possibility you get on with it and any time you're just after another experience you're just getting more hooked on experiences and experiences are all traps. The game is to use a method and then when you're finished with it let it go.' (C)

Hallucinogenic Plants of North America, by Jonathan Ott (Berkeley, CA: Wingbow Press, 1976)
'Curiously, we have come full circle. Although the great Western religions had effectively eliminated the use of hallucinogenic drugs, by making these drugs "tabu" and persecuting users, and although this prohibition of these substances has been enforced for centuries, the advent of the modern chemical age has radically changed this situation. Drugs and drug use have seemingly become the dominant "religion," and the modern preoccupation with pharmacological agents has led to a resurgence in interest in old "tabu" substances.' (C)

Hallucinogens: Cross-Cultural Perspectives, by Marlene Dobkin de Rios (Bridport, Dorset: Prism Press, 1990)
'It is my firm conviction, based on more than fifteen years of specialized study of hallucinogens and culture, that these substances have played more than a minor role in structuring the lives, beliefs, hopes, and values of large numbers of people. Members of preindustrial societies in many cultures with varying epistemological perspectives have always incorporated mind-altering plants into facets of daily activity. The economic behavior, the social organization, and the belief systems of

some societies, for example, have been affected by the use of mind-altering plants.' (C)

Hallucinogens and Culture, by Peter Furst (Chandler & Sharp, 1976)
'Broad overview, by plant, for many cultures, of hallucinogen use. Includes tobacco, Cannabis, ibogaine, ayahuasca, lysergic acids, psilocybin and muscimole mushrooms, Peyote, Datura, the Virola snuffs, toads, and other flora and fauna, all presented in their cultural context. Good introduction to the field; recommended. References and index.' (MB)

Hallucinogens and Shamanism, ed. Michael J. Harner (Oxford: Oxford University Press, 1973)
'Unlike most earlier anthropological reports on shamanism, these essays go beyond objective observation. Most of the authors have succeeded in penetrating the primitive mystical experience by taking the psychotropic catalyst and participating in the native ceremonies.' (C)

Heaven and Hell, by Aldous Huxley (New York: Harper & Row, 1956)
'Today we know how to lower the efficiency of the cerebral reducing valve by direct chemical action, and without the risk of inflicting serious damage on the psychophysical organism...Knowing as he does what are the chemical conditions of transcendental experience, the aspiring mystic should turn for technical help to the specialists – in pharmacology, in biochemistry, in physiology and neurology. And on their part, of course, the specialists (if any of them aspire to be genuine men of science and complete human beings) should turn, out of their respective pigeonholes, to the artist, the sibyl, the visionary, the mystic – all those, in a word who have had experience of the Other World and who know...what to do with the experience.' (C)

High Culture: Marijuana in the Lives of Americans, by William Novak (New York: Knopf, 1980)
'Does Marijuana affect the values of the people who smoke it? For some users, at least, the answer is yes, although this group appears to be in the minority. On the one hand, many smokers have found marijuana the perfect companion to a greater pursuit of pleasure, sensuality, and physical comfort. At the same time, an equally large group, which includes some people from the first group, sees marijuana as the appropriate vehicle for an exploration of spirituality.' (C)

High Priest, by Timothy Leary (Ronin Publishing, 1968)
'Original account of the psychedelic research

and life at Harvard, from 1960 to 1962. Each chapter contains part of the storyline, plus an I Ching hexagram, a guide (R. Gordon Wasson, Allen Ginsberg, William Burroughs, Michael Hollingshead, others), and running marginalia. Much on psychedelics and the religious experience.' (MB)

How to Get High, by Dawn Human (1988) reprint may be forthcoming
'The Use of Drugs as a Spiritual Path. Use of LSD and marijuana as a connection to the Goddess, as well as for self-exploration and relating to the natural world. Includes meditations and exercises. Personal story of the use of entheogens as a spiritual path.' (MB)

The Ibogaine Story, by Paul DiRienzo and Dana Beal (1997)
'Report on the Staten Island Project. Several themes weave through this narrative, about the use of ibogaine for treatment of heroin, cocaine, alcohol, and other addictions, and the politics involved. Cultural history of addictive drug use and Iboga use. Technical speculation on receptor mechanisms of ibogaine and beta carbolines.' (MB)

The Invisible Landscape: Mind, Hallucinogens, and the I Ching, by Terence McKenna and Dennis McKenna (San Francisco: HarperCollins, 1993)
'We believed that the widespread use of psychedelic drugs in modern society was somehow rooted to the intuition that exploration and reassimilation of so-called magical dimensions was the next valid step in humanity's collective search for liberation...It is our contention...that the presence of psychoactive substances is a primary requirement of all true shamanism, and that where such substances are not exogenously available as plants, they must be endogenously available either through metabolic predisposition to their synthesis, as may occur in schizophrenia, or through the various techniques of shamanism: dancing, drumming, singing, and the confrontation of situations of stress and isolation. Where these alkaloids are not present, shamanism becomes ritual alone, and its effectiveness suffers accordingly.' (C)

Journey to Ixtlan, by Carlos Castaneda (Harmondsworth: Penguin, 1973
Third book in the Castaneda series.
Kidnapped in the Amazon Jungle, by Bruce Lamb & Manuel Cordova-Rios (North Atlantic Press (PGW), 1994)
'Most recent version of story of abduction and initiation into the Huni Kui tribe. Fascinating tale, less ethnobotany. Good for younger readers. No index.' (MB)

8

The Long Trip: The Prehistory of Psychedelia, by Paul Devereux (New York: Penguin, 1997)
'One aim of this book is to demonstrate (rather than to merely state) that our modern culture stands out in the long record of human history because of its difficulty in accepting in an orderly and integrated way the role natural substances, primarily from the plant kingdom, have played in aiding mind expansion.' (C)

LSD, Man & Society, ed. Richard C. DeBold and Russell C. Leaf (Middletown, CT: Wesleyan University Press, 1967)
'In the meantime there is an increasing need for organized religion to consider the impact of the psychedelic religious movement. The churches could help people to integrate such profound experiences with the aid of meaningful and appropriate religious symbols. Such people do tend to talk about their drug experiences in religious terms. In our experimental work with divinity students and ministers, those who had a meaningful religious framework were much helped in using positive psychedelic experiences to understand their faith more existentially.' (C)

LSD – My Problem Child: Reflections on Sacred Drugs, Mysticism, and Science, by Albert Hofmann (Los Angeles: J.P. Tarcher, 1983)

The Magical and Ritual Use of Herbs, by Richard Allan Miller (Rochester, VT: Destiny Books (Inner Traditions), 1983)
'Sections on Psilocybe mushrooms, morning glory, fly agaric, other hallucinogens. Background, effects, and ritual uses for each. Drawings, three indices, bibliography.' (MB)

The Man Who Turned on the World, by Michael Hollingshead (London: Blond & Briggs, 1973)
'And how do I think of LSD et al.? – as certain truths about the nature of my inner self came to be manifest in my conscious mind, my interest in psychedelics began to wane proportionately, so that today I do not believe that LSD can help me towards self-realisation. It had never been more than preliminary, one may say, a pretext for me to explore inwardness and unfamiliar mental states for whatever they might reveal. But LSD has nothing more to give me...In relation to any religious beliefs I now hold, I am a confessed Franciscan, though I freely admit that I have a very long way to go before I shall be able to express this outwardly – with my entire being – the love Saint Francis of Assisi showed was for all living creatures, and in respect to love of this kind, I must to this extent be regarded as clumsy...I know that many readers, and by no means the worst

among them, would disapprove of such measures as taking LSD; one should be strong enough, they say, to exist by faith without the aid of drugs. Yes! One should be, but what if one is too weak?' (C)

Maria Sabina: Her Life and Chants, by Alvaro Estrada (Santa Barbara, CA: Ross-Erikson, 1981)
'At the time of my first velada with Maria Sabina, in 1955, I had to make a choice: suppress my experience or resolve to present it worthily to the world. There was never a doubt in my mind. The sacred mushrooms and the religious feeling concentrated in them through the Sierras of Southern Mexico had to be made known to the world, and worthily so, at whatever cost to me personally (G. Wasson).' (C)

Meditation: An Outline for Practical Study, by Mouni Sadhu (Hollywood, CA: Melvin Powers Wilshire *c.* 1967)
'Another twenty minutes elapsed and I felt nothing except more nausea. "Probably this test is also a flop," I said to my friends. "I think I had better take the brandy and finish the business"...Next moment I was as if beyond the room and beyond my own personality. Fully conscious and with eyes closed, I was aware of my body as if from a great distance, while it sat quietly on the divan, but I was in no way connected with it. An overwhelming feeling of happiness, no, much more, of a great bliss embraced all my being...Aloofness, blissful freedom and absolute harmony, this is an infinitesimal part of my present state, which I can describe in words. It is similar to my first experience of spiritual consciousness, experienced in the summer of 1949, at the feet of an Indian Rishi-Ramana. Later, the same state was induced many times by deep meditation, based on complete concentration of the mind, by excluding every thought, but it always required stillness of the body, separation from all the senses and the impossibility of speaking, hearing, or moving.' (C)

Mindscapes, ed. Antonio Melechi (Mono, 1998)
'An Anthology of Drug Writings. Older but interesting essays by famous people. One section on ayahuasca, peyote, and psilocybin, with writings by Artaud, Burroughs, Wasson, Harner, Castaneda, and Terence McKenna. Another on mescaline and LSD features Huxley, Michaux, Nin, Leary, and others. Also has sections on nitrous oxide and hashish. Altered state experiences are hard to describe; these articulate writers help us understand them.' (MB)

The Mythmakers, by Mary Barnard (Athens, OH: Ohio University Press, 1966)
'When we consider the origin of the mythologies and cults related to drug plants, we should surely ask ourselves which, after all, was more likely to happen first: the spontaneously generated idea of an afterlife in which the disembodied soul, liberated from the restrictions of time and space, experienced eternal bliss, or the accidental discovery of hallucinogenic plants that give a sense of euphoria, dislocate the center of consciousness, and distort time and space, making them balloon outward in greatly expanded vistas?...Perhaps the old theories are right, but we have to remember that the drug plants were there, waiting to give men a new idea based on a new experience. The experience might have had, I should think, an almost explosive effect on the largely dormant minds of men, causing them to think of things they had never thought before. This, if you like, is direct revelation.' (C)

The Natural Mind: A New Way of Looking at Drugs and the Higher Consciousness, by Andrew Weil (Boston: Houghton Mifflin, 1972)
'Now it is interesting that people who begin to move in a spiritual direction in connection with drug experimentation sooner or later look for other methods of maintaining their experiences. One sees many long-time drug users give up drugs for meditation, for example, but one does not see any long-time meditators give up meditation to become acid heads. This observation supports the contention that the highs obtainable by means of meditation are better than the highs obtainable through drugs – a contention phrased not in moral terms but simply in practical ones.' (C)

The Nature of Shamanism, by Michael Ripinsky-Naxon (1993)
'Best on beliefs and world-views of native shamans. Much on their mind-states and hallucinogens. How symbols, metaphor, and language define and describe alterations of consciousness. Psychotropic Universe, Ritual Drug Complex, Botanic Experience. Good references and bibliography.' (MB)

The New Religions, by Jacob Needleman (Garden City, NY: Doubleday, 1970)
'it is already clear why the taking of drugs forms no part of the practice at Zen Center. To take drugs is to crave a certain experience. And to crave a certain experience is to deny, now and here, the Buddha nature of oneself. In Zen this is called deluded thinking...almost all of the American students I interviewed spoke with respect of drugs such as LSD. Some said that

without the drug experience they would never have been opened up to the possibilities in themselves which are being realized in their Zen practice...Perhaps the search for an inner life, whether with drugs or without them, is totally misguided without the simultaneous search for a more complete outer life.' (C)

On Being Stoned: A Study of Marijuana Intoxication, by Charles T. Tart (Palo Alto, CA: Science and Behavior Books, 1971)
'For some users, important spiritual experiences have taken place while they were intoxicated with marijuana, or as a result of marijuana use. Some of these have been spontaneous, others deliberately sought through meditation, which many users feel is enhanced by intoxication. Because of these experiences, the use of marijuana has acquired a religious significance to some users' (C)

One Foot in the Future: A Woman's Spiritual Journey, by Nina Graboi (Santa Cruz, CA: Aerial Press: 1991)
'Inevitably, this [Pahnke's] study evoked my interest. Once more I saw to what extent my mind would go to block me from looking at what was unfamiliar. I realized that there was more to these drugs than the sensation-thirsty media let us know. And with all my being, I longed to experience what the divinity students had experienced.' (C)

One Nation Under God: The Triumph of the Native American Church, ed. and compiled by Huston Smith and Reuben Snake (Santa Fe, NM: Clear Light Publishers, 1996)
'That fear escalated in the early 1990s, as a result of the Supreme Court's explicit ruling (on April 17, 1990, in Employment Division of Oregon v. Smith) that the Bill of Rights – specifically the "free exercise of religion" clause in the First Amendment to the United States Constitution – does not extend to the Native American Church because of its sacramental use of Peyote. This book is the story of the Native Americans' response to – and victory over – that ruling. The judicial branch of the United States having deserted them, they resorted to its legislative branch. Without a nickel in their coffers, they challenged the highest court of the land on the Peyote issue and won, reversing (by four years of determined effort) four centuries of prejudice against their sacrament. It is a story that deserves to be documented, remembered, and retold for generations, for it carries hope for freedom lovers the world over.' (C)

8

The One Quest, by Claudio Naranjo (New York: Viking Press, 1972)
'The use of psychedelic substances provides another way of affecting one's experience of the self. Early in the experimentation with these substances, the users described the occurrence of death-rebirth experiences resembling those in mystic literature, and the term egoless has become standard in the description of reactions to LSD. It would seem that different drugs may temporarily suppress one or more aspects of the controlling and censoring mechanisms to which our ordinary sense of identity is linked, so that the person may experience his reality beyond the ordinary self-concept. Interestingly, the resulting experience of the self "when the doors of perception are cleansed" easily leads to the experience of oneness with other beings or forms of life, and this in turn to the mystical realm.' (C)

One River: Explorations and Discoveries in the Amazon Rain Forest, by Wade Davis (New York: Simon & Schuster, 1996)
'Once I tried to explain heaven to a young woman, she said, smiling, as she poured Schultes a cup of tea. I said it was a beautiful place, a place where there are no tears. She asked whether I had been there. I said no. I explained that only the dead know heaven. Then she looked at me with the saddest face. She said she was so sorry for me. And she left almost in tears. How strange, Schultes said. It was only later that I realized that most Mazatec actually claim to have been to heaven. With the mushrooms? Yes...When I first came here I complained about the use of mushrooms to an old man. Do you know what he told me? No, Schultes smiled. He said, "But what else could I do? I needed to know God's will, and I don't know how to read." They both laughed.' (C)

Open Mind, Discriminating Mind: Reflections on Human Possibilities, by Charles T. Tart (San Francisco: Harper & Row, 1989)
'This book looks at waking and dreams, living in clarity and living in illusion, firewalking, delusions about the psychic, mystical experiences, psychic healing, dream yoga, defenses against reality, bodily intelligence, prayer, altered states of consciousness, and many other "strange" and yet familiar experiences. When you disagree and react strongly I encourage you to open your mind to understanding why you disagree. You may still disagree with me but you will have learned more about yourself. When you agree completely I encourage you to open and examine your mind even more strongly. The beliefs we do not examine can be far more dangerous to us than the ones we reject.' (C)

Our Right to Drugs: the Case for a Free Market, by Thomas Szasz (New York: Syracuse University Press, 1996)

Outlawing the Shaman, by Richard Glen Boire (Spectral Mindustries, forthcoming)
'How the West has dealt with religious users of mind-altering substances. By noted expert in psychedelic law.' (MB)

'Pahnke's "Good Friday Experiment": A Long-term Follow-up and Methodological Critique', by Rick Doblin, *Journal of Transpersonal Psychology*, 23, 1, (1985): 1–28)
'In the long-term follow-up even more than in the six-month follow-up, the experimental group has higher scores than the control group in every category.' 'A relatively high degree of persisting positive changes were reported by the experimental group while virtually no persisting positive changes were reported by the control group.' 'All psilocybin subjects participating in the long-term follow-up, but none of the controls, still considered their original experience to have had genuinely mystical elements and to have made a uniquely valuable contribution to their spiritual lives.' 'Pahnke failed to report the administration of the tranquilizer thorazine to one of the subjects who received psilocybin...[and] underemphasized the difficult psychological struggles experienced by most of the psilocybin subjects.' (C)

People of the Peyote, ed. Stacy Schaefer and Peter Furst (Albuquerque: University of New Mexico Press, 1996)
'Huichol Indian History, Religion, and Survival. Extensive, excellent, many faceted study of Huichol Indian development, culture, art, spirit, mythology, and other topics. These eighteen papers from around the world, both scholarly and sensitive, include material from decades of anthropology and directly from Huichols. Schaefer relates the meaning of peyote to Huichols, and describes their temple and its solar geometry. Also Huichol medicine, minority use of a Solanaceae plant, deer–maize–peyote trinity, wolf power, land of the dead, and current political and ecological challenges. Glossary, bibliography, index. Recommended.' (MB)

Persephone's Quest: Entheogens and the Origins of Religion, by Stella Kramrisch, Jonathan Ott and R. Gordon Wasson (New Haven, CT: Yale University Press, 1986)
'I hold that the fruit of the Tree of the Knowledge of Good and Evil was Soma, was the kakulja, was *Amanita muscaria*, was the Nameless Mushroom of the English-speaking

people. The Tree was probably a conifer in Mesopotamia. The serpent, being underground, was the faithful attendant on the fruit.' (C)

The Peyote Book: A Study of Native Medicine, ed. Guy Mount (Cottonwood, CA: Sweetlight Books, 1993)
The Peyote Book is an ongoing, ever-growing publication. Readers are invited to submit stories, personal testimonials, research and illustrations for future editions.
'The largest difference I can see between Indian religion and Christian religion is in interpersonal relationships. Indian religion taught that sharing of one's goods with another human being was the highest form of behavior. I sing my Jewish songs in the tipi, and I wear my father's prayer shawl, the one he wore at his bar mitzvah in Germany. My Indian friends say that it does not matter in what language you sing; there are always at least two people who understand – you and the Creator.' (C)

The Peyote Cult, by Weston La Barre (Norman, OK: University of Oklahoma Press, 1989)
'This is the classical study of the background of the Mexican and American Indian ritual based on the plant that produces profound but temporary sensory and psychic derangements.' (C)

The Peyote Dance, by Antonin Artaud (New York: Farrar, Straus and Giroux, 1976)
'Artaud's experience with the Tarahumara Indians in 1936 was a psychic ordeal and a spiritual revelation. This mosaic work, written over a period of twelve years and spanning Artaud's stay at the Hôpital Psychiatrique in Rodez, documents Artaud's struggle to integrate an overwhelming mystical experience into his own religious and mental being.' (C)

Pharmacotheon: Entheogenic Drugs, Their Plant Sources and History, by Jonathan Ott (Kennewick, WA: Natural Products Co., 1993)
'This book is about those wondrous entheogens, these strange plant sacraments and their contained active principles. The neologism derives from an obsolete Greek word meaning "realizing the divine within," the term used by the ancient Greeks to describe states of poetic and prophetic inspiration, to describe the entheogenic state which can be induced by sacred plant-drugs.'(C)

PIHKAL: A Chemical Love Story, by Alexander Shulgin and Ann Shulgin (Berkeley: Transform Press, 1991)
'There has never been a book like PiHKAL,

and...we may not soon see another of its kind. No library of psychedelic literature will henceforth be complete without it. Some day in the future, when it may again be acceptable to use chemical tools to study the mind, this book will be a treasure-house, a sort of sorcerer's book of spells, to delight and enchant the psychiatrist/shaman of tomorrow.' (Dr David Nichols, Purdue University, Foreword of *PiHKAL*).

Plants of the Gods: Their Sacred, Healing and Hallucinogenic Powers, by Richard Evans Schultes and Albert Hofmann (Rochester, VT: Healing Arts Press, 1992)
'A few plants, however, had inexplicable effects that transported the human mind to realms of ethereal wonder. These plants are the hallucinogens. Plants that alter the normal functions of the mind and body have always been considered by peoples in nonindustrial societies as sacred, and the hallucinogens have been "plants of the gods" par excellence.' (C)

Plants, People, and Culture, by Michael J. Balick and Paul Alan Cox (New York: Scientific American/W.H. Freeman, 1996)
'Overview of people and plants, then sections on healing, eating, building, and visionary plants, ends on conservation. "Entering the Other World" explains ebena snuff preparation; ayahuasca botany and biochemistry; communal kava experience; Cannabis in world history; coca; opium; and peyote use in the Native American Church. Good photos and graphics, suggested reading, index. Excellent introduction.' (MB)

Psychedelia Britannica: Hallucinogenic Drugs in Britain, ed. Antonio Melechi (London: Turnaround, 1997)
'At every stage of history humankind has had a burning desire to achieve wholeness. Formerly this was to be reached by moral and religious means. In our age, more than ever before, humankind wishes "the end of desire" through wealth, power, knowledge and sometimes religion. If we transcribe religion into spiritual knowledge, then the rise of many cultural trends, alternative religions, and the street use of cannabis and LSD, are common ways of attempting to find wholeness in western society.' (C)

Psychedelic Art, by R.E.L. Masters and Jean Houston (New York: Grove Press, 1968)
'Surrealism was exclusive; psychedelic art is inclusive; it does not withdraw from the external world but rather affirms the value of inwardness as complementary awareness. The aim of psychedelic experience is to expand the

consciousness so that it can be a consciousness of more. Unlike surrealism, psychedelic art makes a basic tenet of spiritual harmony with the universe...Much psychedelic art is presently limited by some degree of adherence to these pseudo-theologies and neo-primitive concepts. There is no reason why it must remain so. When circumstances are more favorable, a profoundly spiritual art should be able to emerge.' (C)

Psychedelic Drugs Reconsidered, by Lester Grinspoon and James B. Bakalar (New York: Basic Books, 1981)
'It should not be necessary to supply any more proof that psychedelic drugs produce experiences that those who undergo them regard as religious in the fullest sense. We could introduce quotations from mystics and other religious figures in the same way that we have used the words of poets and psychotics. Every kind of typically religious emotion, symbol, and insight appears during psychedelic drug trips...All we can say is that the testimony of those who have undergone psychedelic religious experiences suggests that the drug-induced kind is not obviously different or inferior in its immediate quality.' (C)

The Psychedelic Experience: A Manual Based on the Tibetan Book of the Dead, by Timothy Leary, Ralph Metzner and Richard Alpert (Secaucus, NJ: The Citadel Press, 1983)
'The drug is only one component of a psychedelic session. Equally important is the mental and spiritual preparation, both before and in the course of taking the drug. This manual uses material from *The Tibetan Book of the Dead* for this preparation. The authors show that it is concerned not with the dead, but with the living. The last section of the manual provides instructions for an actual psychedelic session, under adequate safeguards.' (C)

Psychedelic Prayers and Other Meditations, by Timothy Leary (Ronin Publishing, 1996). First published in 1966.
'Poems/prayers by Leary, based on the Tao Te Ching, to read before, during, and after psychedelic sessions. Helps invoke pure energy flow, cellular consciousness, and external and internal sensations. New edition has nice graphics and notes by Ralph Metzner and Michael Horowitz.' (MB)

Psychedelic Reflections, ed. Lester Grinspoon and James B. Bakalar (New York: Human Sciences Press: 1983)
'For all five of the subjects mentioned here, and many of their students, psychedelic experience

produced a new interest in depth psychology, religion, spirituality, and consciousness, as well as related disciplines and practices such as meditation...In particular, the esoteric core of the great religions and spiritual traditions could be seen as roadmaps to higher states of consciousness, and some of the most profound material in these traditions became especially clear and meaningful during psychedelic sessions.' (C)

The Psychedelic Resurgence: Treatment, Support and Recovery Options, by Richard Seymour and David E. Smith (Hazelden, MN: 1993)

Psychedelic Shamanism: The Cultivation, Preparation and Shamanic Use of Psychotropic Plants, by Jim DeKorne (Port Townsend, WA: Loompanics Unlimited, 1994)
'I am today a psychologically and spiritually enriched person because of psychedelic drug-experiences I had decades ago, yet I'd be the last person to proselytize the use of such materials as a path for everyone. These substances are powerful catalysts for personal insight, yet when absorbed into the metabolism of those who are not ready for them, they have proven to be both individually and socially disruptive. Of course, this is not a characteristic of the drugs, but of the consciousnesses of those who ingest them, and our reactionary laws against psychedelics may be seen as an index of how far we have to go as a culture to attain even minimum levels of psychological sophistication in these matters.' (C)

'Psychedelics & The Path' (topical issue) of *Gnosis: A Journal of the Western Inner Traditions*, 26 (Winter 1993)
'Do psychedelics have a legitimate place on the spiritual path?...we've drawn together a kaleidoscope of perspectives in this special issue' (C) .

'Psychedelics Revisited' (topical issue) of *ReVision: The Journal of Consciousness and Change*, 10, 4 (Spring, 1988)
'Readers of this journal need little introduction to the significance of psychedelic substances for the exploration of consciousness that has occurred in the Western world in the 20th century.' (C)

Psychedelics: The Uses and Implications of Hallucinogenic Drugs, ed. Bernard Aaronson and Humphry Osmond (London: Hogarth Press, 1971)
'Movement within reaches the level of archetype and myth and may transcend these to a

point of ultimate mystical union...[Archetypes] may derive from fundamental perceptions of our own structures and modes of functioning...this manner of thinking and perceiving, the concentration on archetype, the sense of an indwelling, immanent God, and the interest in meditation have correspondingly created an interest in those forms of religion that stress these notions: Hinduism, and Tibetan and Zen Buddhism.'

The Psychology of Religion: An Empirical Approach, by Bernard Spilka, Ralph W. Hood Jr. and Richard L. Gorsuch. (Englewood Cliffs, NJ: Prentice-Hall, 1985)
'It has long been recognized that religious traditions have employed various naturally occurring and synthetic substances in their religious rituals. However, until recently it was rather arrogantly assumed that such concerns were more the domain of the anthropologist dealing with less "advanced" religious traditions...The literature on psychedelic drugs is immense, easily running into many thousands of studies. Curiously, very few studies have been conducted using religious variables or directly assessing the religious importance of drug-induced experiences...Yet if physiological arousal can lead to evaluation in religious terms, clearly any physiological arousal is of potential religious importance.' (C)

Realms of the Human Unconscious: Observations from LSD Research, by Stanislav Grof (London: Souvenir Press (Educational and Academic), 1993)
'When the list of the Great Books is updated, I nominate *Realms* for introducing the LSD method of exploring the human mind and for the resulting map.
'...the material from serial LSD sessions even in its present form is of crucial theoretical significance and represents a serious challenge to the existing concepts of contemporary science. I have attempted to outline the cartography of the human unconscious as it has been manifested in LSD sessions of my patients and subjects. I have been quite encouraged by the fact that in various areas of human culture there are numerous indications that the maps of consciousness emerging from my LSD work are fully compatible and sometimes parallel with other existing systems. Examples of this can be found in C.G. Jung's analytical psychology, Roberto Assagioli's psychosynthesis, and Abraham Maslow's studies of peak experiences, as well as religious and mystical schools of various cultures and ages.This parallel between the LSD experiences and a variety of phenomena manifested without chemical facilitation provides additional supportive evidence for the unspecific and catalyzing effect of LSD.' (C)

Recovery of the Sacred, by Carlos Warter (Florida: Health Communications, 1994)
'Personal spiritual adventure of a doctor, passing through many lands and traditions, including plant shamanism; Sufi, Christian, Jewish, and Islamic mysticism; Buddhism; and others. Claudio Naranjo and Don Hector teach him about magic plants.' (MB)

Religion, Altered States of Consciousness, and Social Change, ed. Erika Bourguignon (Columbus: Ohio University Press, 1973)
'In studying institutionalized altered states of consciousness, for the most part in traditional societies and in a sacred context, are we dealing with a rare and exotic phenomenon of interest only to specialists, a bit of anthropological esoterica? Or are we dealing with a major aspect of human behavior that has significant impact on the functioning of human societies?' (C)

Religion and the Individual: a Social-Psychological Perspective, by C. Daniel Batson, Patricia Schoenrade and W. Larry Ventis (New York: Oxford University Press, 1993)
'We have considered four possible facilitators of religious experience: psychedelic drugs, meditation, religious language, and music. We suggested that although none has the power to produce religious experience, each has the power to facilitate it.' (C)

Religion and the State: Essays in Honor of Leo Pfeffer, ed. James E. Wood Jr. (Waco, TX: Baylor University Press, 1985)
'When the state forbids the use of a substance like marijuana, should any class of potential users be afforded an exemption?...When one asks how any such an exemption would be administered, one realizes that any attempted application of some amorphous standard to individual cases would work serious injustice and would quickly undermine the efficacy of the general prohibition...Any feasible exemption would need to be cast in terms of specialized use. One such use is medical. Another specialized use is in the context of religious services. An exemption that reaches persons who use drugs in corporate religious services, but does not cover either nonreligious group use or individual religious use, can be defended.' (C)

Religious Behavior, by Michael Argyle (London: Routledge & Kegan Paul, 1968)
'The question may be asked – why do these particular physiological states tend to be experienced as "religious"? Why do other drugs like alcohol not produce religious experiences? Perhaps it is only a narrow range of physiological states which come to be defined and interpreted as religious.' (C)

8

Religious Belief and Philosophical Thought: Readings in the Philosophy of Religion, ed. William P. Alston (New York: Harcourt, Brace & World, 1963)

'...there have been many religious men who have believed that they were able to discover that God exists in a more direct fashion, by experiencing His presence in as direct a way as that in which one experiences the presence of trees, buildings, and other human beings. Are experiences of this sort, always or sometimes, really direct apprehensions of an objectively existing personal deity, or are they purely subjective states of feeling which have no reference to anything beyond the subject?' (C)

Religious Ecstasy: Based on Papers Read at the Symposium on Religious Ecstasy Held at Abo, Finland, on the 26th–28th of August 1981, ed. Nils G. Holm (Stockholm: Almqvist & Wiksell International, 1982)

'Mystical experiences are perhaps best described as occurrences through which an individual, in an intensive and unusual way, is afforded new knowledge of the innermost essence of the universe. Not infrequently the experience implies some sort of absorption into the great universal whole. In the case of ecstasy however, interest is more concentrated on certain mental changes without any assumptions being made about the constituent qualities of the experience itself.' (C)

Religious Experience, by Wayne Proudfoot (Berkeley: University of California Press, 1985)

'Given the results of Schachter's experiments, it seems quite plausible that at least some religious experiences are due to physiological changes for which the subject adopts a religious explanation...' (C)

Religious Experience: Its Nature and Function in the Human Psyche, by Walter Houston Clark, H. Newton Malony and Alan R. Tippett (Springfield, IL: Charles C. Thomas, 1973)

'The thrust of Doctor Clark's position is that man has the capacity for religious experience within himself. The book shows that properly directed, profound religious experiences are potent sources of personality change...This is a theory long neglected by psychologists and too often by the churches. The most controversial aspect of the lectures is Doctor Clark's affirmation of the value of induced religious experience through the use of drugs.' (C)

The Religious Experience: A Social-Psychological Perspective, by C. Daniel Batson and W. Larry Ventis (New York: Oxford University Press, 1982)

'What, then, does our review of the available research suggest about the effect of psychedelic drugs on religious experience? Although the research is not conclusive, we believe it suggests that psychedelic drugs can and do facilitate religious experience.' (C)

Religious Movements in Contemporary America, ed. Irving Zaretsky and Mark P. Leone (Princeton, NJ: Princeton University Press, 1974)

'My mind was a field in autumn. Naked branches were studded with black cocoons. Suddenly, one cocoon split and a butterfly with poppy-scarlet wings emerged, then another cocoon split and another, first here, then there, then everywhere, and all space was filled with the fluttering scarlet wings. (Image After Psilocybin)...let us now try to tie down a little more firmly the particular religious movement we are here trying to describe and interpret. Let us, for a start, give the movement a name: Neotranscendentalism. It includes the ever increasing number of people who (1) reject traditional Western acquisitive and economic values, (2) are concerned with the mystical, (3) wish to develop more direct, less role-oriented interpersonal relationships, and (4) are interested in communal and cooperative styles of living rather than isolationist, competitive patterns.' (C)

The Religious Situation: 1968, ed. Donald R. Cutler (Boston: Beacon Press, 1968)

'There is, on the other hand, the "pelagian" prejudice that spiritual achievement is proportionate to personal effort. Those who share this prejudice cannot conceive of the possibility that the Creator may have graced his creation with drugs which, discovered in due time, might be instrumental in preparing people to understand the gentleness, brotherhood, and peace of the gospels. Spiritual achievement is not won only through will and effort; often, it is a grace. Drugs humble the spiritual pretensions of men, effecting through the psychoneural organism what conscious effort does not bring about...Escape rituals are important social safety-valves: when traditional escape rituals have died out or been suppressed, safety-valve rituals spring up to take their place, sometimes ludicrously orgiastic like Beatlemania, sometimes socially anti-adaptive like teenage gang rivalry: one of the tasks of present-day industrialized societies is to provide adequate escape rituals for their members.' (C)

Restless Is the Heart: A Perspective on Love and Violence and Their Relationship, Robert Kimball (Bristol, IN: Wyndam Hall, 1988)

The author is Professor of Theological Ethics and Dean of the Thomas Starr King School for the Ministry, Berkeley, California, and a member of the doctoral faculty of The Graduate Theological Union. 'I had an interesting day back in 1964, when Sam, Bill and I took advantage of an offer by a psychiatrist friend to take some carefully produced and measured Swiss LSD. It was my one experience with this powerful drug...The back and forth rhythm both continued and built, and suddenly a knowing-feeling happened, the rhythm stopped, there was a oneness of all. Different as both ends of the pendulum rhythm were, all of a moment, they were one and the same. There was no distinction of East or West, thinking or feeling, laughter or anger.' (C)

Rio Tigre and Beyond, by Bruce Lamb (Berkley: North Atlantic Press, 1985)
'Second in the Lamb series, most useful ethnobotany, continues Cordova-Rios story after he leaves Huni Kui and becomes a curandero. Describes ayahuasca and other healing methods, and Materia Medica appendix lists 81 Amazon plants, their uses, and tentative botanical identification. Good index.' (MB)

The Road to Eleusis: Unveiling the Secret of the Mysteries, by R. Gordon Wasson, Carl A.P. Ruck and Albert Hofmann (twentieth anniversary edition, William Dailey Rare Books, 1998)
'In July 1975 I was visiting my friend Gordon Wasson in his home in Danbury when he suddenly asked me this question: whether Early Man in ancient Greece could have hit on a method to isolate an hallucinogen from ergot that would have given him an experience comparable to LSD or psilocybin. [Albert Hofmann] In conclusion I now answer Wasson's question. The answer is yes, Early Man in ancient Greece could have arrived at an hallucinogen from ergot.' (C)

Rolling Thunder, by Doug Boyd (New York: Dell, 1974)
'Rolling Thunder, the subject of this book, is a keeper of tribal secrets – a modern medicine man. Boyd's book is an account by a contemporary white man of the inner experience of American Indians...Rolling Thunder, like Swami Rama and perhaps all "medicine people," gives priority to the capacity to control the attention, to maintain "one-pointedness of mind." There can be no healing, no meditation, no meaningful spiritual experience without that highest of disciplines – particularly if drugs are to be used and not dangerously distracting or defeating.' (C)

Sacred Leaves of Candomblé: African Magic, Medicine, and Religion in Brazil, by Robert A. Voeks (Austin: University of Texas Press, 1997)
'Originally expecting to document the origin and use of a few African plants in Brazil, I discovered in short order that the story of the Candomblé flora not only was rich and complex, but was in many respects a metaphor for the African–American diaspora. Neither can be comprehended without understanding the subtle interplay between history, geography, culture, and political economy.' (C)

Sacred Mirrors: The Visionary Art of Alex Grey, by Alex Grey with Carlo McCormick. (Rochester, VT: Inner Traditions International, 1990)
'Inspiration for the Sacred Mirrors emerged after I had a series of mystical experiences that caused me to redefine my view of consciousness and the self. I felt that my body was no longer just a solid, isolated object in the world of separate forms and existential anxiety, but more like a manifestation of the primordial energy of awareness that was everywhere present. I wanted my paintings to visually chart the spectrum of consciousness from material perception to spiritual insight; and to function, if possible, as symbolic portals to the mystic domain.' (C)

Sacred Mushrooms and The Law by Richard Glen Boire (Spectral Mindustries, 1997)
'Describes federal and all state laws on psilocybin mushrooms and compounds. California law against spores; legal difference between mushrooms and their active compounds. Religious Freedom Restoration Act as defense for religious use. By noted lawyer and author of the fine *Entheogen Law Reporter* newsletter. Recommended.' (MB)

The Sacred Mushroom Seeker: Essays for R. Gordon Wasson, ed. Thomas J. Riedlinger (Portland, OR: Dioscorides Press, 1990)
' "Imagine the feeling!" he challenged me. "The darkness was total except for the glowing red embers." Now I was the one who sat wide-eyed, listening carefully, as Gordon recalled the amazing events of that evening..."Have you ever taken them?" "Yes," I admitted. Then I told him of something peculiar I had experienced when doing so. Though I do not believe in conventional spiritual entities, the mushrooms had induced a strong feeling that some kind of spirit was present, an invisible, silent entity that stood at the opposite verge of my consciousness. I sensed it to be, not an angel or devil, but something connected in some way to earth and the physical realm; perhaps a tutelary spirit such as primitive societies

8

believed to be dwelling in trees, rocks and rivers. "Have you ever had a similar experience?" I wondered.' (C)

Scandal: Essays in Islamic Heresy, by Peter Lamborn Wilson (Brooklyn, NY: Autonomedia, 1988)
'a great many people in Iran, Afghanistan, Pakistan, India and elsewhere use preparations of cannabis for various spiritual reasons. Very little has been published on this subject, and of that little almost nothing of value. Between 1968 and 1978 I had occasion to observe and participate in such hemp use, and I consider my own observations of some small value.' (C)

The Science and Romance of Selected Herbs Used in Medicine and Religious Ceremony, by Anthony Andoh (San Francisco: North Scale Institute, 1986)

The Scientific Study of Religion, by Milton J. Yinger (New York: Macmillan, 1970)
'From the perspective we have adopted, we must ask: What combination of structural, cultural, and character sources supports the use of drugs in religious activities?' (C)

Scrapbook of a Haight Ashbury Pilgrim: Spirit, Sacraments and Sex in 1967/68, by Elizabeth Gips (Santa Cruz, CA: Changes Press, 1991)
'The ground, the fabric, the underlying basis of the Haight Ashbury and the Summer of Love was spirit. We traveled to the heart of godhead, reveled in the ecstasy of union. We experienced ourselves as gods and goddesses and put our consciousness beyond form, into the magical rainbow that is the molecular flow...Nothing is hidden; there is still the amazing contrast between spiritual ecstasy and inter-relationship trauma. I mean, it was hard, man, and it was heaven. It was groovy, and it was sad. It was a pendulum swing between nirvana and hell. But through it all we were reaching for spirit.' (C)

The Secret Chief, by Myron Stolaroff (MAPS, 1997)
'Story of a pioneering therapist (now deceased) who used psychedelics in his practice. Fascinating narrative/interview; early excitement in the 50s, group and ceremonial uses, therapy techniques, various compounds compared. Stan Grof, Albert Hofmann, Ann Shulgin, and Sasha Shulgin also contribute.' (MB)

The Seduction of the Spirit: The Use and Misuse of People's Religion, by Harvey Cox (New York: Simon & Schuster, 1973)

'I don't believe for a minute that all those terrifying "drug education" spots on TV will scare kids out of trying drugs. In fact, they may have the opposite effect. Everyone longs, sometimes secretly, to experience altered states of consciousness. The renewed quest for interiority is a way of fighting the violation of our marrow we experience in an acquiring-consuming-competing society.' (C)

To Seed the New Planet, by John Walker (Beyond All Publications, 1996)
'A Story of Self-Realization and Divine Union through Psychedelic Transformation in Nature. Story of a man's search for enlightenment and community in Northern California. He reaches insights through psychedelics and otherwise about the planetary ecology and the relation of local and global communities. He realizes his nature as a spiritual being and as an aspect of the Eternal One. Interesting writing and dialog.' (MB)

A Separate Reality, by Carlos Castaneda (Harmondsworth: Penguin, 1971)
Sequel to *The Teachings of Don Juan*.

The Shaman: Voyages of the Soul – Trance, Ecstasy and Healing from Siberia to the Amazon, by Piers Vitebsky (London: Macmillan, 1995)

Shamanic Voices, by Joan Halifax (Harmondsworth: Arkana (Penguin), 1979)
'Shamans talk directly about their visions and work. Many plant shamans speak: Maria Sabina about mushrooms, Manuel Cordova-Rios about ayahuasca, several Huichol about Peyote. Stories of journeys to other worlds, healing, and personal transformation. References and bibliography (no index).' (MB)

Shamanism: Archaic Techniques of Ecstasy, by Mircea Eliade (New York: Pantheon, 1964)
Classic text on the subject.

Shamanism, by Nevill Drury (Shaftesbury: Element)
'Good introduction to shamans and sacred plants. Richly illustrated. Talks with shamans, cosmologies, rituals, and Western shamanism. Concise, easy to read.' (MB)

Shaman Woman, Mainline Lady: Women's Writings on the Drug Experience, ed. Cynthia Palmer and Michael Horowitz (New York: William Morrow, 1982)
'*Shaman Woman, Mainline Lady* is the first collection of women's writings on their experiences with mind-altering drugs. These

powerful memoirs, poems, short stories, and book excerpts span the Victorian to the present post-psychedelic eras...' (C)

Simulations of God: The Science of Belief, by John C. Lilly (New York: Simon & Schuster, 1975)
'I rather resent the fact that when I take a drug, I have signed a contract with a chemical for the specific period of time that it exerts powerful influences upon everything I do, think, feel, or am. Then the effect wears off, leaving me in a state of wonderment that such a small quantum of a substance could so profoundly affect my being. They are merely chemical tools useful in the proper context for those who are exploring the human brain and the human mind and the possible parameters and variations of its states of being.' (C)

SOMA: Divine Mushroom of Immortality, by R. Gordon Wasson (The Hague: Mouton, 1968) New York: Harcourt Brace Jovanovich
'In a word, my belief is that Soma is the Divine Mushroom of Immortality, and that in the early days of our culture, before we made use of reading and writing, when the RigVeda was being composed, the prestige of this miraculous mushroom ran by word of mouth far and wide throughout Eurasia, well beyond the regions where it grew and was worshipped.' (C)

Sorcery and Shamanism: Curanderos and Clients in Northen Peru, by Donald Oralemon and Douglas Sharon (Salt Lake City, University of Utah Press, 1993)

The Speed Culture: Amphetamine Use and Abuse in America, by Lester Grinspoon and Peter Hedblom (Cambridge, MA: Harvard University Press, 1975)
'There was a strong emphasis on religion, particularly small or arcane cults, and astrology; many abusers have adapted traditional studies of the zodiac to fit private, complex, and incessantly discussed "systems"...conventional or systematically rigorous religion holds very little appeal for amphetamine abusers, because these stimulants so easily give one aspect of the religious experience to the abuser, namely, intensity of feeling toward the sacred.' (C)
Spirits, Shamans, and Stars, ed. David L. Browman and Ronald A. Schwarz (1979)
'Three parts. Perspectives on Psychotropic Drugs with chapters on yage, and espingo, a possible hallucinogen, as well as coca and tobacco. Medical Anthropology discusses cannabis use in Brazil and other healing techniques, and Spirits, Structures, and Stars has a nice chapter on a San Pedro curandero from Peru. Name and subject indices.' (MB)

Spiritualität und Drogen, by Hans-Heinrich Taeger (Markt Erlbach: Raymon Martin Verlag, 1988)

The Spiritual Nature of Man: A Study of Contemporary Religious Experience, by Alister Hardy (Oxford: Clarendon Press, 1979)
'Over the years my colleagues and I have collected together over four thousand first-hand accounts which show that a large number of people even today possess a deep awareness of a benevolent non-physical power. Which appears to be partly or wholly beyond, and far greater than, the individual self...Pahnke may have been over-optimistic in his ideas of what such research may do, but there can be little doubt that the altered states of consciousness induced by the taking of drugs do indeed facilitate an experience that could not otherwise be achieved under normal conditions.' (C)

The Still Point: Reflections on Zen and Christian Mysticism, by William Johnston (New York: Fordham University Press, 1970)
'But if religious experience is so important, it might be a good idea to stimulate it, and thus arises the use of drugs as a way to mysticism...As for the drugs, if they do not induce mysticism in the philosophical sense, a fortiori, they have nothing to do with theology. It seems true, indeed that certain drugs can touch the same level of psychic life as does mysticism, accentuating the same faculties and enabling one to see into the essence of things in a way similar to Zen...There is as yet no evidence for the existence of a drug that effects the detachment and the serenity resulting from silent meditation. And all this indicates a profound difference between the experiences.' (C)

The Storming of the Mind, by Robert Hunter (Garden City, NY: Doubleday, 1971)
'It is worth noting, as several writers have pointed out, that what is existentially astonishing about the LSD experience is the "discovery" that, mentally, most of us have been operating within the confines of a quite narrow and sharply restricted level of consciousness...the consciousness which the drug experience offers is not unique; it is not 'new'; it is not unnatural; there is nothing "freaky" or "far-out" or weird about it all, except in the context of contemporary society.' (C)

Tales of the Yanomami, by Jaques Lizot (Cambridge University Press, 1985)
'Daily Life in the Venezuelan Forest. Author lived with this tribe for fifteen years, and describes their lifestyle, magic realms, and

politics, often using stories told by members of the tribe. Interesting chapter on shamanic use of Virola and Anadenanthera snuffs. Includes photos, Yanomami glossary, bibliography.' (MB)

The Teachings of Don Juan, by Carlos Castaneda (Harmondsworth: Penguin, 1970)
Originally presented as an anthropological study but now considered by many to be a fictional account.

Thanatos to Eros: Thirty-five Years of Psychedelic Exploration, by Myron J. Stolaroff (Berlin: Verlag für Wissenschaft und Bildung, 1994)
'...the revelations also included profound realizations that God is absolutely real, and that there is only One Person, of which we are all a part. I held LSD to be the most important discovery man has ever made, and would devote my life to learning more about it and how to use it effectively, not only for myself but for others.' (C)

This Timeless Moment: A Personal View of Aldous Huxley, by Laura Archera Huxley (New York: Farrar, Straus, & Giroux, 1968)
'After half an hour, the expression on his face began to change a little, and I asked him if he felt the effect of LSD, and he indicated no. Yet I think that something had taken place already...The twitching [of Huxley's lower lip] stopped, the breathing became slower and slower, and there was absolutely not the slightest indication of contraction, of struggle. It was just that the breathing became slower – and slower – and slower; the ceasing of life was not a drama at all, but like a piece of music just finishing so gently in a *sempre piu piano*, *dolcemente*...and at five twenty the breathing stopped.' (C)

Three Halves of Ino Moxo, by Cesar Calvo (Rochester, VT: Inner Traditions, 1981)
'Evokes the images and feelings of the ayahuasca jungle; colorful, dark, intense. High quality literature by noted Peruvian author, translated by one who knows these realms well. Lyrical, mythical, the story of Calvo's search for Cordova-Rios, now Ino Moxo, and the three ayahuascaros who help him. Brings forth the worlds and realities of the plant sorcerers. Acclaimed as literature. Photos and glossary. Recommended.' (MB)

TiHKAL: The Continuation, by Alexander Shulgin and Ann Shulgin (Berkeley, CA: Transform Press, 1997)
'The personal story continues, along with an excellent guide to many "places in the mind"

and how to use them, psychedelic psychotherapy, and long chapters on DMT plants and ayahuasca. Comprehensive appendices on drug laws, cactus alkaloids, carbolines, tryptamines. Truly great!' (MB)

Toads and Toadstools, by Adrian Morgan (Berkley: Celestial Arts (Ingram), 1995)
'Mostly about the European use of toads and mushrooms (especially Amanita) in witchcraft and shamanism; also some on use in the Americas (but no *Bufo alvarius*). Lovely, detailed illustrations by the author, and a short description of his efforts at toad intoxication. Notes, bibliography, no index.' (MB)

Tobacco and Shamanism in South America, by Johannes Wilbert (New Haven, CT: Yale University Press, 1987)
'Tobacco drinking occurs among the principal Panoan tribes and, as elsewhere, primarily in association with shamanism. As documented in the ethnographic sections of the book, there remains no doubt that through action on the central nervous system nicotine is apt to produce altered states of consciousness akin to hallucination. Religious practitioners among South American Indians...consider hunger for food characteristic of man and hunger for tobacco typical of spirits.' (C)

Toltecs of the New Millennium, by Victor Sanchez (Bear & Co., 1996)
'*Publishers Weekly* says it's a compelling spiritual autobiography, by an anthropologist who studies the Wirrarika in Mexico and then finds manifested an alteration of reality. He examines the way substances such as LSD and peyote generate religious states of consciousness. An interesting read and a revealing examination of sacred territory.' (MB)

Tricycle: The Buddhist Review, (fall, 1996)
Buddhism and Psychedelics.
Quarterly periodical, this issue focuses on the subject: 'Psychedelics: Help or Hindrance?'

The Unfolding Self: Varieties of Transformative Experience, by Ralph Metzner (Novato, CA: Origin Press, 1989)
'So I had the first six or so psychedelic experiences of my life behind the bars of a maximum security prison. To this day, I vividly remember the extraordinary experience of having my visual field expanded until it became a 360-degree circle or sphere, within which the prison walls, the bars on the windows, and the locks on the doors had become meaningless. Though still visible and real, they seemed inef-

fectual in imprisoning the human spirit, which soared unconstrained that day.' (C)

Uses of Marijuana, by Solomon H. Snyder (New York: Oxford University Press, 1971)
'As a mind-altering substance, cannabis seems to have come of age in India, where the Hindu used cannabis as an aid in meditation. The community had some paradoxical attitudes toward the two most prevalent intoxicants, daru, a potent alcoholic beverage distilled from the flowers of the mahwa tree, and bhang. The warrior caste, the Rajputs, used daru exclusively, and seemed to regard cannabis as an indulgence fit only for sissies. The Brahmins, on the other hand, employed cannabis in both religious and social settings. Rajputs, of course, represent the temporal aristocracy as Brahmins do the spiritual.' (C)

Vine of the Soul, by Richard Evans Schultes and Robert F. Raffauf (Synergetic Press (Atrium), 1992)
Medicine Men, Plants and Rituals in the Colombian Amazonia Focuses on native use of ayahuasca, the 'vine of the soul', and other plants in this region. Extensive photos of plants, their preparation, and the medicine men who use them. Beliefs, dances, art, and other cultural expressions of plants and their spirits. (MB)

The Violet Forest, by Foster Perry (Santa Fe: Bear & Co, 1998)
Shamanic journeys in the Amazon. The author's journey on his path as a modern shaman participating in Ayahuasca rituals.

Where Science and Magic Meet, by Serena Roney-Dougal (Shaftesbury, Dorset: Element Books, 1991)
Looks at common ground that links developments in the new sciences with the ancient wisdom of various occult and spiritual traditions.

White Rabbit, ed. John Miller and Randall Koral (1995)
'Reports from writers, artists, visionaries, and others about their experiences with psychedelics and other drugs. From Lewis Carroll to William Burroughs, Charles Dickens to Philip K. Dick, and Florence Nightingale to Timothy Leary, these 38 excepts span centuries of mystical drug use.' (MB)

Wizard of the Upper Amazon, by Bruce Lamb (Berkley: North Atlantic Press, 1974)
'The story of Nanual Cordova-Rios who was captured by the South American Indians at the beginning of the century and his experiences with ayahuasca. First in the Lamb series, overlaps much with *Kidnapped in the Amazon Jungle*.' (MB)

The World is As You Dream It, by John Perkins (Destiny Books, 1994)
'Shamanic Teachings from the Amazon and Andes. Personal story of inner quest and ayahuasca use, in Colombia, Ecuador, and the Andes. Perkins leads tours to shamans, and started the Earth Dream Alliance to purchase and conserve rain forests to help protect indigenous cultures.' (MB)

Zen and the Brain, by James H. Austin (Cambridge, MA: MIT Press, 1998)
'Toward an Understanding of Meditation and Consciousness. Professor of Neurology and Zen practitioner explains what we know about the brain mechanisms and anatomy of altered states of consciousness. Focus is on Zen mental states, but includes several chapters on psychedelic states and various others. Also includes background on neurotransmitters and brain anatomy. For general readers. Glossary, references, notes, index.' (MB)

Notes

Introduction

1. Alex Kershaw, 'Fighting for the Unborn', *Observer Magazine*, 7 March 1999.
2. C.T. Tart (ed.), *Altered States of Consciousness*, Garden City, NY: Anchor Books, Doubleday, 1972.
3. Ram Dass, recorded lecture 'The Path of Service – Here and Now in the 90s'. Recorded live in Denver, Colorado, during a Seva Foundation Tour (1990). Tape by Sounds True Recordings, Boulder, Colorado. ISBN: 1-56455-032-x.
4. 'Let's Get Cerebral', *Independent on Sunday*, 11 January 1998.
5. Mansuch Patel and Helen Waters, *Crisis and the Miracle of Love: Mastering Change and Adversity at any Age*, Bilston, W. Midlands: Life Foundation Publications, 1997

Drugs and Spirituality?

1. A. Weil, *The Natural Mind*, Boston: Houghton Mifflin, 1986.
2. A. Hofmann, 'The Message of the Eleusinian Mysteries', in R. Forte (ed.) *Entheogens and the Future of Religion*, San Francisco: Council on Spiritual Practices, 1997.
3. R.G. Wasson, A. Hofmann and C.A.P. Ruck, *The Road to Eleusis*, New York: Harcourt Brace Jovanovich, 1978.
4. Hofmann, 'The Message of the Eleusinian Mysteries'.
5. The 1961 recipient of the American Psychological Association William James Memorial Award for contributions to the psychology of religion.
6. D. Steindl-Rast ,'Explorations into God', in Forte (ed.) *Entheogens and the Future of Religion*.
7. S. Roney-Dougal, *Where Science and Magic Meet*, Dorset: Element Books 1993.
8. J.C. Callaway, M.M. Airaksinen and J. Gynther, 'Endogenous Beta-Carbolines and Other Indole Alkaloids in Mammals', *Integration: Journal for Mind-moving Plants and Culture*, 5 (1995).
9. Dr Dave Nichols, pers. comm., 2 March 1999.
10. Ian Cotton, *The Hallelujah Revolution*, London: Little Brown 1995.
11. Weil, *The Natural Mind*.
12. Contact high: 'a common occurrence in a group experiment with a psychedelic drug is that a drug-free observer becomes aware that he is experiencing some effects of the material being used by others. The altered state has become contagious. Animals in the household are especially prone to this kind of unintentional participation, usually appearing to enjoy it immensely. There is no known scientific explanation for this phenomenon' (A. and A. Shulgin *PiHKAL*, Berkeley, CA: Transform Press, 1991).
13. W.N. Pahnke, *International Journal of Parapsychology*, 8, 2 (Spring 1966): 295–313.
14. W.H. Clark, *Chemical Ecstasy: Psychedelic Drugs and Religion*, New York: Sheed & Ward (1969).
15. R. Doblin, *Journal of Transpersonal Psychology*, 23, 1 (1991): 1–28.
16. A. Huxley, *The Doors of Perception* and *Heaven and Hell*, HarperCollins 1954.

A Different Kind of Church

1. G.D. Richman, 'The Santo Daime Doctrine', *Shaman's Drum*, Winter 1990–91: 30–41.
2. Santo Daime Official Homepage: http://www.geocities.com/RainForest/5949/
3. UDV Official Homepage: http://www.udv.org.br/udvpag01-ing.htm
4. Ibid.
5. C.S. Grob *et al.*, 'Human Psychopharmacology of Hoasca, a Plant Hallucinogen used in Ritual Context in Brazil', *Journal of Nervous and Mental Disease*, 184 (1996): 86–94.
6. Ibid.

7. Ibid.
8. Ibid.
9. G. Samorini, 'The Initiation Rite in the Bwiti Religion (Ndea Narizanga Sect, Gabon)'. Paper presented at the 2nd Congres Internacional per a l'Estudio dels Modicats de Consciencia, 3–7 October 1994, Lleida (Spain).
10. J.W. Fernandez, *Bwiti: An Ethnography of the Religious Imagination in Africa*, Princeton, NJ: Princeton University Press.
11. Samorini, 'The Initiation Rite in the Bwiti Religion'.
12. Ibid.
13. Thanks to Leo Mercado of the Peyote Foundation for much of the information in this section.
14. Information from the *Entheogen Law Reporter*, compiled and edited by Richard Glen Boire, Esq.
15. T. Lyttle, 'Drug Based Religions and Contemporary Drug Taking', *Journal of Drug Issues*, 18, 2 (1988): 275.
16. Temple of the True Inner Light flyer found on the Internet newsgroup alt.psychoactives
17. M. Rose, 'Psychedelic Eden', *Spirit Magazine*, 6, June/July (1997).
18. Lyttle, 'Drug Based Religions and Contemporary Drug Taking, 175.
19. From p. 84–86 © Peter Gorman. A longer version of this article was first published in *High Times*, January 1990.

Psychoactives in World Religions

1. There is a view that this attitude is softening with the arrival of the antidepressant, Prozac. Otherwise orthodox American evangelicals have praised Prozac for its value in treating Christians suffering from depression and have warned fellow evangelicals not to assume that God could not work through Prozac.
2. *The Misuse of Drugs: Report by the Board for Social Responsibility*, General Synod GS1300, July 1998.
3. R.G. Wasson, *Soma: Divine Mushrom of Immortality*, New York: Harcourt Brace Jovanovich, 1971.
4. Marco Polo recorded the best-known version of the story.
5. R.A. Wilson, *Sex and Drugs: A Journey beyond Limits*, Phoenix, AZ: New Falcon Publications, 1982.
6. J.M. Allegro, *The Sacred Mushroom and the Cross*, New York: Doubleday, 1970.
7. *Tricycle* magazine, fall 1996.
8. K. Leech, *Drugs and Pastoral Care*, London: Darton, Longman, Todd, 1998.
9. P. Lamborn Wilson, *Scandal: Essays in Islamic Heresy*, Brooklyn, NY: Autonomedia, 1988.

Contemporary Shamanism for Westerners

1. By 'Westerner' we refer to people from the industrialised societies, mainly Europe and the United States.
2. Paper by Enriques Gonzalez Rubio, 'The Flesh of God: Sacred Mushroom Traditions among the Mazatec Shamans'.
3. Paper by Pedro Fernandes Leite da Luz, translated into English by Joshua Callaghan.
4. Gonzalez Rubio, 'The Flesh of God'.

Home Users of Psychoactives

1. *Tricycle: the Buddhist Review*, fall 1996.

Rave Spirituality

1. Russell Newcombe has written a number of books about drugs and harm reduction, and is Director of the 3D Research Bureau, an independent drugs research and consultancy service.
2. *Release Drugs and Dance Survey: An Insight into the Culture* (1997) Release, 388 Old Street, London EC1V 9LT.
3. See 'Rave on the Internet', p. 244 of the present book, for details of these clubs.
4. Return to the Source Website at http://www.rtts.com
5. R. Howard, *The Rise and Fall of the Nine O'Clock Service*, London: Mowbray, 1996.

6. R. Griffin, CD sleevenotes, *Return to the Source*, 1996.

7. Fraser Clark, http://www.algroup.co.uk/wpb/people/fraser.htm

8. *Release Drugs and Dance Survey: An Insight into the Culture*, Release, 388 Old Street, London EC1V 9LT, 1997, p.23.

9. R. Griffin, pers. comm., 10 October 1998, London.

10. See the Prayer for Peace on p. 167.

11. http://www.rtts.com/earthdance.html

Before, During and After

1. T. Leary *et al.*, *The Psychedelic Experience, a Manual based on the Tibetan Book of the Dead*, New York: Citadel, 1964.

2. A. and A. Shulgin, *TiHKAL: The Continuation*, Berkeley, CA: Transform Press, 1997.

3. Ibid.

Medical and First Aid

1. C. Jones in N. Saunders, *Ecstasy Reconsidered*, London, Nicholas Saunders Publishing, 1997.

Glossary

1. A. and A. Shulgin, *PiHKAL: A Chemical Love Story*, Berkeley CA: Transform Press, 1991.

2. Ibid.

3. Ibid.

4. Myron Stolaroff, *The Secret Chief*, MAPS, 1997.

5. Shulgin and Shulgin, *PiHKAL*.

We welcome feedback and are keen to receive accounts and hear of any books, contacts or other resources that you feel we should have included.

You can email us at: ultimatehigh@ndirect.co.uk or through our website at http://www.csp.org/nicholas/spiritualindex.html

Index